COAST LINES

Fleet List and History

IAN COLLARD

AMBERLEY

First published 2015

Amberley Publishing
The Hill, Stroud
Gloucestershire, GL5 4EP

www.amberley-books.com

Copyright © Ian Collard 2015

The right of Ian Collard to be identified as the Author
of this work has been asserted in accordance with the
Copyrights, Designs and Patents Act 1988.

ISBN 978 1 4456 4674 9 (print)
ISBN 978 1 4456 4675 6 (ebook)

British Library Cataloguing in Publication Data.
A catalogue record for this book is available from the British Library.

Typeset in 10pt on 13pt Celeste.
Typesetting and Origination by Amberley Publishing.
Printed in the UK.

CONTENTS

COAST LINES: FLEET HISTORY

Hopeful.

Coast Lines Ltd was formed on Merseyside in 1913 by the merger of Powell, Bacon and Hough Lines. An interest in the Bacon Line had been acquired by Powell in 1910, and Hough in 1912. The new fleet consisted of sixteen coastal ships operating in the Irish Sea. The company grew from a small fleet of vessels to the world's largest coastal fleet, which pioneered the coordination of coastal sea and road transport from the 1950s onwards and was eventually taken over by P&O in 1971.

At its peak, the line comprised of Powell, Bacon & Hough Lines, British Channel Islands Shipping, Queenship Navigation, Belfast Steamship Company, Burns & Laird Lines, British & Irish Steam Packet, North of Scotland, Orkney & Shetland Shipping, Tyne Tees Shipping and the Zillah Shipping Company.

The coastal services provided by Coast Lines can be traced back to the early nineteenth century, when small sailing ships provided a service for merchants between London and Liverpool. In 1793, services were maintained between Bristol and thirty other coastal ports. The Liverpool firm of Swainson & Cram provided services to Bristol and were also shipbuilders. In 1830 a Bristol merchant named Frederick Hillman Powell, who regularly shipped cargo from Bristol to Liverpool, took an interest in the company, which later became Cram, Powell & Company.

The company operated a fleet of sailing vessels and the schooner *Ann Powell* was added, which was named after Powell's wife. The *Ann Powell* was employed in the Bristol trade, and the brigs *Locomotive* and *Queen of Avon* and barques *Chrystaline* and *Eliza Ann* were operated in the foreign trade. The brig *Pearl* sailed on the service from Canning Dock, Liverpool, to Redcliffe Backs, Bristol, from 1845 to 1860. George Cram retired from the business in the early 1850s to develop a shipbuilding operation at Chester; the partnership with Harry Cram was dissolved and the company became the Powell Line.

In the early 1850s, the company decided to experiment with steam and *Amelia* was purchased to operate between Liverpool and Bristol. She was later joined by *Athlete*, which had a cargo capacity of 300 tons and was commanded by Captain Laver until 1875. *Athlete* introduced the Powell Line's regular service between Liverpool and Bristol, leaving Liverpool every Tuesday and Bristol on a Saturday. It was reported at the time that all of her voyages under the command of Captain Laver were 'entirely without accident of any kind', and that the merchants were so confident in his ability that they did not insure cargoes carried by her.

The steamer *Augusta* was introduced in 1862 for the Liverpool–Bristol and the Liverpool–London direct services. *Augusta* also operated to Nantes, Le Havre, Dunkirk and Spanish ports with general cargo on the outward journey and grain and sugar on return. The original London agents were Wallis & La Thangur, which became Charles Wallis on the death of his partner. John Allen was later made agent and remained as the company's representative in the capital for many years. In the 1860s David Muir Barry, Frederick Honey and Col. Alfred Read joined the company.

The *Edith Owen* initially operated on the London route and later to Bristol. The *Marley Hill* joined the fleet in 1864 and was a sister to the *Augusta*. She was driven ashore in bad weather off Whitehaven but was later salvaged and refloated. The *Northumberland* and *William France* carried coal from South Wales to Liverpool for the Cunard liners. *Mersey* and *Edith Cowan* operated to London with cargo and also carried several passengers. Frederick Powell owned the barque *Staffordshire*, which was operated in the foreign trade and commanded by Captain John Honey.

The *Ethel Cane* was renamed *Cheerful*, becoming the first of the vessels to bear the '-ful' suffix. She was later lost in the Bristol Channel after colliding with HMS *Hekla* in dense fog. *Truthful* was built in 1870, and *Faithful* was built for the London–Liverpool route and later the Liverpool–Bristol service. The *Voltaic* was not renamed, but the *Point Clear* became *Hopeful*, *Morgan Richard* was renamed *Truthful* and the *African* was given the name *Graceful*. The other members of the fleet were the *Mary*, *Monica* and *Hispania*.

In 1880, the fleet consisted of *Truthful*, *Faithful*, *Hispania*, *Swan*, *Elaine* and the *Asia*. Sailings were offered from Liverpool to Dunkirk and a deed of partnership was drawn up under the title of F. H. Powell & Company. The partnership included John Ellis, Ferdinand Honey and Alfred Read. John Ellis retired in 1890 and George R. Pritchard was appointed freight manager, with George F. Honey as his assistant. L. E. Penn was appointed to the London office in 1886, being employed there until his retirement in 1938.

The coastal voyages were becoming very popular, and *Powerful*'s sailings from London on Wednesdays carried an average of forty to fifty passengers for the trip to Liverpool. The *Masterful*, on her scheduled Saturday sailing, usually carried seventy to eighty passengers.

The *Hispania* was lost with all hands while on charter and a service to Manchester was offered following the opening of the Manchester Ship Canal. *Swan* arrived at Manchester with a cargo of 1,200 tons, which was the largest to enter the canal up to that time. Arrangements were made for the mutual alternative sailing of the Hough Line. *Masterful* and *Powerful* were built and equipped with submarine signalling equipment. The ships were built with unusually large hatches that enabled them to accommodate the large mahogany logs which were discharged by the West African steamers at Liverpool.

Samuel Hough had been a purser on a vessel during the Crimean War and he founded the Bacon Line with the steamers *Genova* and *East Anglian* and offered a service from Liverpool, Falmouth, Plymouth, Southampton, and Portsmouth to London. Around 1840, he had obtained a position at the firm of Tamplin & Company, agents for the British & Irish company in Liverpool, and on his return from the Crimea he was offered a partnership in the company. He later acquired the *El Dorado*, *Maggie Warrington*, *Baidar* and another tramp steamer that he renamed the *Edith Hough*. *El Dorado* was lost in Hudson's Bay while on charter, but her crew managed to reach Quebec by foot after walking 600 miles with an Indian guide.

The *Samuel Hough* carried seventy-five passengers, and the *Mary Hough* had a capacity of seventy on the service from Liverpool to London. The *Mary Hough* was also lost while on charter off Newfoundland and the *Dorothy Hough* was the final steamer built for the line. When Samuel Hough died in 1902, the company was taken over by Richard G. Hough and his brothers Samuel, William, Ernest and Robert. The company was incorporated on 1 January 1904 with offices at 25 Water Street, Liverpool.

John Bacon was employed as a clerk by Fitzsimon, Appleby & Company before forming the Bacon Line around 1850. He offered services from Liverpool and Preston to Wexford and Bristol Channel ports with the steamers *Sovereign*, *Jane Bacon*, *Rocket*, *Sir Walter Bacon*, *Sunlight*, *Brunswick*, *Stuart*, *Prestonian* and *Montague*. *Montague* had been the Tsar of Russia's yacht for a number of years. John Bacon died in 1886 and for three years the business was carried out by Joseph Wright. John Bacon Ltd was incorporated in 1889.

On 30 September 1913, the three lines were merged and incorporated as Powell, Bacon & Hough Lines Ltd. The fleet consisted of *Powerful*, *Cornish Coast*, *Faithful*, *Sussex Coast*, *Dorset Coast*, *Graceful*, *Norfolk Coast*, *Hampshire Coast*, *Stonehenge* and *Hopeful* from Powell's. *Edith*, *Sir George Bacon*, *Sir Edward Bacon*, *Sir Roger Bacon*, *Sir Walter Bacon* and the barges *Harfat* and *Pennar* came from the Bacon Line and the *Annie Hough* and *Dorothy Hough* from Hough's. The ships' total tonnage was over 16,000 tons and the company's name was changed to Coast Lines Ltd in May 1917, becoming a public company in June 1919. The company was acquired by the Royal Mail Line in March 1917 for £800,000, with Sir Owen Phillips as its chairman and Alfred H. Read as managing director. The shareholdings were distributed in preference and ordinary shares in the Royal Mail Line, Elder Dempster & Company Ltd, Union Castle Line, McGregor, Gow, Norris & Joyner Ltd, Lamport & Holt Line and James Moss & Company Ltd. Sir Alfred Read had purchased shares in the British & Irish Steam Packet Company Ltd in 1914 and in 1918/19 he gained a controlling interest in the City of Dublin Steam Packet Company Ltd and the City of Cork Steam Packet Company Ltd. The City of Dublin Steam Packet Company Ltd withdrew their services from the Liverpool–Dublin route in 1919, and after it lost the Holyhead–Dun Laoghaire mail contract in 1920, it went into liquidation in 1924. The City of Cork Steam Packet Company Ltd was finally merged with the British & Irish Steam Packet Company in 1936, but the vessels retained their funnel colours.

Graceful.

The British & Irish Steam Packet Company Ltd had been established in 1836, providing a service from Dublin to London, and in 1848 it also offered sailings from Waterford to Liverpool. In 1851, services to Limerick were provided but these were discontinued three years later. The Belfast Steamship Company Ltd was founded in Belfast in 1824 by local merchants and was registered under that name on 25 May 1852, with a capital of £50,000 and based at 33 Donegall Quay, Belfast. It acquired the Liverpool–Belfast service from Langtry's in 1859 after providing a joint service with them from 1854.

Coast Lines Ltd managed Burns & Laird Lines Ltd; Belfast Steamship Company Ltd; British & Irish Steam Packet Company Ltd; Michael Murphy Ltd; British Channel Islands Shipping Company Ltd and Island Shipping Company Ltd with their subsidiaries in Jersey and Guernsey; Tyne Tees Steam Shipping Company and its associate, Aberdeen Steam Navigation Company Ltd; Queenship Ltd; A. Coker & Company Ltd; Coast Lines (Africa) Ltd and its South African subsidiaries; North of Scotland, Orkney & Shetland Shipping Company Ltd; and jointly with the LMS (later part of British Railways) David MacBrayne Ltd and its subsidiary the Clyde & Campbeltown Shipping Company Ltd.

In 1918, the firm of Stocks, Turnbull & Company Ltd was acquired with their steamers *Abbotshall*, *New Abbotshall* and *Kirkaldy*. They were originally known as the London & Kirkcaldy Steamship Company Ltd. M. Langlands was taken over in 1919, a company that dated back to the 1836 when the Glasgow & Liverpool Royal Steam Packet Company was formed. Following the acquisition, M. Langlands & Sons Ltd was registered to act as agents for Coast Lines Ltd at Ardrossan and other ports. It maintained the Glasgow–Liverpool and Glasgow-Manchester cargo services and in 1924 it acquired the Glasgow–Stranraer–Preston services of the Grahamston Shipping Company Ltd. The Stranraer–Preston route lasted until the end of April 1924 and the Glasgow/Greenock to Stranraer closed on 1 August that year.

Tedcastle, McCormick & Company Ltd were taken over in 1919 with some vessels allocated to the British & Irish Steam Packet Company and others to Coast Lines Ltd. The Volana Shipping Company Ltd operated the *Volana*, *Volga*, *Voltaire*, *Volpone*, *Volante*, *Volvey*, *Volhynia*, *Volturous* and *Volscian* from Liverpool to Llanelly, Cardiff and Barryport. The company was also acquired by the Coast Lines Group in 1919. In March 1920, the Little Western Steamship Company of Penzance and their managers, G. Bazeley & Sons, and steamers *Mercutio*, *Cadoc* and *Cloth* became part of the Coast Lines Group.

The London Welsh Steamship Company operated vessels from West Quay, London Docks, for import and Denmark Shed, South Quay, for export. Services were offered to Cardiff, Swansea, Llanelly and to Port Talbot by the steamers *Welsh Trader*, *Cardiff Trader*, *Swansea Trader* and *Tay 1*. Furness Withy & Company Ltd took an interest in the company in 1911 when all vessels except *Tay 1* were replaced by *Channel Trader*, *London Trader* and *Llanelly Trader*. The company was acquired by Coast Lines Ltd in 1924.

Henry Burden Junior & Company Ltd provided a service from London to Poole. Vessels trading on the route had operated since the early part of the nineteenth century and steamers were introduced by the Poole, Isle of Purbeck, Isle of Wight & Portsmouth Steam Packet Company, which was registered in 1845. The route became the South Coast Shipping Company in 1887, managed by John Carter and operated by the steamer *Basic*, carrying American flour from London to the local millers. The South Coast Shipping Company was replaced by the London, Isle of Wight & Poole Steamship Company Ltd in 1901 and the routes operated by the *Blanche*, *Orleans*, *Nantes* and *Bessimer*. Two years later the service was taken over by the London & Poole Steamship Company Ltd, but this company soon went into liquidation. Henry Burden Junior & Company Ltd was registered in 1906 and operated the service until 1937, when Coast Lines Ltd took over the route.

In 1824, the firm of Robert Gilchrist & Company was formed as the Glasgow & Liverpool Shipping Company, operating a fleet of fast, rantapike, schooners. The firm's headquarters were transferred to Liverpool in 1862, and in 1873 and 1883 steamers were purchased and the firm of F. R. Harrison & Company was acquired, followed by James Harrison & Company. The canal vessels were used as feeders to the coastal and ocean-going ships. Following the introduction of a service to the Bristol Channel, they acquired two small companies and established the South Wales & Liverpool Steamship Company Ltd. Henry Lamont & Company was purchased in 1910, with the right of reversion of the Bristol and Hayle trade in 1913, which was exercised in 1923 and Richard Burton & Son were taken over in 1922. The company traded with their steamers *Fire King*, *Fire Queen*, *Madge Wildfire* and *Portia* until they were acquired by Coast Lines in 1943.

Michael Murphy Ltd and the Dublin General Steam Shipping Company Ltd were merged into the British & Irish Steam Packet and the steamers *Enda* and *Patricia* were bought by Coast Lines in 1929 for £10,000. The Antrim Iron Ore Company Ltd operated a passenger and cargo service from Belfast to the Tyne and Tees via Stornoway. The company and its two vessels *Glentaise* and *Glendun* were bought by Coast Lines in 1929.

A nightly passenger service from the North Wall, Dublin, to Liverpool was introduced by the British & Irish Steam Packet in 1923, with *Lady Louth* and *Lady Limerick* and joined by the *Lady Longford* in 1924. In 1930 they were replaced by *Heroic* and *Graphic* from the Belfast Steamship Company, which were renamed *Lady Connaught*, *Lady Munster* and *Lady Leinster* respectively. In 1929 the Burns & Laird Lines altered their nomenclature by naming their ships beginning with the word 'Laird'. John Westcott Ltd of Plymouth had been acquired in 1925, the Liverpool Cartage Company Ltd, Thomas Allen Ltd of London and Huxham & Company Ltd all became part of the Coast Lines Group.

Owen Philipps, 1st Baron Kylsant, was born on 25 March 1863 as the third of five sons of the Reverend Sir James Erasmus Philipps, 12th Baronet of Picton Castle, and his wife the Hon. Mary, daughter of the Hon. Reverend Samuel West. He was educated at Newton College, Newton Abbot, Devon, and became an apprentice with the shipping firm Dent & Company of Newcastle upon Tyne in 1860. In 1886, he moved to the shipping firm of Allan & Gow in Glasgow and set up his own shipping firm two years later. By the end of the nineteenth century, he and his brother John owned the King Line Ltd, the Scottish Steamship Company (a finance company), the London Maritime Investment Company and the London & Thames Haven Petroleum Wharf.

The brothers purchased shares in the Royal Mail Steam Packet Company, and in 1902 Owen was made chairman and managing director of the company. In the first twenty years of the twentieth century, the Royal Mail Steam Packet acquired a controlling interest in more than twenty companies, including the Pacific Steam Navigation Company, the Union Castle Line and White Star Line in 1927. He was a Member of Parliament until 1922 and was created a peer as Baron Kylsant the following year. In 1924, he became chairman of shipbuilders Harland & Wolff. In February 1931 it was revealed that for several years the company had been paying dividends to stockholders, despite trading at a loss. Kylsant was arrested and charged with making false statements with regard to company accounts for 1926 and 1927, contrary to Section 84 of the Larceny Act 1861. Harold John Morland, the company auditor, was charged with aiding and abetting the offences. Kylsant resigned as chairman of the Royal Mail Steam Packet in November 1930 and Sir Alfred Read was appointed in his place.

Both he and Morland pleaded not guilty when they were committed to trial at the Old Bailey in July 1931 and were found not guilty of the first two charges. However, Kylsant was found guilty of the final charge of issuing a document with intent to deceive. Morland was discharged and Kylsant was sentenced to twelve months imprisonment. He spent one night in prison and was released on bail pending an appeal. This was heard in November 1931, and when it was dismissed he served ten months in Wormwood Scrubs prison and was released the following August. Following his conviction he resigned all his knighthoods and lieutenancies and died on 10 June 1937 at his home in Pembroke.

It was left to Sir Alfred Read and his financial advisor, Sir John Mann, and board of directors to manage Coast Lines Ltd through this difficult period, and at the end of 1935, Hambros Bank purchased two million ordinary Coast Lines shares, ensuring the future of the company as an independent body. Sir Alfred Read was the elder son of Col. Alfred Read of Chester and began his shipping career in Anchor Line, becoming a partner in F. H. Powell & Company. He was the first chairman in 1913 when the three companies were amalgamated, was a member of the Mersey Docks & Harbour Board and chairman of the Liverpool Steam Ship Owners' Association in 1912. He was appointed to the Ministry of Shipping and served as director of Home Trade Services from 1917 to 1919. He was knighted in 1919, was a member of the Port of London Authority from 1934 to 41 and the president of the Institute of Transport in 1936.

Arnet Robinson, the managing director of Coast Lines for many years, was born in Stanmore, Middlesex, in 1898 and was educated at Westminster School. During the First World War he served in France with the 1st Battalion 60th Rifles, and in 1918 he was attached to the Royal Air Force as an adjutant. He joined Coast Lines' London office in 1920 and was later appointed assistant manager at Bristol. In 1931, he became commercial manager at Liverpool, and joint manager with J. W. Lester the following year. At the outbreak of the Second World War in 1939, he became deputy general manager and managing director in 1948. He was also a director of the Belfast Steamship Company Ltd, Grayson, Rollo & Clover Docks Ltd and the Reliance Marine Insurance Company Ltd. He became the chairman of the Liverpool Steam Ship Owners' Association in 1946, and was a member of the Mersey Docks & Harbour Board and the Institute of Transport. He was president of the Liverpool Shipping Staff's Association and a Liverpool committee member of the National Lifeboat Institution.

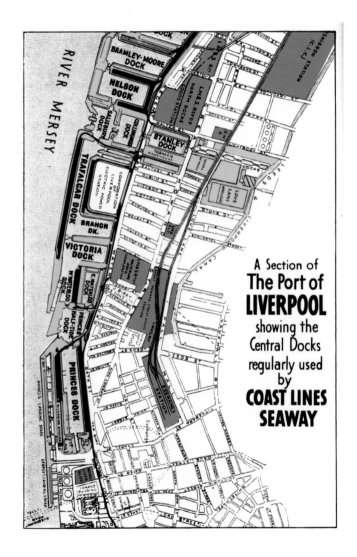

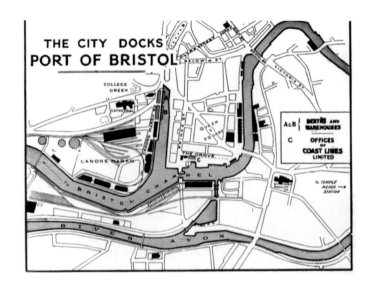

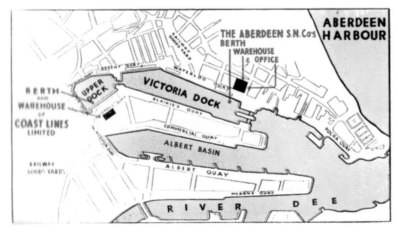

Coast Lines Seaway maps of Liverpool, Bristol and Aberdeen Harbour.

A small minority holding was taken in David MacBrayne Ltd in 1928, in partnership with the London, Midland & Scottish Railway Company. The Clyde & Campbeltown Shipping Company Ltd was acquired in 1931 and sold to the Caledonian Steam Packet Company Ltd in 1949. The British & Irish Steam Packet Company (1936) Ltd was created in 1936, incorporating the City of Cork Steam Packet Company and Michael Murphy Ltd. The Sligo Navigation Company Ltd was purchased by Burns & Laird Lines and the Plymouth, Channel Islands & Brittany Steamship Company Ltd in 1936. The London & Channel Islands Steamship Company Ltd was acquired in 1937, becoming the British Channel Islands Shipping Company Ltd. Its tramping interests became British Channel Traders Ltd in 1943 and Queenship Navigation Ltd four years later. Fisher Renwick Manchester–London Steamers Ltd, who provided a cargo service from Manchester to London, were taken over in 1939.

The Ardrossan Dockyard was originally designed for the building of ships made of wood. By 1900, the shipbuilding yard had three berths for building ships, a graving dock for ships up to 1,000 tons and a repair slip for vessels up to 400 tons. Equipment was renewed in 1888 and in 1898 the yard changed hands and became the Ardrossan Dry Dock & Shipbuilding Co. Ltd. The yard was further modernised in 1907, and by 1912 was enjoying great prosperity. The new shipyard was completed in about 1916. It covered 22 acres and had five building berths capable of accommodating 400- to 500-foot vessels of up to 9,000 tons. This new shipyard allowed vessels to be built and launched directly into the Firth of Clyde. The yard was closed in 1930 but was taken over by Coast Lines Ltd during the 1930s. It was sold in 1962 and by 1969, some of the South Yard land was acquired by the McCrindle Group and some small-scale shipbuilding work took place.

At the beginning of the 1930s, three twin-funnelled motor passenger ships were introduced to the Liverpool–Belfast service. They were the *Ulster Monarch*, *Ulster Queen* and *Ulster Prince* and they replaced the *Graphic*, *Heroic* and *Patriotic* on the route, which were transferred to the British & Irish Steam Packet Company. They were the first diesel-driven cross-channel passenger ships, being equipped with two 10-cylinder Burmester & Wain type diesel engines of a four stroke, trunk piston, airless injection version with direct reversing gear. Each ship had accommodation for 418 First Class and 486 Third Class passengers and was also designed to carry 700 tons of cargo. A similar vessel, *Innisfallen*, was delivered to the City of Cork Steam Packet Company in 1930 for the Fishguard–Cork service.

Ulster Monarch, *Ulster Queen* and *Ulster Prince* were built and engined by Harland & Wolff Ltd in Belfast. On the day of the launch of *Ulster Monarch*,

Ulster Monarch.

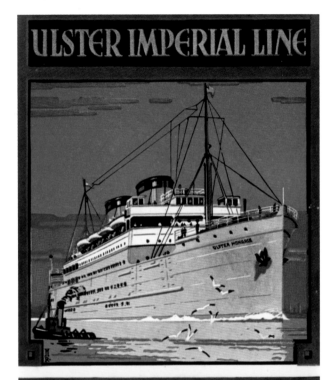

Above and right: 1930s advertisements.

24 January 1929, the Belfast newspaper carried the headline 'Wonder Ship launched by Messrs. Harland & Wolff'. The accompanying article said,

> Yesterday when the Ulster Monarch slipped out from under the great gantries where for month's men and machines have hammered her from an ugly hulk into a creature of beauty, there was no cheer from the crowds which assembled to see her take to the water. It was not an occasion for applause of that sort. Rather was one overpowered by her dignity and majesty as she entered the waters of the Abercom basin, and slowly but proudly settled on an even keel. Even now before she gets her final "polish" she looks, and is a work of art, and will bring nothing but honour to her builders, Messrs. Harland & Wolff.

Following the launch of Ulster Prince on 25 April 1929 the guests were given a trip on *Ulster Monarch* down Belfast Lough.

The three ships later entered service, providing a reliable and regular service on the Liverpool–Belfast route until the outbreak of the Second World War in 1939. *Ulster Prince* was lost at Nauplia in 1941. *Ulster Queen* was requisitioned by the Admiralty as a landing ship infantry and then converted to a fighter direction ship and was broken up at Belgium in 1949. *Ulster Monarch* carried troops to France and became a combined operations ship, taking part in the Norwegian invasion, the Dunkirk evacuation and the occupation of Iceland. She was later fitted with landing craft and participated in the North African landings. She circumnavigated Africa and took part in the Italian campaign. While at Tripoli she was set on fire, was later hit by a torpedo and had a bomb pass through her that failed to explode. She was returned to the Liverpool–Belfast service in 1946, operating with the *Ulster Prince*, which had been built as *Leinster* in 1938. They were both withdrawn in 1966 in preparation for the arrival of the new car ferries *Ulster Prince* and *Ulster Queen* on the route. *Ulster Monarch* was sold to Van Heyghen Freres and broken up at Ghent. It was estimated that during her lifetime she covered nearly 1¼ million miles and carried more than 3½ million passengers.

Royal Scotsman and *Royal Ulsterman* were delivered to the Burns & Laird Lines overnight Glasgow–Belfast service by Harland & Wolff in 1936. They could accommodate 550 First Class and 650 Third Class passengers and were single funnelled and powered by two 8-cylinder B&W oil engines, which produced 10,400 bhp. *Royal Scotsman* was requisitioned by the Admiralty as a landing ship infantry and commissioned as HMS *Royal Scotsman*. She and her sister ship *Royal Ulsterman* were returned to their owners in 1946 and continued to operate on the Glasgow–Belfast route until 1967. *Royal Scotsman* was purchased by L. Ron Hubbard, who used her as a floating college in the Mediterranean. She was later renamed *Apollo* and broken up in Texas in 1984.

Royal Ulsterman operated as a Royal Navy Reserve troop transport, participating in the Dunkirk evacuation and the liberation of the Channel Islands in 1945. She embarked 2,800 troops at St Nazaire on 18 June 1940 and transported them to Falmouth. She carried French personnel to Casablanca, refugees from the Mediterranean to Glasgow and landed 700 troops on Iceland. She was holed in a collision with the destroyer HMS *St Mary's* on 29 August 1941 off the west coast of Scotland, and was sent to the Mersey to be repaired. *Royal Ulsterman* also participated in Operation Torch when she landed United States Army Rangers of the 1st Battalion on the Algerian coast on 8 November 1942. She was attacked by five Luftwaffe aircraft on 14 November while carrying troops from Oran to Algiers but escaped undamaged. She took part in the Sicily Landings in July 1943 and Operation Overlord, the Allied invasion of Normandy, on 6 June 1944. Following her sale by Burns & Laird Lines in 1967 she operated as *Cammell Laird* as an accommodation vessel and was sold to Med-Link Lines Shipping Company Ltd, Cyprus, and renamed *Sounion*.

She sank at Beirut following an explosion on 3 March 1973 and was towed to Piraeus, where she was broken up.

Leinster and *Munster* were introduced in 1937/38 for the Liverpool–Dublin service provided by the British & Irish Steam Packet Company. They were also fitted with B&W oil engines which gave them a speed of 18 knots. On 22 December 1936, the British & Irish Steam Packet was reconstituted when the company, the City of Cork Steam Packet, and Michael Murphy Ltd as well as their interests in the Dundalk & Newry Steam Packet Company, were brought together. Following her delivery in November 1937, *Leinster* was placed on charter to the Belfast Steamship Company while a new passenger terminal was completed at the North Wall, Dublin, the following March. The British & Irish Steam Packet Company also took delivery of the cattle/cargo vessels *Kilkenny*, in 1937, and *Dundalk*, two years later.

The passenger vessel *Riviera* was purchased from the South Eastern & Chatham Railway Company by Burns & Laird Lines in 1932, renamed *Lairds Isle* and placed on the Ardrossan–Belfast route. *Lairdswood*, *Lairdscrest* and *Lairdsbank* were delivered by Harland & Wolff in 1936 for the Heysham–Londonderry and Ardrossan/Ayr–Belfast services, and were designed to carry 290 cattle and 600 tons of cargo. *Killarney* became popular as a cruise ship in the 1930s and sailed from Liverpool to the Western Isles and Hebrides until the outbreak of the Second World War in 1939. The popularity of cruising in coastal cargo vessels declined during this period and *Southern Coast* was sold for further trading; *Hadrian* and *Bernicia* were laid up and sold. *Western Coast*, *Ocean Coast*, *Pacific Coast*, *Atlantic Coast* and *British Coast* continued to provide this service but with a reduced capacity of twelve passengers. Several

Above: Royal Scotsman.

Below: Munster.

Riviera, later *Lairds Isle*.

property acquisitions were made during this time, such as the Atlantic Hotel in Liverpool, another in Stornoway and Carrollstown Estates Ltd.

An agreement was made with the London, Midland & Scottish Railway and the Great Western Railway to work closely together and coordinate the services provided by them all in the Irish Sea trade. At the end of the decade, West Coast Airways (Holdings) Co. Ltd was established, with a capital of £50,000, with the London, Midland & Scottish Railway holding half of the shares, British & Foreign Aviation Ltd with 34½ per cent and Coast Lines and the Great Western Railway with 7¾ per cent each. A standing committee of the railway executives of the railway and coastal liner companies was formed, with Coast Lines Ltd being represented in this group. Unsuccessful attempts were made to take over the Bristol Steam Navigation Company and Palgrave Murphy of Dublin, but the Group did negotiate the takeover of the Belfast, Mersey & Manchester Steamship Company Ltd at the end of the Second

World War in 1945. It was purchased from the joint managing owners, Samuel Lawther & Sons Ltd of Belfast and John J. Mack from Liverpool. The three-ship business of the Belfast, Mersey & Manchester Steamship Company was merged into the Belfast Steamship Company in 1960. Coast Lines Ltd operated a fleet of 127 vessels at the beginning of the Second World War in 1939. Thirty-three of these were lost and five sold. Ten ships were built during the war and seven purchased second-hand. Coast Lines vessels took part in the evacuations of Dunkirk and Brest, the expedition to Norway and the North African, Italian and Normandy campaigns. There were 123 of the company's personnel who received honours and awards for their actions during the war.

The Liverpool shipowners and agents A. Coker & Company Ltd were taken over in 1943 together with R. Gilchrist & Company Ltd. The Tyne Tees Steam Shipping Company followed in 1943 when it became part of the Coast Lines Group. It was formed in 1904, bringing together the Tyne Steam Shipping Company Ltd, the Tees Union Steamship Company Ltd, the Free Trade Wharf Company Ltd and the coastal shipping interests of Furness Withy & Company Ltd. Services were provided from Newcastle and Sunderland to London, Antwerp, Rotterdam, Amsterdam, Dordrecht, Hamburg, Bremen, Ghent and northern French ports. The company also provided services from Middlesbrough to Bremen and Hamburg.

Burns & Laird Lines took delivery of *Lairds Loch* in 1944, which was designed for the Glasgow–Londonderry service. She was initially used to carry cargo but was later modified to enable her to carry forty-eight berthed and 300 passengers in saloons. *Moray Coast* was delivered in 1940 and *Southern Coast* in 1943. The *Leinster* was transferred to the Belfast Steamship Company in 1946, becoming *Ulster Prince* running alongside *Ulster Monarch* on the Liverpool–Belfast service. A new *Leinster* and her sister *Munster* were built by Harland & Wolff for the Liverpool–Dublin route and *Innisfallen* was introduced for the service from Fishguard to Cork.

The Aberdeen Steam Navigation Company Ltd was acquired in 1946. It was established in 1821 to carry livestock, cargo and passengers from Aberdeen to Hull and London. In addition to shipbuilding, John Duffus manufactured engines for steam vessels and traded as the Aberdeen & London Steam Navigation Company with his own ships between Aberdeen and London. The company originally operated sailing ships and the first steamship was introduced in 1827, with a service to Sunderland being introduced in 1837. The service to Hull was discontinued in 1854. The passenger services were operated until 1945 but were discontinued in 1948 following the company's takeover by the Tyne Tees Steam Shipping Company Ltd. The cargo service continued until 1962 after suffering competition from road and rail operators.

On 20 June 1947, the *Lady Killarney* sailed from Liverpool on a cruise programme to the west coast of Scotland and the Hebrides. She had been built as the *Patriotic* for the Belfast Steamship Company by Harland & Wolff, at Belfast. Cruises had been operated by Coast Lines in the 1930s by the *Killarney*, which had been sold to Greek operators following her war-time service. The *Lady Killarney* proved popular as a cruise ship and continued in service until 1956, when she was laid up and broken up at Port Glasgow.

The British Channel Islands Shipping Company Ltd made an application in 1946 for a monopoly of a service between Guernsey, Alderney and Sark. The following year a service was provided by Islands Shipping Company Ltd with *Robina*, *Sark Coast* and *Herm Coast* and an agreement was entered into with the Vectis Shipping Company Ltd for the carriage of cargo between Southampton, Portsmouth and the Isle of Wight.

In 1946, Sir Alfred H. Read, chairman of Coast Lines Ltd wrote,

I hope that the public and the merchants will not forget the good service our ships rendered to them before the war and to the nation during the war, and will continue to support us in the future to enable us to secure our fair share of the transport of the country. An efficient transport system is essential for the prosperity of the nation, and the coastal carriage of goods by sea always has been and should continue to be a cheap and efficient form of transport. We are actively engaged with the operators of other modes of transport in evolving an arrangement whereby all forms of internal transport shall be used to the best advantage of merchants and shippers.

The Zillah Shipping Company Ltd and William A. Savage Ltd were taken over in 1949 and purchased for £450,000. The Zillah Shipping & Carrying Company Ltd dated from 1891, when the steamer *Zillah* was built for the Warrington flatman William Savage. He soon moved to Liverpool where he was able to expand his tramping business. A major share was purchased in Thesen's Steamship Company Ltd of South Africa in 1949. The Norwegian Thesen brothers established the business in 1869 after sailing to the Cape to repair a damaged schooner. The Thesen Line became Thesen's Steamship Company in 1916, but with the opening of the George–Knysna railway line in 1926, and cheaper road and rail charges, the family sold its vessels and the company. It was purchased by the Houston Line and later by Mitchell, Cotts.

The policy of the Coast Lines board at the time was to slowly build up a share-holding in a company they were interested in taking over and gradually become the major investor. It was this strategy that was followed with their interest in Thesen's, which eventually led to them holding the controlling interest in Coast Lines Africa (Pty) Ltd. *Carrick Coast* and *Dorset Coast* were refitted and sent to Cape Town where their names were changed to *Zulu Coast* and *Matabele Coast* respectively. Thesen's other vessels were renamed with the 'Coast' nomenclature. The Hawthorndene Hotel in Cape Town was purchased for use by passengers on Coast Lines Africa (Pty) services. Coast Lines' interest in

Above: Lady Kildare.

Below: Vessels loading at Belfast Harbour.

Coast Lines Group companies in 1947.

this trade was sold to Safmarine in November 1966, when the fleet was merged into Unicorn Shipping Lines of South Africa, a subsidiary of the Durban-based Grindrod Company.

The next ten years was obviously a period of consolidation for the Coast Lines Group as it was not until 1958 that they looked at adding William Sloan & Company Ltd to their portfolio. The company had been formed in 1825 by William Sloan and operated small sailing schooners, including *Glasgow Packet, London Packet, Hope, St Rollox, Charles Tennant, John Tennant, Ann Gibson, Thames, Christina, Countess of Mar* and *James Paxton*. Sloan had joined his uncle, Charles Tennant, in the ownership of the St Rollox Chemical Works, Glasgow. The Glasgow Screw Steam Ship Company offered a service from Glasgow to London in January 1851, with McCallum, Graham & Company as agents. However, William Sloan & Company was soon acting as agents for this service.

In 1858, Sloan started a service from Glasgow to Belfast, Bristol and Swansea, which was later extended to include calls at Newport and Cardiff. He acquired the firm of Robert Henderson & Company of Belfast in 1891, which included the cattle-carrying routes between Silloth, Douglas and Dublin. The passenger service declined and the ships had their passenger accommodation removed early in the 1930s. William Sloan & Company Ltd were taken over by Coast Lines Ltd in 1958, but following competition from rail and road operators, the sailings to the Bristol Channel ceased in 1968 and were succeeded by a daily express unit-load service through Preston. This was operated by Northern Ireland Trailers Ltd, which had been purchased from the British Transport Commission in 1959.

Above: Tay.

Below: Irish Coast (3).

A. Coker & Company Ltd was disposed of in 1951 for £12,000, with an agreement from its three directors not to engage in any activity for ten years that would compete with Coast Lines services. Captain A. R. S. Nutting succeeded Sir Alfred Read as chairman of the company in 1950, and together with the board, authorised the refinancing of the company by the Hambros Bank to cover the costs of a ship replacement programme. Consequently, it was decided to borrow £500,000 from the Ship Mortgage Finance Company Ltd at 4¾ per cent rate of interest. *Irish Coast* was built at a cost of £816,000 as a relief ship for the Irish Sea services. A second fleet replacement programme took place from 1953 with *Herero Coast* joining the fleet from Thesen's, *Cheshire Coast*, *Lancashire Coast*, *Western Coast*, *Essex Coast*, *Fife Coast* and *Cambrian Coast*. *Sandringham Queen* was delivered to the Queenship Navigation Ltd in 1955, and *Ulster Pioneer* and *Ulster Premier* to the Belfast Steamship Company the same year. *Somerset Coast* was delivered in 1958 at a cost of £227,500.

The passenger service from Liverpool to Dublin had commenced again in 1946 with *Longford* and *Louth*. However, within two years the new *Leinster* and *Munster* were delivered and *Innisfallen* for the Fishguard–Cork route. The cargo vessels *Glengariff*, *Inniscarra* and *Wicklow* were transferred to the British & Irish steam Packet Company in the 1950s.

It was at this time that the Atlantic Steam Navigation Company Ltd provided some worrying competition to Coast Lines services. They were operating a war-built Landing Ship Tank (LST) from Preston to Larne, and by the end of the decade were planning to introduce new purpose-built roll on/roll off vessels to the service. A strike by Irish seamen in 1951 affected the profitability of the services at the time, and the Coast Lines board looked at the possibility of a link with the Atlantic Steam Navigation Company. However, it was decided to provide a joint container service between Preston and Drogheda with *Noach*, in

Wicklow (2).

Link Line colours, and *Stream Fisher*, chartered by the Atlantic Steam Navigation Company from James Fisher & Sons Ltd.

Coastal Airways Ltd was established in 1955 with Hunting Clan Air Transport Ltd and Elder Dempster & Company Ltd, with Coast Lines having a third interest. Coast Lines had also taken an interest in John Foreman Ltd, Coastal Roadways Ltd, British Polar Engines Ltd, British Wheeler Process Ltd, the Piel & Walney Gravel Company Ltd and the Ardrossan Trawling Company Ltd. It was also decided to provide bulk oil storage at Liverpool docks for mineral and vegetable oils.

Scottish Coast was delivered in 1957 and operated on the Burns & Laird Lines service from Glasgow to Belfast or Dublin. She was also engaged on the daylight summer service from Ardrossan to Belfast, replacing *Lairds Isle*. In 1958, the two Zillah ships *Birchfield* and *Brentfield* were converted into unit-load vessels and renamed *Pointer* and *Spaniel* respectively for a service between Liverpool and Belfast. These were followed by two new purpose-built vessels, *Buffalo* and *Bison*, in 1961/62. A Liverpool–Londonderry via Portrush, and a Manchester–Belfast service were also provided. Vessels were placed on the Ardrossan–Belfast service to convey containers, lorries, trailers and flats.

In 1959 the Coast Lines Group owned 102 ships, including eleven passenger ships, thirteen cargo/livestock carriers and seventy-eight cargo ships. Coast Lines took control of the North of Scotland, Orkney & Shetland Shipping Company Ltd in November 1961. The company had been established in 1875 to operate services from Scotland to the Orkney and Shetland islands. In 1820, the Leith & Clyde Shipping Company joined with the Aberdeen, Dundee & Leith Shipping Company to form the Aberdeen, Leith, Clyde & Tay Shipping Company. Their fleet of sailing ships operated initially to Glasgow, Edinburgh, London, Rotterdam and Liverpool. Their first steamer, *Velocity*, competed with the *Tourist*, which operated between Leith and Aberdeen. Their services were extended to Wick in 1833 and to Kirkwall and Lerwick in 1836. The company became the North of Scotland, Orkney & Shetland Steam Navigation Company in 1975.

The Clyde Shipping Company's Belfast–London business was acquired in 1961 and Irish Road Ferry Services Ltd was established by renaming the former Dundalk & Newry Steam Packet Company Ltd. Ulster Ferry Transport Ltd was taken over in 1962 and Anglo-Irish Transport Ltd

Cheshire Coast at Leith.

Above: Left to right: *Irish Coast* (3), *Ulster Monarch, Kilkenny, Meath* (3) and *Munster* (2) at Princes Dock, Liverpool.

Left: *Irish Coast* was advertised to undertake six thirteen-day cruises from Liverpool, commencing 7 June 1957. However, records show that she was relieving *Ulster Monarch* on the Liverpool–Belfast service until 28 July, and she then replaced *Lairds Isle* on the Ardrossan–Belfast service on 7 August. In September that year, she was operating on the Glasgow–Belfast route while *Scottish Coast* was receiving her overhaul, and was employed on relief sailings on other Coast Line services from October to April 1958.

Innisfallen (2) taken from the bridge of *Irish Coast* (3) in Princes Dock, Liverpool.

Hibernian Coast approaching the Needles on 11 June 1961.

in 1964. In March 1962, the company set up the Liverpool Road Haulage Board, which covered the services provided by Thomas Allan Ltd, Liverpool Cartage Company Ltd, John Foreman Ltd, A. S. Jones & Company Ltd, Northern Ireland Trailers Ltd and James Hemphill Ltd, which had been acquired in 1960. Another board was also set up, which reported to the main executive board.

Eurofreight Ltd was formed by the Tyne Tees Steam Shipping Company in 1960 to provide express container services to the Continent with John Forman Ltd. Dent's Wharf was purchased from T. Roddam Dent & Sons Ltd at Middlesbrough. Vessels loaded at Newcastle Quayside and Hillgate Wharf, Gateshead, Sunderland and Middlesbrough to London, Bremen, Hamburg, Amsterdam, Rotterdam, Dordrecht, Antwerp, Ghent, Dunkirk, Calais, Boulogne, Le Havre, Cherbourg and the Channel Islands ports. By 1967 the fleet was reduced to five vessels, with only *Yorkshire Coast* and *Stormont* remaining the following year. The services of the Tyne Tees Steam Shipping Company were finally closed down in 1976.

Link Line (Continental) operated under the control of the Tyne Tees Steam Shipping Company to offer economical transport for large containers, lift-vans, Lancashire flats, trailers and portable tanks between Newcastle and Rotterdam. The *Frisian Coast* was converted to carry containers and flats and sailed from the Tyne to Rotterdam on her inaugural voyage on 21 November 1963.

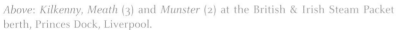

Above: *Kilkenny*, *Meath* (3) and *Munster* (2) at the British & Irish Steam Packet berth, Princes Dock, Liverpool.

Above right: *Leinster* (2) and *Ulster Prince* (3) in Princes Dock, Liverpool.

Below right: *Lancashire Coast* (3) sails to Belfast from the Waterloo Dock entrance, Liverpool.

The unit-load cargo ship *Buffalo* was launched at the yard of the Ardrossan Dockyard Company on 2 May 1961. She was specially designed to carry vehicles and container cargo between Liverpool and Belfast. *Buffalo* was the twenty-seventh ship built at the Ardrossan Dockyard for the Coast Lines Group. She was designed to carry vehicles in the large hold and the tween deck was built throughout the length, so vehicles carrying very high loads could be accommodated at the forward end. The decks were specially strengthened to carry container cargo, and by omitting the athwart-ship bulkhead they could be carried in the hold and tween deck. She was fitted with MacGregor hatch covers operated by two 3-ton electrically driven winches. At her launch, Coast Lines stated that the decision to build the ship followed the success of the Link Line service which began in 1959. *Buffalo* was followed by the *Bison*, which was built by Charles Hill & Son Ltd at Bristol.

The steamships *Ulster Herdsman* and *Glengariff* were sold in 1963. Agreements had been made covering the transportation of coal to the Republic and Northern Ireland with Cawood, Wharton & Company Ltd. Coast Lines Republic of Ireland's coal interest involved Tedcastle, McCormick & Company Ltd and the Dublin General Steam Shipping Company Ltd, joint owners of the shares in Michael Murphy Ltd. The Ardrossan Dockyard Ltd was sold in 1962 and the *Wirral Coast* was delivered by Cammell Laird of Birkenhead. At the launch of *Wirral Coast* on 17 July 1962, Arnet Robinson, vice chairman and managing director of Coast Lines, mentioned that his company were engaged in some trades in direct competition with land routes that could not stand increased prices in costs and may not be able to justify replacing an existing ship with a new vessel, as there would be no expectation of earning even the depreciation. He added that, 'Since costs have risen even further, which means that some of our trades will have to get more revenue or the services will have to be withdrawn'. The traditional general cargo service between the Mersey and Newry, which had operated since the middle of the nineteenth century, ended on 4 April 1964. It was replaced by a unit-load service operating three times weekly in each direction between Liverpool and Newry. *Inniscarra* was converted to carry containers, flats and trailers and a new loading bay and 25-ton crane were installed at the port of Newry.

The British & Irish Steam Packet introduced special winter weekend fares on the Liverpool–Dublin route early in 1964. These allowed passengers to travel out on a Friday evening and return on Monday. Day return fares were also introduced, which enabled passengers to travel out on a Friday night and return on Saturday. The company had trailed the fares the previous November and they had proved popular, especially for Irish people working in England who wanted to go home for the weekend. The company said that, 'At this time of year the passenger ships are comparatively quiet so we are able to offer this concession which is not practicable during the peak summer months.'

Glengariff approaches Woodside Landing Stage in 1961.

Above: Wirral Coast.

Right: Coast Lines Seaway advert.

The *Caledonian Coast* and *Hibernian Coast* provided cruises from London to Liverpool from the beginning of May until the end of September in the 1960s. One ship departed from East India Dock, London, every Friday afternoon, while the other left East Trafalgar Dock, Liverpool, every Friday or Saturday before noon. Depending on cargo commitments, the ship would also call at a south coast port or Dublin, and occasionally Cork on the return trip. H. H. Fry described a cruise he had taken in 1964:

The food, which can make or mar a holiday, is excellent. Plenty of it, very well cooked and tastefully served:

0730 hrs	Cup of tea and biscuits.
0830 hrs	Breakfast.
1100 hrs	Coffee and biscuits.
1300 hrs	Four-course lunch.
1600 hrs	Tea.
1900 hrs	Five-course dinner.
2200 hrs	Tea and sandwiches.

The cost of the cruise was £26 5s, £57 10s for the round voyage for a single cabin or £23 5s for a single cruise, £50.15s for a round voyage in a double berth cabin.

Captain A. R. S. Nutting, the chairman of Coast Lines Ltd, died in March 1964. He had held the role since 1950 and was educated at Eton and Trinity Hall, Cambridge. He served with the Irish Guards in the

Above: Cars loading onto *Ulster Prince* (2) at Princes Landing Stage, Liverpool.

Below: *Hibernian Coast*.

First World War, was military assistant to the Chief of the Imperial General Staff in the Second World War and was awarded the OBE for his services. A former governor of the Bank of Ireland, he was chairman of several companies and a director of companies in the Coast Lines Group. Sir Arnet Robinson was appointed chairman of Coast lines Ltd and retained his executive responsibilities.

At the fifty-first annual general meeting of Coast Lines in 1964, the trading profit of the company amounted to £1,059,269, which was an increase of £44,408 over the result for the previous year. The net profit amounted to £743,438, as compared to £686,891 for the year 1962. The total number of vessels owned by the Group at the end of 1963 was eighty-eight, of which fifteen were passenger ships, eleven cargo/livestock carriers and sixty-two cargo vessels. *Swazi Coast* was built specifically for the South African trade and was completed at the end of the year. Chairman Sir Arnet Robinson noted that,

> The passenger services were reasonably supported, but there are signs that the numbers travelling by sea, particularly First Class, are likely to be smaller than in previous years. The steps we took to cater for additional numbers of passengers cars met with a good response and we are continuing our efforts to provide for this important movement.

At the end of 1964 Coast Lines announced changes in the itineraries of vessels on the Portrush and Londonderry unit-load services. From 2 November the two services were amalgamated and both operated to and from Preston. The direct sea service between Liverpool and Portrush ceased after the sailing from Liverpool on 30 October. The combined services were as follows: Preston and Londonderry – four sailings weekly in each direction. Preston to Portrush – two sailings weekly (Monday and Thursday). Portrush to Preston, two sailings weekly (Tuesday and Friday), with extra sailings as required.

Leinster (2) in dry dock at Liverpool.

Sark Coast (2) at Liverpool.

Munster (2) laid up in Morpeth Dock following her final sailing.

At the beginning of 1965 it was announced that from 1 July until 28 August, *Scottish Coast* would operate a daylight car ferry service between Ardrossan and Belfast. A 'drive-on' ramp on the vessel would facilitate the loading and discharge of motor vehicles, and there would be accommodation for twenty-five vehicles aboard as well as passengers. She would leave Montgomerie Pier at 9:15 a.m., arriving at Donegall Quay, Belfast, six hours later. She would return at 3:15 p.m. daily, arriving at Ardrossan at 8 p.m.

In 1965, the board of Coast Lines Ltd announced that it had entered into an agreement with the Government of the Republic of Ireland for the sale to the government of the whole of the issued share capital of the British & Irish Steam Packet Company Ltd (B&I), a wholly owned subsidiary of

Coast Lines, less certain assets not directly related to the shipping services of the B&I. The British & Irish Steam Packet, together with its subsidiary the City of Cork Steam Packet Company Ltd, had a fleet of nine ships with a total gross registered tonnage of 17,545 tons. All of the ships sailed under the Irish flag, and the two companies operated shipping services for many years on the trunk routes between the Republic of Ireland and Great Britain. Coast Lines Ltd continued to act as agents in Britain.

After allowing for the transfer to Coast Lines of the assets and the re-payment of inter-group loans, the net amount received by Coast Lines under the agreement was £2,750,000. In the negotiations with the government, the board had the benefit of the advice of Baring Brothers & Company Ltd, who supported it with its advice that the transaction was in

Above: *Scottish Coast* (2) was sold in 1969 and renamed *Galaxias*, operating cruises on the Mediterranean.

Above right: The new B+I car ferry *Leinster* (3) sails from Langton Lock, Liverpool.

Below right: *Munster* (3) sails from Liverpool on her maiden voyage on 15 May 1968.

the best interests of the Coast Lines Group. The new management of the B&I Line instigated a programme of modernisation and fleet replacement. *Leinster*, *Munster* and *Innisfallen* were sold and replaced by new roll on/roll off car ferries for the Liverpool–Dublin and a new Cork–Swansea route.

A road-sea cargo assembly depot was established at Hope Street, Salford, as one of a number of similar centres being developed throughout Britain for the purpose of bulking merchandise into containers or other forms of unit-loads, which would then be transported by road and sea to Ireland.

The vessels of Queenship Navigation Ltd were disposed of and the company ceased to trade. The staff were transferred to other units in the Group in London. *Norwave*, the first vessel owned by North Sea Ferries Ltd, was launched from the yard of A. G. Weser, West Seebeck, Bremerhaven, on 2 July 1965. She was named by Mrs D. L. J. Mortelman, wife of the chairman of the General Steam Navigation Company Ltd who, with the Tyne Tees Steam Shipping Company Ltd, were the British partners in the consortium. She was registered in Hull to maintain a service between Rotterdam (Europort) and Hull, with a sister ship, *Norwind*.

The service operated initially with three sailings a week from the King George V Dock at Hull to Rotterdam (Europort) in 1965, developing to a daily service the following year. It was a partnership between two British, two Dutch and two German concerns to operate roll-on/roll-off services for cars, coaches and freight vehicles. The maximum capacity of each vessel was 200 cars, or sixty-five trailers and twenty-five cars, while 240 passengers were accommodated in berths and seats. The berth at Rotterdam, covering an area of 16 acres, was specially built. In addition to the parking area, a customs and handling shed and an office block were provided. A berth was constructed at Hull by the British Transport Docks board, with similar facilities and equipment to that at Rotterdam. Tyne Tees Steam Shipping Company Ltd retained its share in North Sea Ferries until the Coast Lines

Group were taken over by P&O in October 1972. Companies within the Coast Lines Group also maintained unit-load sea services between Preston–Larne, Preston–Londonderry, Preston–Newry and Ardrossan–Larne.

Munster was delivered to the B&I Line from the Nobiskrug yard in Rendsburg and sailed on her maiden voyage from Liverpool to Dublin on 15 May 1968. *Innisfallen* inaugurated the new route between Cork and Swansea and *Leinster* was the first ferry to be built in the Republic of Ireland. She cost £2,500,000 and her delivery by the Verolme Cork shipyard marked the full implementation of the Line's £10,000,000 plan of investing in new ferries and terminals. A new ferryport was built at Dublin on reclaimed land to accommodate the new car ferries, and was able to unload and load a ship in less than an hour. The other terminals at Cork and Swansea were soon operational, but a temporary terminal at Carriers Dock, Liverpool, was used prior to the opening of one at Canada Dock. In her first seven months of operation, *Munster* carried 37,500 cars and 175,000 passengers in addition to a considerable quantity of freight.

Dorset Coast was converted to a container ship in 1966 and was chartered to British Rail to operate on the Folkestone–Boulogne service. In October 1965, Coast Lines sold the tramping interests of the Queenship Navigation Ltd to Watts, Watts & Company Ltd and the Britain Steamship Company. The Zillah Shipping Company was sold outright to Coast Lines in 1967; two ships were sold and six others were transferred to Coast Lines routes and services. The Channel Islands trade of the British Channel Islands Shipping Company was transferred to a unit-load service via Newhaven in 1966. Two years later this was transferred to the Commodore Shipping Company Ltd, who purchased the subsidiary in 1969, together with the unit-load assets of Thomas Allen Ltd.

Ulster Prince and *Ulster Queen* entered service on the Belfast Steamship Company's Liverpool–Belfast route in 1967, and the *Lion* sailed on her maiden voyage from Ardrossan to Belfast early the following year.

LIVERPOOL
DAILY POST
COAST LINES SUPPLEMENT
WEDNESDAY, APRIL 19, 1967

Bon voyage!

TONIGHT, the new BELFAST STEAMSHIP CO. LIMITED ferry ship ULSTER PRINCE sails from LIVERPOOL to BELFAST on her maiden voyage and so inaugurates the first ever passenger and drive-on/drive-off ferry between the two cities. Soon she will be joined by ULSTER QUEEN, and together they will operate every weeknight and, additionally, every Sunday during the period 9th July—17th September.

Whether travelling on business or on holiday, First or Second Class, this is the overnight route for the discerning passenger from city centre to city centre. De Luxe suites, cabins and sleeping berths, lounges, restaurants, cafeterias and bars.

If you are not taking your car, there are now fast electric train connections between Liverpool, London and the Midlands.

And remember, there are NO CURRENCY RESTRICTIONS in travelling to and from Northern Ireland.

Above: *Belfast Steamship Company car ferry brochure, 1968.*

Right: *Liverpool Daily Post*, Coast Lines supplement, 19 April 1967.

CAMMELL LAIRD AND COMPANY (Shipbuilders & Engineers) LIMITED.

Launch of

M. V. "ULSTER QUEEN"

on

THURSDAY 1st December 1966 at 12-15 p.m.

ADMIT ONE TO SHIPYARD

GREEN LANE ENTRANCE ONLY

FOR CONDITIONS SEE BACK.

---

71. BELFAST STEAMSHIP CO. LTD. 14

SPECIAL EXCURSION TICKET

M.V. ST. CLAIR

ABERDEEN to LIVERPOOL

Depart Aberdeen SUNDAY, 8th FEBRUARY, 1970

FARE (including use of Berth) - £7 0s 0d

CONDITIONS OF CARRIAGE

Passengers, vehicles and luggage are only carried subject to the Company's Standard Conditions of Carriage as exhibited in the Company's offices and on board their ships. All sailings are subject to alteration or cancellation without prior notice. Fares and rates subject to revision.

Link Line and Ulster Ferry Transport Ltd became Ulster Ferry Link Line Ltd in 1969. Northern Ireland Trailers (Scotland) Ltd was established in 1968 and began operations from a new depot at Polmadie, Glasgow. The company ran a fleet of road vehicles and equipment, catering primarily to the door-to-door movement of traffic in containers, flats or pallets between all parts of Scotland and Ireland. Northern Ireland Trailers Ltd, with headquarters at Albert Edward Dock, Preston, also operated from depots at London, Bristol, Stoke-on-Trent, Liverpool, Belfast and Larne. The road transport organisation moved well in excess of 1,000 tons of cargo every twenty-four hours. In 1967 Link Line Ltd was operated by Coast Lines and was absorbed into the road haulage business of the Liverpool Cartage Company Ltd. In addition to Link Line Ltd and Northern Ireland Trailers Ltd operations, another associated company, Ulster Ferry Transport Ltd and its subsidiary Leinster Ferry Transport, offered similar facilities. A. S. Jones & Company was engaged in the transport of bulk liquids, powders and gases and provided transport for these commodities in demountable tanks.

Companies within the Coast Lines Group also maintained unit-load sea services between Preston–Larne, Preston–Londonderry, Preston–Newry and Ardrossan–Larne. At the annual general meeting of Coast Lines Ltd in September 1968, Chairman Sir Arnet Robinson emphasised that radical changes in methods of operations involved time and expense,

Above: *Cammell Laird* launch ticket for *Ulster Queen* (2) on 1 December 1966.

Below: Special Coastal Cruising Association excursion for a positioning voyage from Aberdeen to Liverpool on *St Clair* (3). She sailed from Aberdeen at 1.00 a.m. on 8 February 1970 and spent the following day cruising around the Scottish coast. *St Clair* arrived at the Waterloo entrance on 10 February and berthed in Princes Dock, Liverpool, at noon.

and that in some cases the full benefits do not accrue immediately. He said that it was one of the difficulties of reorganising and expanding a group of companies, but in the case of Coast Lines the operation was being carried out with the minimum of interference to the Group's operation. He emphasised his confidence that 'substantial improvements would be achieved in 1969, barring unforeseen circumstances'.

At the annual general meeting on 24 July 1969, the board reported a trading profit for the year 1968 amounting to £747,178, compared to £229,721 the previous year. After taxation (including £75,384 in respect of prior years and the increased rate for corporation tax and the interest of minority shareholders) the net profit attributable to Coast Lines Ltd was £482,859. This was largely absorbed by the cost of dividends on the Cumulative Preference Stocks and the first interim dividend of 7½ per cent, which was paid in January 1969 on the ordinary stock.

The board also reported that they would continue the reorganisation of certain trades in line with developments in the movement of traffic in unit loads, and this meant the closure of some long established shipping services and the setting up of more road transport depots. They reported that the service from Ardrossan to Belfast using the *Lion* was well supported and that they were optimistic for the future. The conventional cargo service operated by Burns & Laird Lines between Glasgow and Londonderry, and also between Glasgow and Belfast, was terminated. Alternative arrangements were made by Northern Ireland Trailers (Scotland) Ltd to unitise traffic formally passing by these services at the new Polmadie depot, and to forward it by the shipping services between Ardrossan/Larne and Belfast.

Above: *Ulster Queen* (2).

Below: *Lion* and *Scottish Coast* (2) at Belfast.

It was stated that the passenger and car services between Liverpool and Belfast had a satisfactory year and the building of the ships *Ulster Queen* and *Ulster Prince* had been fully justified. A new award-winning passenger terminal at Donegall Quay, Belfast, was opened to service both car-ferry services from Liverpool and from Ardrossan, and improvements were made to the passenger terminal at South West Princes Dock, Liverpool. The meeting was told that the road haulage activities continued to expand and had a successful year. A. S. Jones & Company Ltd had opened a new depot at Bromborough, incorporating modern workshop and tank cleaning equipment. Both Northern Ireland Trailers Ltd and Ulster Ferry Transport Ltd, together with its subsidiary Leinster Ferry Transport Ltd, had leased additional land at Preston Docks. Ulster Ferry Transport had also developed a 2½-acre site there as a marshalling area with offices and lifting facilities.

John Forman Ltd had acquired sites at both Hull and Middlesbrough and it was anticipated that these would be developed in 1969, probably in conjunction with the Group's other road transport activities. Thomas Allen Ltd and James Hemphill Ltd had continued to operate successfully. Further developments were taking place in the field of commercial unit-load services and it was considered that there would be expansion in this sector through the new depots being developed at Hull, Middlesbrough and Felixstowe. Henry Smither & Son Ltd had been reconstituted to provide a road haulage service to the Overseas Containers Ltd Depot at Orsett and OCL had taken a 20 per cent interest in that company. It was noted that there was considerable pressure in the road haulage industry to increase drivers' basic rates of pay and Group subsidiaries were affected by strike action in London, Hull, Middlesbrough and Merseyside and these stoppages caused considerable shortfalls in operating revenue to a number of companies. However, the Group had been able to negotiate a number of successful productivity deals with the trade unions.

Chairman K. W. C. Grand stated that,

When we announced our second Interim Dividend in May, 1968 we indicated that we hoped to be able to return to a Group trading profit level of about £1 ¼ million in 1969. At the end of April, our trading results were, in fact ahead of forecast. Unfortunately, during May, labour disputes caused some stoppages, particularly in Liverpool where our shipping services were halted for a time. This affected the earnings not only of the shipping companies operating from Liverpool, but also the road transport companies linked to them.

He hoped that given 'reasonable trading conditions and freedom from industrial disputes that the Group would obtain the target figure mentioned above.' *ASD Meteor* was chartered in February 1973 to be employed on the Belfast–Heysham joint service.

In February 1971, an offer of £5.6 million in deferred stock was made by the P&O Steam Navigation Company Ltd for Coast Lines Ltd. This was accepted by the board with Coast Lines and the General Steam Navigation Company Ltd becoming P&O Short Sea Shipping in February 1971, and later P&O Ferries. *Bison* and *Buffalo* were transferred from the Belfast–Liverpool service to North Sea Ferries' Hull–Rotterdam route. *Norbrae*, the former *Buffalo*, was later placed on P&O's London Continental services as *Roe Deer*. *Spaniel* and *Pointer* were employed on the unit load service from Liverpool to Belfast and were registered in the name of the Belfast Steamship Company Ltd. However, the service was closed in 1973.

Donautal and *Isartal* were chartered to the Belfast Steamship Company from 1970 and were purchased by P&O in 1977. *Donautal* became *St Magnus* and *Isartal* was renamed *Pointer* for the Ardrossan–Belfast route. This arrangement was the first time that the Belfast Steamship Company had chartered a foreign flag vessel in peacetime. *Donautal* operated between Donegall Quay at Belfast and South Nelson Dock,

Ulster Prince (3) in the Mersey awaiting the departure of Munster (3) from Waterloo Dock.

Viking Trader (1977/3,809 grt) at Fleetwood. She became Leopard in 1996, European Navigator in 1998, Black Iris in 2003 and Black Horses in 2012. She was broken up in 2014.

Liverpool. She was purchased in 1974, becoming Ulster Sportsman, and was the last vessel to be registered by the Belfast Steamship Company Ltd. However, the service was brief as she was taken on a bare-boat charter by Truck Lines for their Poole services in 1976. Her sister, Saaletal, was chartered in 1971 for the Ardrossan–Belfast route but was soon operating on a new service from Belfast to Heysham, jointly with British Rail.

ASD Meteor was chartered in February 1973 to be employed on the Belfast–Heysham joint service.

The Belfast Steamship Company and Burns & Laird Lines were amalgamated as Belfast Steamship Company, and the Tyne Tees Steam Shipping Company continued to provide a service from Newcastle to the Continent with Stormont until 1976. Ferrymasters chartered the Embdena for the Preston–Londonderry service and she was renamed British Unit. She was purchased by the Belfast Steamship Company Ltd in 1973 and renamed Ulster Merchant. Ferrymasters also introduced a new Fleetwood–Larne service and Bison and Buffalo were placed on the route under the Pandoro name. The Preston–Londonderry route was closed down in July 1975 and the goodwill of the Warrenpoint services was sold to the Coastal Container Group in June 1977.

The Belfast Steamship Company and Burns & Laird Lines became P&O Ferries Irish Sea Services from 1 October 1975. Ulster Prince and Ulster Queen were painted in P&O colours during their overhauls in

1976 with 'P&O Ferries' painted on their hulls. It was announced on 30 October 1975 that *Lion* would be withdrawn from the Ardrossan–Belfast service, and she was later introduced on P&O's route from Dover to Boulogne. *Union Melbourne* was chartered for the Pandoro service and was renamed *Puma* for the Liverpool–Larne service.

P&O continued to operate the Belfast–Liverpool passenger service and were planning to replace *Ulster Prince* and *Ulster Queen* with larger vessels. Attempts were made to advertise the passenger vessels in 1980 by offering special fares and offers. In 1981, the National Union of Seamen lodged a claim for a 16 per cent increase in wages, and this was followed by a series of stoppages on the passenger vessels. The ships were occupied by union members and services were brought to a halt. Soon after the resumption of services, efforts were made to obtain some form of assistance from the government for the construction of replacement vessels and new port facilities at Belfast and Liverpool. The company also made attempts to negotiate new working arrangements with the trade unions and looked at ways in which economies could be made in the operation of the ships. At the beginning of October 1981, it was announced that the Belfast–Liverpool service would close on the 12th of that month. However, the closure was postponed until 11 November and early that month the crew of both passenger vessels held a 'sit in' at Liverpool and all sailings were cancelled. Staff working for Pandoro came out in sympathy and sailings from Ardrossan and Aberdeen were also affected. The occupation of the vessels ended in early December and both ships were sent to Ostend and were later sold.

On 19 January 1987, P&O took over the European Ferries Group who were trading as Townsend Thoresen. The Group operated services from Dover, Portsmouth, Felixstowe and Cairnryan, and also included the ports of Felixstowe and Larne in Northern Ireland. The services were renamed P&O European Ferries on 22 October and operated routes

Saint Colum (1) (1973/5,285 grt) operated on Belfast Car Ferries' service from Liverpool to Belfast from 1982 to 1990.

from Dover, Felixstowe and Portsmouth. In 1997, P&O became the sole owner of North Sea Ferries and the Group was later divided into P&O Portsmouth, P&O North Sea and a joint venture between P&O and the Stena Line, as P&O Stena Line, in Dover. In August 2002, P&O acquired Stena Line's 40 per cent share of P&OSL and it was merged with the Portsmouth and North Sea operations under the P&O Ferries Ltd brand. The Zeebrugge service was closed in 2002 and the Fleetwood–Larne route was sold to the Stena Line Group in 2004, together with the *European Leader*, *European Pioneer* and *European Seafarer*. An experimental Mostyn–Dublin service had been introduced but this was closed in 2004.

The Irish Government had privatised the British & Irish Steam Packet in 1995 as Irish Ferries Ltd, and it was sold to a consortium

Above: *Mersey Viking* (1997/21,856 grt) and *Lagan Viking* (1997/21,856 grt) on Norse-Merchant Ferries' service from Liverpool to Belfast.

Above right: P&O's *Norbank* (1993/17,464 grt) and *European Leader* (1975/3,484 grt) in the River Mersey.

Below right: *Stena Mersey* (2005/27,510 grt) arriving at Twelve Quays, Birkenhead, from Belfast in 2015.

of P&O, Maersk Line and some other parties. In 2004, P&O decided to close several of its Portsmouth routes, and on 15 January 2010, the company announced that it would cease operations on the Portsmouth–Bilbao service. P&O branded the services from Scotland to Orkney and the Shetland Islands as P&O Ferries until 1989, when the name was changed to P&O Scottish Ferries. From 2002 the routes were operated by Northlink Orkney & Shetland Ferries, and Northlink Ferries Ltd from 2006. Following a re-tendering process, the Serco Group was awarded the contract to operate the service from 5 July 2012.

In March 2006, P&O Ferries, P&O Estates and P&O Maritime Services were sold to Dubai World. On 8 August 2008, the company placed an order for two new ships for the Dover–Calais service. They were named *Spirit of Britain* and *Spirit of France* and are the largest ferries operating in the English Channel. *Spirit of Britain* entered service on 21 January 2011, and *Spirit of France* on 9 February the following year. In 2015, P&O Ferries operate services from Dover to Calais, Hull to Rotterdam and Zeebrugge, Liverpool to Dublin and Larne to Troon and Cairnryan.

Above: Irish Ferries' *Ulysses* (2001/50,938 grt) operates on the Dublin–Holyhead service.

Below: Representative vessels from the fleets of Coast Lines and associated companies. 1. *Lairds Oak*, 2. *Freshfield*, 3. *Saxon Queen*, 4. *British Coast*, 5. *Matabele Coast*, 6. *Inniscarra*, 7. *Rowanfield*, 8. *Channel Coast*, 9. *Adriatic Coast*, 10. *Iberian Coast*, 11. *Dundalk*, 12. *Cheshire Coast*, 13. *Ulster Weaver*, 14. *Northumbrian Coast*, 15. *Fife Coast*, 16. *Hadrian Coast*, 17. *Brookmount*, 18. *Lairdsglen*, 19. *Jersey Coast*, 20. *Balmoral Queen*, 21. *Brentfield*, 22. *Innisfallen*, 23. *Ulster Prince*, 24. *Irish Coast*, 25. *Munster*, 26. *Royal Scotsman*, 27. *Ulster Premier*, 28. *Lairds Loch*, 29. *Caledonian Coast*, 30. *Netherlands Coast*, 31. *Kilkenny*.

FLEET LIST

1. *Devon Coast* (1909) O.N. 128001

782 grt   59.43 × 9.14 m

B. W. Harkess & Son Ltd, Middlesbrough. Yard No. 179.

Single screw, triple expansion, steam engine.

31.8.1909   Launched as *Graceful* for the British & Continental Steam Ship Company Ltd (F. H. Powell & Company as managers), Liverpool.

1910   Renamed *Devon Coast* for F. H. Powell & Company Ltd.

1913   Powell, Bacon & Hough Lines Ltd, Liverpool.

1917   Coast Lines Ltd, Liverpool.

1934   Sold to Brook Shipping Company Ltd (Comben Longstaff & Company Ltd as managers), London. Renamed *Devonbrook*.

1937   Owned by Cia de Navegação Norte Sul, Rio de Janeiro. Renamed *Sao Pedro*.

1943   Cia Comércio de Navegação, Rio de Janeiro.

1952   Broken up at Rio de Janeiro.

2. *Monmouth Coast* (1906) O.N. 124007

874 grt   64.5 × 10.16 × 4.22 m

B. W. Harkess & Son Ltd, Middlesbrough. Yard No. 167.

Single screw, triple expansion, steam engine, 149 nhp, 3 cylinder. By Richardsons, Westgarth & Company, Middlesbrough. 11 knots.

2/10/1906   Launched as *Faithful* for F. H. Powell & Company Ltd, Liverpool.

1914   Renamed *Monmouth Coast* for Coast Lines, Liverpool. (Powell, Bacon & Hough, Liverpool).

1919   Sold to Miller Steam Ship Company Ltd (W. H. Miller as managers), Hull. Same name.

1921   Sold to Soc. Geral De Comércio, Industria E. Transporte, Lisbon, Portugal. Renamed *Silva Gouveia*.

23.12.1927   On a voyage from Hamburg to Oporto she was wrecked at Paya Rostro Peton Pardas near Cabo Toriñana.

3. *Somerset Coast* (1911) O.N. 131401

1,149 grt   76.3 × 11 × 4.4 m

B. Sir Raylton Dixon & Company Ltd, Middlesbrough. Yard No. 565.

Single screw, triple expansion, steam engine, 178 nhp. By builder.

1911   Built as *Graceful* for F. H. Powell & Company Ltd, Liverpool.

1913   Renamed *Somerset Coast* for Coast Lines Ltd.

21.4.1917   On a voyage carrying general cargo from Bristol to Liverpool she was in collision with the *Sound Fisher* and sank 1½ miles west-south-west of Bardsey Light.

4. *Eastern Coast* (1903) O.N. 118034

1,607 grt   860 nrt   2,125 dwt   82.4 × 11 × 5.88 m

B. Swan Hunter & Company Ltd, Walker. Yard No. 404.

Single screw, triple expansion engine, 238 nhp, 3 cylinder. By Wigham, Richardson & Company Ltd, Walker. 13 knots.

Passengers: Fifty First Class.

25.7.1903   Launched as *Powerful* for F. H. Powell & Company Ltd, Liverpool.

1914   Renamed *Eastern Coast* for Coast Lines Ltd (Powell, Bacon & Hough Ltd, Liverpool).

1919   Sold to the British Hispano Line Ltd, London, renamed *Perez*.

1920   Sold to the Harken Steam Ship Company Ltd (Davies, David & Daniel Ltd as managers), renamed *Eaton Grove*.

1923   Purchased by the Standard Fruit Company (Vaccaro Brothers & Company Ltd, Honduras, as managers). Became *Algeria*.

1924   Owned by the Mexican American Fruit Steam Ship Corporation, La Ceiba, Honduras. Same name.

1925   Owners restyled American Fruit Steam Ship Corporation (Standard Fruit & Steam Ship Corporation as managers).

1934   Sold to the Seaboard Steam Ship Corporation, La Ceiba. Same name.

1936   Purchased by J. S. Webster & Sons Ltd, Kingston, Jamaica. Renamed *Allister*.

Powerful.

29.5.1942   On a voyage from Kingston to Tampa, with a cargo of 500 tons of bananas, she was sunk 50 miles south-west of Port au Prince, Haiti, by a torpedo from the German submarine *U-504*.

5. *Sussex Coast/Wirral Coast* (1907) O.N. 124086

640 grt   54.9 × 8.7 m

B. W. Harkess & Son Ltd, Middlesbrough. Yard No. 170.

Single screw, triple expansion, steam engine, 3 cylinder.

8.8.1907   Launched as *Truthful* for the Watchful Steamship Company Ltd (F. H. Powell & Company Ltd), Liverpool.

1907   Renamed *Sussex Coast* for F. H. Powell & Company Ltd, Liverpool.

1913   Renamed *Wirral Coast* for Coast Lines Ltd (Powell, Bacon & Hough Ltd).

1916   Sold to the Limerick Steam Ship Company Ltd, renamed *Claddagh.*

1917   Claddagh Steam Ship Company (Kater & Robinson Ltd), London.

1918   Sold to the City of Cork Steam Packet Company Ltd, same name.

1924   Purchased by Ellerman's Wilson Line, renamed *Nero.*

1928   Owned by Ada Cristina Piazza in D'Arrigo, Catania. Renamed *Cristina.*

1930   Sold to A. Patane & Company, Trieste. Renamed *Gagliardo.*

1931   Sold to Ivo Vacchi Suzzi, Trieste. Renamed *Imola.*

1933   Purchased by Pompei, Dante, Ancona. Renamed *Marchigiano.*

1935   Soc Italiana ATIL, Genoa.

13.3.1936   On a voyage from Genoa to Assab with a cargo of benzene, she sank following an explosion off Cape Elba in the Red Sea.

6. *Western Coast* (1913) O.N. 135502

1,165 grt   76.3 × 11 × 4.5 m

B. W. Harkess & Son Ltd, Middlesbrough. Yard No. 202.

Single screw, triple expansion, steam engine, 202 rhp, 3 cylinder. By Richardsons, Westgarth & Company Ltd, Middlesbrough.

6.8.1913   Launched as *Hopeful* for F. H. Powell & Company Ltd, Liverpool.

1914   Renamed *Western Coast* for Coast Lines Ltd (Powell, Bacon & Hough, Liverpool).

24.2.1915   On a voyage with general cargo from London to Liverpool, she was torpedoed and sunk 8 miles south-east of Beachy Head by the German submarine *U-8.*

7. *Suffolk Coast* (1913) O.N. 135526

780 grt   59.4 × 9.1 m

B. W. Harkess & Son Ltd, Middlesbrough. Yard No. 203.

Single screw, triple expansion, steam engine, 3 cylinder, by builder.

20.10.1913   Launched as *Suffolk Coast* for Powell, Bacon & Hough Lines Ltd, Liverpool.

7.11.1916   On a voyage from Glasgow to Fécamp she was captured and scuttled by German *U-17* off Cape Barfleur.

8. *Norfolk Coast* (1910) O.N. 131290

782 grt   59.44 × 9.14 × 3.66 m

B. W. Harkess & Son Ltd, Middlesbrough. Yard No. 182.

Single screw, triple expansion, steam engine, 128 nhp, 3 cylinder. By Richardsons, Westgarth & Company Ltd, Middlesbrough. 10 ½ knots.

3.9.1910   Launched as *Norfolk Coast* for F. H. Powell & Company Ltd, Liverpool.

1913   Powell, Bacon & Hough Lines Ltd, Liverpool.

1917   Coast Lines Ltd, Liverpool.

18.6.1918   On a voyage from Rouen to the Tyne in ballast, she was torpedoed and sunk 23 miles south-east of Flamborough Head by *UB-30.* Eight of her crew of fifteen lost their lives. Captain, H. R. E. Thomas.

9. *Hampshire Coast* (1911) O.N. 131387

787 grt   59.4 × 9.1 m

B. W. Harkess & Company Ltd, Middlesbrough. Yard No. 190.

Single screw, triple expansion, steam engine, 3 cylinder. By Richardsons, Westgarth & Company Ltd, Middlesbrough.

7.9.1911   Launched as *Hampshire Coast* for F. H. Powell & Company Ltd, Liverpool.

1913   Powell, Bacon & Hough Lines Ltd, Liverpool.

1917   Coast Lines Ltd, Liverpool.

1936   Sold to Kyle Shipping Company Ltd (Monroe Brothers Ltd as managers). Renamed *Kylebay*.

16.6.1950   Arrived at Dunston and broken up.

10. *Cornish Coast* (1904) O.N. 118136

676 grt   54.9 × 8.5 × 3.7 m

B. W. Harkess & Company Ltd, Middlesbrough. Yard No. 162.

Single screw, triple expansion, steam engine, 3 cylinder. By MacColl & Pollock Ltd, Sunderland.

24.9.1904   Launched as *Cornish Coast* for F. H. Powell & Company Ltd, Liverpool.

1913   Powell, Bacon & Hough Ltd, Liverpool.

3.3.1915   On a voyage with a cargo of cement from Rochester to Birkenhead and Liverpool, she sank following a collision with *Jeannette Woermann* off Birkenhead.

11. *Dorset Coast* (1908) O.N. 127912

672 grt   54.86 × 8.96 m

B. W. Harkess & Company Ltd, Middlesbrough. Yard No. 173.

Single screw, triple expansion, steam engine, 3 cylinder. By Blair & Company Ltd, Stockton-on-Tees.

30.5.1908   Launched as *Dorset Coast* for F. H. Powell & Company Ltd, Liverpool.

1913   Powell, Bacon & Hough Lines Ltd, Liverpool.

1915   Sold to Thomas C. Steven & Company Ltd, Leith. Renamed *Arbonne*.

26.2.1916   On a voyage from Le Havre to Newcastle in ballast she was torpedoed by *U-2*, 3 miles east of Kentish Knock.

12. *Stonehenge* (1876) O.N. 73735

784 grt   61.2 × 9.4 m

B. S. P. Austin & Son Ltd, Sunderland. Yard No. 116.

Single screw, compound steam engine.

21.10.1876 Launched as *Fenton*.

1913   Renamed *Stonehenge*.

1916   Sold to John Harrison Ltd, London. Same name.

1921   Owned by Italian interests. Same name.

1926   Renamed *Adone*.

6.3.1932   On a voyage from Cotrone to Licata in ballast she was wrecked near Pozzallo.

13. *Pennar* (1907) I.D. 1124099

132 grt

B. Barge built by W. J. Yarwood & Sons Ltd, Northwich. Yard No. 95.

21.9.1907   Launched.

1913   Acquired.

1.1948   Sold.

14. *Harfat* (1911) I.D. 1131386

128 grt

B. Barge built by W. J. Yarwood & Sons Ltd, Northwich. Yard No. 163.

12.8.1911   Launched.

1913   Acquired.

1940   Sold.

15. *Edith* (1880)

919 grt

1880   Barge built at Northwich by W. J. Yarwood & Sons Ltd.

1913   Acquired.

1916   Sold to H. & E. Grayson Ltd and later to the Kymo Shipping Company Ltd.

16. *Gloucester Coast* (1913) O.N. 135448

919 grt   64.06 × 10.11 × 4.05 m

B. George Brown & Company Ltd, Garvel Yard, Greenock. Yard No. 81.

Single screw, triple expansion, steam engine, 96 rhp, 3 cylinder. By Ross & Duncan Ltd.

22.2.1913   Launched as *Sir Walter Bacon* for John Bacon Ltd, Liverpool.

1913   Powell, Bacon & Hough Lines Ltd, Liverpool. Renamed *Gloucester Coast.*

1917   Coast Lines Ltd, Liverpool.

1936   Sold to the Bristol Steam Navigation Company Ltd, Bristol. Renamed *Alecto.*

2.5.1937   On a voyage from Swansea to Rotterdam, she collided with the Yugoslavian vessel *Plavnik* off Noord Hinder lightship in fog and sank.

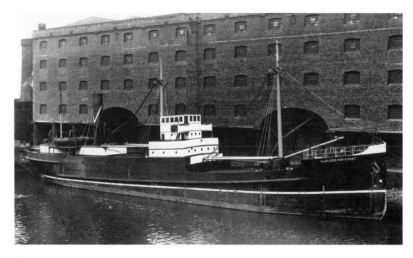

Gloucester Coast.

17. *Pembroke Coast* (1912) O.N. 135432

809 grt   354 nrt   60.71 × 9.17 × 3.41 m

B. Fullerton & Company Ltd, Merksworth Works, Paisley. Yard No. 225.

Single screw, triple expansion, steam engine, 99 nhp, 3 cylinder. By Ross & Duncan Ltd.

13.11.1912 Launched as *Clydeholm* for J. B. Couper Ltd and delivered as *Sir Roger Bacon* for John Bacon Ltd, Liverpool.

1913   Powell, Bacon & Hough Lines Ltd, Liverpool. Renamed *Pembroke Coast.*

1917   Coast Lines Ltd, Liverpool.

1930   Transferred to the City of Cork Steam Packet Company Ltd. Renamed *Blarney.*

1933   Sold to the Wexford Steamship Company Ltd (J. J. Stafford Ltd, Wexford, as managers). Renamed *Wexfordian.*

29.2.1936   On a voyage with a cargo of coal from Ayr to Wexford, she was wrecked off Dogger Bank, 7 miles north-east of Rosslare.

14.10.1936 Towed to Dalmuir to be broken up by W. H. Arnott Young & Company Ltd.

3.1937   Broken up.

18. *Gower Coast* (1899) O.N. 105238

804 grt   60.4 × 9.2 × 4 m

B. Dundee Shipbuilding Company Ltd, Dundee. Yard No. 127.

Single screw, triple expansion, steam engine, 98 nhp. By builder.

1899   Launched as *Prestonian* for John Bacon Ltd, Liverpool.

1913   Renamed *Sir George Bacon.*

1914   Renamed *Gower Coast.*

1915   Sold to Ford Shipping Company Ltd (Mann, Macneal & Company Ltd, Glasgow, as managers). Same name.

5.4.1917   On a voyage with a cargo of coal from the Tyne and Boulogne to Tréport, she was sunk by a mine from the German submarine *U-71* in the English Channel. Fifteen of her crew were lost.

19. *Sir Edward Bacon* (1899) O.N. 102467

483 grt   160 nrt   50.29 × 7.65 × 2.95 m

B. Irvine Shipbuilding & Engineering Company Ltd, Irvine. Yard No. 12.

Single screw steam engine, 69 nhp, 2 cylinder. By builder.

28.2.1899   Launched as *Birker Force* for Birker Force Steam Ship Company Ltd (W. S. Kennaugh & Company, Whitehaven, as managers).

Southern Coast.

1905   West Coast Shipping Company Ltd (W. S. Kennaugh & Company as managers).

12.1913   Sold to John Bacon Ltd, Liverpool.

1914   Sold to J. H. Bennetts & Company, Penzance. Renamed *Pivoc.*

1920   Owned by Holman Coal & Shipping Ltd (F. W. Holman, Penzance, as managers).

22.1.1922   On a voyage from Swansea to Rouen she was beached after striking a submerged object off Rouen. She was later declared a total loss.

20. *Southern Coast* (1911) O.N. 131348

1,872 grt   86.3 × 11 × 5.8 m

B. Greenock & Grangemouth Dockyard Company Ltd, Greenock. Yard No. 330.

Single screw, triple expansion, steam engine, 3 cylinder. By J. G. Kincaid & Company Ltd, Greenock.

1911   Built as *Dorothy Hough* for Samuel Hough Ltd, Liverpool.

1913   Coast Lines Ltd (Powell, Bacon & Hough Ltd, Liverpool). Renamed *Southern Coast.*

1936   Sold to the Falkland Islands Company Ltd, Liverpool. Renamed *Lafonia.*

26.3.1943   In collision when two convoys converged. Sank off Warkworth.

21. *Lancashire Coast* (1900) O.N. 110785

1,109 grt   68.7 × 10.4 m

B. J. Scott of Kinghorn Ltd. Yard No. 109.

Single screw, triple expansion, steam engine.

14.3.1900   Launched as *Delta.*

1904   Renamed *Annie Hough.*

1914   Renamed *Lancashire Coast*.

1919   *Arwyco*.

1934   *Corsisco*.

1941   *Corinto*.

1949   Broken up at Fieldsboroug, New Jersey, USA, by the North American Smelting Company.

22. *Northern Coast* (1913) O.N. 133548

1,189 grt   76.35 × 10.97 m

B. Sir Raylton Dixon & Company Ltd, Middlesbrough. Yard No. 585.

Single screw, triple expansion, steam engine, 3 cylinder. By Richardsons, Westgarth & Company Ltd, Middlesbrough.

13.12.1913   Launched for Powell, Bacon & Hough Lines Ltd, Liverpool.

1917   Coast Lines Ltd, Liverpool.

1920   Transferred to the British & Irish Steam Packet Company Ltd, renamed *Lady Martin*.

1938   Sold to A/S Eesti Laevaliinid, Tallinn. Renamed *Pearu*.

6.1940   Seized by the USSR in the Baltic Sea.

1940   Renamed *Vodnik*, USSR.

14.8.1941   Lost east of Prangli Island.

23. *Irish Coast* (1904) O.N. 119091

603 grt   238 nrt   54.95 × 8.26 × 3.26 m

B. Murdoch & Murray Ltd, Port Glasgow. Yard No. 193.

Single screw, compound steam engine, 80 nhp, 2 cylinder. By Muir & Houston Ltd.

18.1.1904   Launched as *Rosslyn* for the Rosslyn Steam Ship Company Ltd (Murray, McNab & Company Ltd, Glasgow, as managers).

1915   Powell, Bacon & Hough Lines Ltd, Liverpool. Renamed *Irish Coast*.

6.1916   Sold to Associated Portland Cement Manufacturers (1900) Ltd.

1917   Renamed *Landport*.

1918   Sold to Albert Chester, Liverpool.

1923   Purchased by the Iona Shipping Company Ltd (Jos H. Cubitt & Company as managers).

9.12.1925   On a voyage with coke from the Tyne to Portsmouth, she sank following a collision with the Swedish vessel *Mathilda* off Flamborough Head.

24. *Welsh Coast* (1915) O.N. 137457

1,070 grt   64.7 × 10.4 m

B. Charles Hill & Sons Ltd, Bristol. Yard No. 122.

Single screw, triple expansion, steam engine. 10 knots.

Welsh Coast.

1915	Built as *Welsh Coast*.

1920   Renamed *Macroom*.

1922   Renamed *Welsh Coast*.

1936   Sold to Monroe Brothers Ltd, renamed *Kyleglen*.

1937   Sold to the Bristol Steam Navigation Company Ltd. Renamed *Melito*.

1950   Sold to Fairwood Shipping Company Ltd. Renamed *Fairwood Oak*.

1956   Owned by Holderness Steam Ship Company Ltd, renamed *Holdervale*.

19.5.1957   Arrived at Charleston, Fife, and broken up.

25. *Wexford Coast/Pentland Coast* (1915) O.N. 137466

423 grt   164 nhp   45.78 × 7.28 × 3.20 m

B. Fullerton & Company Ltd, Merksworth Works, Paisley. Yard No. 239.
Single screw, compound, 87 nhp, 2 cylinder. By Ross & Duncan Ltd.

31.3.1915   Launched for Powell, Bacon & Hough Lines Ltd, Liverpool.

1917   Coast Lines Ltd, Liverpool.

1920   Transferred to the City of Cork Steam Packet Company Ltd, renamed *Blarney*.

1930   Coast Lines Ltd, renamed *Pentland Coast*.

1934   Sold to John S. Monks Ltd, renamed *Coastville*.

21.11.1940   On a voyage from Bangor to Liverpool in ballast she was stranded at Ballymacormick Point, Bangor

26.12.1940   Refloated, towed to Belfast and broken up.

26. *Kentish Coast* (1908) O.N. 137435

758 grt   56.4 × 9.2 m

B. Dundee Shipbuilding Company Ltd. Yard No. 199.
Single screw, triple expansion, steam engine.

14.5.1908   Launched.

1908   Delivered as *Hinderton*.

1915   *Kentish Coast*.

1928   *La Flandre*.

10.11.1928   Wrecked Jennycliffe Bay, Plymouth.

12.1928   Broken up at Lelant by T. W. Ward Ltd.

27. *Western Coast* (2) (1916) O.N. 137530

1,394 grt   73.2 × 11 × 5.6 m

B. Dublin Dockyard Company Ltd, Dublin. Yard No. 90.
Single screw, triple expansion, steam engine, 172 nhp. By builder. 8½ knots.

1916   Delivered to Coast Lines Ltd (Powell, Bacon & Hough Lines Ltd, Liverpool).

17.11.1917   On a voyage from Portsmouth to Barry Roads she was torpedoed by *UB-40* and sank 10 miles west-south-west of the Eddystone Lighthouse, Cornwall. Seventeen lives were lost.

28. *Suffolk Coast* (2) (1917) O.N. 140511

870 grt   60.3 × 9.4 m

B. W. Harkess & Son Ltd, Middlesbrough. Yard No. 212.
Single screw, 3 cylinder engine. By MacColl & Pollock Ltd, Sunderland.

22.3.1917   Launched as *Suffolk Coast* for Powell, Bacon & Hough Lines Ltd, Liverpool.

8.1918–7.1919   Requisitioned by the Admiralty as a Q-ship and collier, renamed HMS *Suffolk Coast*. As a decoy ship she was disguised as a tramp steamer or other lone vessel, but was actually heavily armed to lure U-boats within firing range.

1918–1919   Open to the public at St Katherine Docks, London.

7.1919   Returned to owners.

1939   Sold to the Kyle Shipping Company Ltd (Monroe Brothers Ltd, Liverpool). Renamed *Kylebank* and later sold to Consolidated Fisheries Ltd, Grimsby, renamed *East Anglian*.

1940   Geo. W. Grace & Company Ltd, Lowerstoft.

1946   Became *Sussex Oak*.

1953   Grace & Chancellor Ltd (Geo W. Grace & Company Ltd).

3.1954   Broken up at Gateshead.

29. *Durham Coast* (1911) O.N. 131864

783 grt   65.5 × 9.8 m

B. Goole Shipbuilding Company Ltd. Yard No. 146.

Single screw, triple expansion, steam engine, 209 nhp, 3 cylinder. By builder.

7.12.1911 Launched.

1912   Delivered as *New Abbotshall* to H. L. Stocks (Turnbull & Company), Kirkcaldy.

1920   Renamed *Durham Coast*.

7.6.1924   Beached at Wallasey following a collision in the Mersey with *Sunoil*.

10.6.1924 Refloated and repaired.

1948   Sold and renamed *Rama Raja*.

8.1957   Broken up at Calcutta.

30. *Kirkcaldy* (1903) O.N. 117571

525 grt   54.9 × 8.2 m

B. Gourlay Brothers Ltd, Dundee. Yard No. 206.

Single screw, triple expansion, steam engine, 134 nhp, 3 cylinder. By builder.

1903   Delivered as *Kirkcaldy* to H. L. Stocks (Turnbull & Company), Kirkcaldy.

3.1918   Coast Lines Ltd, Liverpool.

Durham Coast in dry dock.

3.1919   Sligo Steam Navigation Company Ltd.

7.1935   Broken up at Ardrossan.

31. *Volturnus* (1913) O.N. 135434

615 grt   53.3 × 8.3 m

B. R. Williamson & Son Ltd, Workington. Yard No. 215.

Single screw, triple expansion, steam engine, 110 rhp. By builder.

1913   Delivered to Volana Shipping Company Ltd (Rogers & Bright Ltd, Liverpool).

9.1914–1.1919 Requisitioned by the Admiralty as a store carrier.

1918   Coast Lines Ltd, Liverpool.

1.11.1919   On a voyage from Copenhagen to London with a cargo of Royal Navy stores she was mined and sank 5 miles south-east of the Shaw Lightship.

32. *Volpone* (1907) O.N. 124058
555 grt   50.2 × 8.1 m
B. Workman, Clark & Company Ltd, Belfast. Yard No. 206.
Single screw, triple expansion, steam engine. By builder.
13.12.1907   Launched.
1907   Delivered to Volana Shipping Company Ltd, Liverpool, as *Volpone*.
1919   Coast Lines Ltd, Liverpool (Powell, Bacon & Hough Lines Ltd, Liverpool), same name.
1919   Regis Shipping Company Ltd, London. Renamed *Lyme Regis*.
1925   British Lines Ltd, London, same name.
Continental Lines Ltd, renamed *Continental Coaster*.
1928   William A. Wilson Ltd, London, same name.
1936   Don David Coastal Shipping Company Ltd, London, same name.
1940   British Isles Coasters Ltd, Bideford. Same name.
24.9.1940   On a voyage from London to the Tyne with scrap iron she was torpedoed and sunk by a German E-boat, *S-30*. Four of her crew lost their lives.

33. *Cornish Coast* (2) (1913) O.N. 135527
616 grt   53.3 × 8.3 m
B. Williamson & Company Ltd, Workington. Yard No. 223.
Single screw, triple expansion, steam engine. 9 knots.
1913   Delivered as *Volana*.
1920   Renamed *Cornish Coast*.

1935   Became *Kyle Queen*.
1951   Renamed *Kardesler*.
1955   *Meso*.
1957   *Emel*.
1983   *Aksel-I*.
1997   *Sile-I*.
3.5.2004   Arrived at Aliaga and broken up.

34. *Gower Coast* (2) (1911) O.N. 131370
617 grt   51.8 × 8.2 × 3.4 m
B. Williamson & Company Ltd, Workington. Yard No. 207.
Single screw, triple expansion, steam engine, 110 nhp. By Ross & Duncan Ltd, Govan.
1911   Delivered as *Volhynia* to Rogers & Bright Ltd.
1919   Renamed *Gower Coast* for Coast Lines Ltd, Liverpool (Powell, Bacon & Hough Lines Ltd).
1932   Sold to John Kelly Ltd and became *Millisle*.
21.3.1941   On a voyage with a cargo of coal from Cardiff to Cork, she was sunk by aircraft bombs 2 miles east of Helwick Light Buoy in the Bristol Channel.

35. *Fife Coast* (1908) O.N. 99953
665 grt   61.3 × 8.9 m
B. McIlwaine & MacColl Ltd, Belfast. Yard No. 51.
Single screw, triple expansion, steam engine.
24.9.1992   Launched as *Glengariff*.
1908   Renamed *Princess Ena* for M. Langlands & Sons Ltd, Glasgow.
1920   Became *Fife Coast*.
1932   Renamed *Siciliano*.
1937   Renamed *Mino*.

1939   Became *Amalia Messina*.

1947   Broken up in Italy.

36. *Cheshire Coast* (1915) O.N. 137790

1,122 grt   73.15 × 10.63 m

B. Sir Raylton Dixon & Company Ltd, Middlesbrough. Yard No. 591.

Single screw, triple expansion, steam engine. By Richardsons, Westgarth Ltd, Middlesbrough.

13.2.1915   Launched as *Princess Irma* for M. Langlands & Sons Ltd, Glasgow.

1919   Coast Lines Ltd, Liverpool.

1920   Renamed *Cheshire Coast*.

1946   Sold to Union d'Entreprises Marocaines, Casablanca. Renamed *Caid Allal*.

1951   Sold to Simon D. Attar, Casablanca. Renamed *Rab*.

28.2.1955   Arrived at Savona and broken up.

37. *Princess Beatrice* (1893) O.N. 99898

974 grt   387 nrt   71.93 × 10.39 × 4.51 m

B. D. & W. Henderson & Company Ltd, Glasgow. Yard No. 365.

Single screw, triple expansion, steam engine, 179 nhp. By builder.

8.3.1893   Launched as *Princess Beatrice* for M. Langlands & Sons Ltd, Glasgow.

6.1919   Coast Lines Ltd, Liverpool.

4.1920   Sold to The Carron Company Ltd, Carron. Renamed *Avon*.

9.7.1928   Arrived at Bowness and broken up.

38. *Silver City* (1915) O.N. 114186

313 grt   103 nrt   41.0 8x 7.04 × 3.04 m

B. Ardrossan Shipbuilding Ltd, Ardrossan. Yard No. 183.

Single screw, compound steam engine, 55 nhp, 400 ihp, 2 cylinder. By builder.

30.3.1901   Launched for the Aberdeen, Leith & Moray Firth Steam Shipping Company Ltd (J. Crombie), Aberdeen.

1915   M. Langlands & Sons Ltd (Alexander & Mathew Langlands), Aberdeen.

1919   Coast Lines Ltd.

1920   Cullen, Allen & Company Ltd (T. S. Wilson, Belfast).

1924   Wilson & Reid Ltd, Belfast.

1927   Edmund Vardy, Hickmans Harbour, Newfoundland.

1928   William A. Munn, St Johns, Newfoundland.

1937   Silver City Steamship Company Ltd, St Johns, Newfoundland.

1938   Job Brothers & Company Ltd, St Johns, Newfoundland.

1939   Sold to Venezuelan interests and converted to a motor vessel. Motor 6 cylinders, 4SA, 300 bhp, by the Sterling Engine Company, Buffalo, NY.

1944   Re-engined, M8 cylinder, 320 bhp, 9 knots, by Vivian Diesel & Munitions Ltd, Vancouver, BC.

1951   Deleted from Lloyd's Register.

39. *Highland Coast* (1912) O.N. 133072

1,094 grt   76.2 × 10.4 × 4.9 m

B. Ramage & Ferguson Ltd, Leith. Yard No. 231.

Single screw, triple expansion, steam engine, 175 nhp. By builder. 12 knots.

1912   Launched as *Princess Melia* for Langlands & Sons Ltd, Glasgow.

1919   Coast Lines Ltd, Liverpool (Powell, Bacon & Hough Lines Ltd).

1920   Renamed *Highland Coast*.

1938   Sold to Tripcovich D. & Company, Sa Di Nav. Rimorchi E Salvataggi Servizi Marittimi Del Mediterraneo, Trieste. Renamed *Tripolino*.

1.11.1942   On a voyage from Benghazi to Tobruk she was bombed and sank by RAF aircraft in the Gulf of Bomba.

40. *Lancashire Coast* (2) (1920) O.N. 143635

1,104 grt   73.18 × 10.63 m

B. Sir Raylton Dixon & Company Ltd, Middlesbrough. Yard No. 611.
Single screw, triple expansion, steam engine, 3 cylinder. By Richardsons, Westgarth & Company Ltd, Middlesbrough.

3.1920   Launched as *Princess Olga* for M. Langlands & Sons Ltd, Glasgow.

18.5.1920   Coast Lines Ltd, renamed *Lancashire Coast*.

7.10.1948   Transferred to the Belfast Steamship Company Ltd, renamed *Ulster Hero*.

9.12.1954   Arrived at Barrow-in-Furness and broken up.

41. *Moray Coast* (1905) O.N. 121226

677 grt   64.2 × 9.5 m

B. Celedon Shipbuilding & Engineering Company Ltd. Yard No. 181.
Single screw, triple expansion, steam engine. By Lilibank Foundry (Builders) Ltd.

21.3.1905   Launched.

1905   Delivered as *Princess Helena* to M. Langlands & Sons Ltd, Glasgow. Cost £26,000.

1920   Coast Lines Ltd, renamed *Moray Coast*.

1935   To J. M. Vlassopould, Ithaca, Greece. Renamed *Olga*.

1936   *Olga M.*

1937   Cape Line Ltd, London. Renamed *Pacifico*.

1939   Requisitioned by the Admiralty.

1940   Sunk as a block ship at Dunkirk harbour.

42. *Lady Tennant/Elgin Coast* (1903) O.N. 119083

452 grt   118 nrt   50.29 × 7.95 × 3.07 m

B. Napier & Miller Ltd, Yoker yard, Glasgow. Yard No. 132.
Single screw, triple expansion, steam engine, 93 nhp, 3 cylinder. By David Rowan & Company Ltd.

7.12.1903   Launched as *Lady Tennant* for M. Langlands & Sons Ltd, Glasgow, to carry explosives for Nobel Explosives Ltd.

1914   Stornoway Shipping Company Ltd, Stornoway.

1916   M. Langlands & Sons Ltd, Glasgow.

1918   M. Langlands acquired by Coast Lines Ltd, Liverpool.

1920   Transferred to the British & Irish Steam Packet Company Ltd.

1923   Renamed *Elgin Coast*.

1930   Renamed *Kilkenny*.

1936   Sold to Captain H. W. B. Ohlmeier, Hamburg. Renamed *Lisa*.

1962   Owned by Theodoros Orestis Vavatsioulas and Helene Theodoru Vavatsioulas, Salonica. Renamed *Oretis*.

1969   Sold to A. Pastrikos and Papageorgiu, Thesalaiki, Greece. Renamed *Mario*.

1974   Broken up in Greece.

43. *Orkney Coast* (1908) O.N. 128245

781 grt   64.00 × 9.60 × 4.02 m

B. Russell & Company Ltd, Kingston Yard, Port Glasgow. Yard No. 597.
Single screw, triple expansion, steam engine, 116 nhp, 3 cylinder. By Dunsmuir & Jackson Ltd.

4.12.1908   Launched as *Princess Thyra* for M. Langlands & Sons Ltd, Glasgow.

29.10.1916   Submarine opened fire on her in the English Channel but she escaped.

1919   Coast Lines Ltd, Liverpool (Powell, Bacon & Hough Ltd). Renamed *Orkney Coast*.

1921   Registered at Liverpool.

1937   Sold to O/Y Wirma (A. Wihuri), Kulosaari.

29.12.1939   Wrecked off Vaasa, Finland, and later fired upon and damaged by Russian submarine *SHCH-311*.

44. *Clyde Coast* (1888) O.N. 95050

817 grt   332 nrt   68.88 × 9.78 × 4.26 m

B. D. & W. Henderson & Company Ltd, Glasgow. Yard No. 333.

Single screw, triple expansion, steam engine, 121 nhp, 3 cylinder. By builder.

15.3.1888   Launched as *Princess Louise* for M. Langlands & Sons Ltd.

1902   New engines installed, triple expansion steam, 3 cylinders, 135 nhp, 800 ihp, by Clyde Shipbuilding & Engineering Company Ltd, Port Glasgow. 10½ knots.

1919   Coast Lines Ltd, Liverpool. Renamed *Clyde Coast*.

1923   Transferred to Burns & Laird Lines Ltd. Renamed *Setter*.

1925   Coast Lines Ltd, Liverpool. Reverted to *Clyde Coast*.

Transferred to the City of Cork Steam Packet Company Ltd. Renamed *Macroom*.

1929   Broken up at Port Glasgow.

45. *British Coast* (1919) O.N. 140639

1,943 grt   88.4 × 13 × 6.1 m

B. Swan, Hunter & Wigham Richardson Ltd, Wallsend. Yard No. 1113.

Single screw, triple expansion, steam engine, 324 nhp, 3 cylinder. By Richardsons, Westgarth Ltd. 10 knots.

1919   Launched as *Etrib* for Moss Steamship Company Ltd (James Moss & Company), Liverpool.

Requisitioned by the Shipping Controller, renamed *War Shannon*.

Coast Lines Ltd, Liverpool. Renamed *British Coast*.

1923   Moss Steamship Company Ltd (James Moss & Company), Liverpool.

14.6.1942   On a voyage from Cartagena and Gibraltar to Liverpool she was torpedoed and sunk by the German submarine *U-522* in the North Atlantic.

46. *Western Coast* (3) (1919) O.N. 140654

1,938 grt   88.39 × 12.95 × 5.73 m

B. Swan Hunter Ltd, Walker. Yard No. 1133.

Single screw, triple expansion, steam engine. 10 knots.

2.8.1919   Launched as *Western Coast*.

26.2.1922   Renamed *Esneh*.

1948   Became *Tefkros*.

1958   Renamed *Shun On*.

27.2.1959   Arrived at Hong Kong and broken up by United Overseas Enterprises Ltd.

47. *Blackwater* (1907) O.N. 123129

678 grt   251 nrt   56.41 × 8.41 × 3.35 m

B. Ailsa Shipbuilding Company Ltd, Troon. Yard No. 181.

Single screw, compound steam, 87 rhp, 2 cylinder by builder.

12.10.1907   Launched as *Blackwater* for Tedcastle, McCormick & Company Ltd, Dublin.

9.8.1915–28.3.1919   British Expeditionary Force Transport *E2610*, transporting cross-Channel stores.

10.1919   Coast Lines Ltd.

1921	Samuel Kelly Ltd, Dublin, and later John Kelly Ltd, Belfast.
20.4.1944–31.8.1945	Requisitioned by the Admiralty.
8.6.1944	Supplied to Sword Beach during the D-Day landings.
1952	Renamed *Ballygowan* (J. G. Christie as managers).
1.10.1954	Arrived at Rainham and broken up by Shaw of Kent Ltd.

48. *Cardigan Coast* (1904) O.N. 117516

711 grt   272 nrt   60.96 × 8.83 × 3.44 m

B. Fullerton & Company Ltd, Paisley. Yard No. 175.

Single screw, triple expansion, steam engine 156 nhp, 3 cylinder. By Ross & Duncan Ltd.

17.2.1904	Launched as *Dublin* for Tedcastle, McCormick & Company Ltd, Dublin.
1919	Tedcastle, McCormick & Company Ltd acquired by the British & Irish Steam Packet Company Ltd.
1920	Coast Lines Ltd, Liverpool. British & Irish Steam Packet Company Ltd.
1922	Coast Lines Ltd, renamed *Cardigan Coast*.
1928	Sold to R. & D. A. Duncan Ltd (William Clint as managers), Belfast. Renamed *Dublin*.
1940	Sold to S. Instone & Company Ltd, London. Renamed *Themston*.
1950	Owned by Tyson, Edgar Shipping Ltd, London.
18.9.1952	Arrived at Rosyth and broken up by Metal Industries Ltd.

49. *Somerset Coast* (2) (1919) O.N. 143620

1,353 grt   73.1 × 11 m

B. Harland & Wolff Ltd, Govan. Yard No. 592.

Single screw, triple expansion, steam engine, 203 nhp, 3 cylinder. By A. & J. Inglis Ltd.

27.12.1919	Launched as *Somerset Coast*.
1935	Converted to shelter deck type.
1950	Renamed *Mountstewart*.
16.11.1955	Arrived up at Troon and broken up by the West of Scotland Shipbreaking Company.

50. *Norfolk Coast* (2) (1894) O.N. 102157

979 grt   616 nrt   67.05 × 9.69 × 4.38 m

B. Archibald McMillan & Son Ltd, Dumbarton. Yard No. 330.

Single screw, triple expansion, steam engine, 129 nhp, 3 cylinder. By David Rowan & Son Ltd.

31.5.1894	Launched as *Valencia* for the Valencia Steamship Company Ltd (James H. Goodyear & Company Ltd as managers), Liverpool.
1910	George Bazeley & Sons Ltd, Penzance.
1912	Renamed *Cadoc*.
4.3.1920	Coast Lines Ltd, Liverpool. Renamed *Norfolk Coast*.
8.4.1932	Sold to Vincenzo Mirabella, Catania. Renamed *Resurrectio*.
1949	Owned by Maurizio Rossi, Venice. Renamed *Daniela*.
3.1949	Reported laid up.
1959	Deleted from Lloyd's Register.

51. *Cloch* (1883) O.N. 87721

762 grt   373 nrt   65.83 × 8.74 m

B. Dobie & Company Ltd, Govan. Yard No. 133.

Iron, single screw, compound steam engine, 105 nhp, 2 cylinder. By John & James Thomson & Company Ltd.

17.9.1883	Launched as *Cloch* for G. J. Kidston & James M. Cuthbert Ltd, Glasgow, and the Glasgow, Cork & Waterford Steam Navigation Company Ltd (G. J. Kidston as managers), Glasgow.

17.2.1893   Clyde Shipping Company Ltd (J. M. Cuthbert as managers), Glasgow.

11.5.1893   George P. Bazeley, Penzance.

15.12.1905   George Bazeley & Sons Ltd, Penzance.

3.3.1920   George Bazeley & Sons Ltd, Penzance acquired by Coast Lines Ltd, Liverpool.

28.5.1920   Sold to Carron Company Ltd, Grangemouth. Renamed *Grange*.

12.6.1925   Arrived at Bowness and broken up.

52. *Mercutio* (1879) O.N. 79154

855 grt   552 nrt   60.99 × 8.86 × 4.87 m

B. James & George Thomson Ltd, Clydebank. Yard No. 169.

Iron, single screw, compound steam engine, 95 rhp, 2 cylinder. By W. V. Lidgerwood, Glasgow.

11.3.1879   Launched as *Mercutio* for Gedhill & Dishart Ltd, Leith.

1884   Marshall, Dodson & Company Ltd, Leith.

1888   Dodson & Craig Ltd, Leith.

1890   Dodson & Company Ltd, Leith.

1891   G. Bazeley & Sons , Penzance.

1910   G. Bazeley & Sons Ltd, Penzance.

1920   Coast Lines Ltd.

8.7.1925   Arrived at Preston and broken up by T. W. Ward Ltd.

53. *Northern Coast* (2) (1920) O.N. 144976

1,220 grt   557 nrt   1,844 dwt   73.18 × 11 × 4.45 m

B. A. & J. Inglis Ltd, Pointhouse. Yard No. 600.

Single screw, triple expansion, steam engine, 203 nhp, 3 cylinder by builder.

29.11.1920   Launched.

1921   Delivered as *Lady Valentia* to the British & Irish Steam Packet Company Ltd.

21.5.1922   Coast Lines Ltd, Liverpool. Renamed *Northern Coast*.

4.1954   Broken up at Passage West by Haulbowline Industries Ltd.

54. *Irish Coast* (2) (1900) O.N. 110519

265 grt   39.3 × 6.7 m

B. Larne Shipbuilding Company Ltd, Larne. Yard No. 12.

Single screw, compound steam engine, 50 rhp, 2 cylinder. By Muir & Houston Ltd.

26.4.1900   Launched as *Mayflower*.

5.1922   Sold to Coast Lines Ltd. Renamed *Irish Coast*.

1930   Converted to a barge.

9.193   Sold to Charles S. Kendall, Portsmouth.

5.1940   Sold to Vectis Transport Company Ltd (E. W. Gilbert Ltd), Portsmouth.

3.1942   Purchased by BISCO (Salvage) Ltd as a scrap metal barge.

31.3.1949   Renamed *Arcliff*.

2.1951   Broken up at Troon.

55. *Lydia* (1890) O.N. 97217

1,059 grt   193 nrt   77.11 × 10.69 × 4.51 m

B. James & George Thomson Company Ltd, Clydebank. Yard No. 251.

Twin screw, triple expansion, steam engine, 360 nhp, 3 cylinder. By builder.

16.7.1890   Launched as *Lydia* for the London & South Western Railway Company, Southampton.

1920   Sold to Montague Yates, Southampton.

Operated as an accommodation ship for James Dredging Towing & Transport Ltd.

3.1921   Sold to M. Yates for a Malta–Syracuse service.

1922   Coast Lines Ltd, Liverpool, to operate the Preston–Dublin service.

1923   Sold to Nav. a Vap. Ionienne G. Yannoulato Frères, Argostoli. Renamed *Ierax*.

1929   Purchased by Hellenic Coast Lines Company Ltd, Piraeus, Greece.

1933   Broken up in Italy.

56. *Eastern Coast* (2) (1922) O.N. 145938
1,220 grt   568 nrt   1,844 dwt   62.17 × 11 × 11 m
B. A. & J. Inglis Ltd, Pointhouse. Yard No. 601.
Single screw, triple expansion, steam engine, 204 nhp, 3 cylinder. By builder.

10.3.1922   Launched as *Eastern Coast* for Coast Lines Ltd, Liverpool.

1954   Hamilton Bermuda Steam Ship Navigation Company Ltd, Hamilton (Donald J. Shanks). Renamed *Pamela Shanks*.

1955   African Coasters (Pty) Ltd (Grindrod Gersigny & Company (Pty) Ltd), Durban.

1955   Became *Margin*.

1.1964   Broken up at Durban after grounding at Port Elizabeth.

57. *Ayrshire Coast* (1922) O.N. 145979
774 grt   332 nrt   61.11 × 9.47 × 3.74 m
B. A. & J. Inglis Ltd, Glasgow. Yard No. 607.
Single screw, triple expansion, steam engine, 123 rhp, 3 cylinder. By builder.

22.8.1922   Launched. Ordered by G. & J. Burns Ltd. Taken over by the British & Irish Steam Packet Company with the intention of naming her *Lady Olive*.

1922   Completed for Coast Lines Ltd, Liverpool.

6.10.1922   Transferred to Burns & Laird Lines Ltd, Glasgow.

1923   Renamed *Spaniel*.

1925   Coast Lines Ltd, renamed *Ayrshire Coast*.

1947   Belfast Steamship Company Ltd, renamed *Ulster Mariner*.

22.7.1955   Arrived at Passage West and broken up by Haulbowline Industries Ltd.

58. *Western Coast* (4) (1919) O.N. 143050
1,434 grt   82.60 × 11.61 × 4.93 m
B. Caledon Shipbuilding & Engineering Company Ltd, Dundee. Yard No. 265.
Single screw, triple expansion, steam engine, 278 rhp, 196 nhp, 3 cylinder. By builder. 12 knots.

17.1.1919   Launched as *War Leven* and completed for the Shipping Controller (J. Moss & Company Ltd, London) as *Limoges*. Sold to Moss Steamship Company Ltd, Liverpool.

16.2.1922   Coast Lines Ltd, Liverpool. Renamed *Western Coast*.

31.3.1941   To Burns & Laird Lines Ltd.

1946   Renamed *Meath*.

1948   Transferred to the British & Irish Steam Packet Company Ltd.

1952   To Burns & Laird Lines Ltd. Renamed *Lairdscastle*.

5.6.1958   Arrived at Hendrik-Ido-Ambacht and broken up.

59. *Carmarthen Coast* (1921) O.N. 147175
964 grt   468 nrt   64.77 × 10.27 × 3.81 m
B. Ardrossan Dockyard Ltd, Ardrossan. Yard No. 316.
Single screw, triple expansion, steam engine, 142 nhp, 3 cylinder. By Plenty & Son Ltd.

23.3.1921   Launched as *Langfjord* for A/S Den Norske Amerikalinje, Christiania.

1.12.1921   Delivered as *Nova* for the Bergen Line.

1922   Coast Lines Ltd, Liverpool. Renamed *Carmarthen Coast*.

Carmarthen Coast.

7.11.1939   On a voyage from Methil to London with, 1,000 tons of general cargo, she was mined and sunk 3 miles off Seaham. The mine was laid by the German submarine *U-24*. Two of her crew were lost.

60. *Glamorgan Coast* (1912) O.N. 132835

684 grt   60.96 × 9.60 m

B. Smith's Dock Company Ltd, South Bank, Middlesbrough. Yard No. 524. Single screw, triple expansion, steam engine, 171 nhp, 3 cylinder. By Richardsons, Westgarth & Company Ltd.

23.11.1912   Launched as *Channel Trader* for the London Welsh Steam Ship Company Ltd (Furness Withy Ltd), West Hartlepool.

5.1923   Coast Lines Ltd, Liverpool. Renamed *Glamorgan Coast*.

13.9.1932   On a voyage from Bristol to Penzance with a general cargo she was wrecked on North Point, Cape Cornwall.

61. *Yorkshire Coast* (1913) O.N. 135884

702 grt   61.05 × 9.60 × 3.71 m

B. Dundee Shipbuilding Company Ltd, Dundee.

Single screw, triple expansion, steam engine, 171 nhp, 3 cylinder. By Richardsons, Westgarth Ltd.

1913   Delivered as *Llanelly Trader* to the London Welsh Steam Ship Company Ltd (Furness Withy Ltd), West Hartlepool.

5.1923   Coast Lines Ltd, Liverpool. Renamed *Yorkshire Coast*.

10.1938   Sold and renamed *Solin*.

1941   *Marino*.

1946   *Solin*.

23.8.1963   Arrived at Split and broken up.

62. *Truro Trader* (1912) O.N. 133061

94 grt   56 nrt   19.99 × 5.60 × 2.65 m

B. Peter McGregor & Sons Ltd, Kirkintilloch. Yard No. 58.

Single screw, oil 2SCSA engine, 23 nhp, 2 cylinder. By J. & C. G. Bolinders Company, Stockholm.

11.6.1912   Launched as *Inniscroone* for Coasting Motor Shipping Company Ltd, Glasgow.

1918   London & Paris Marine Express Company Ltd, Hull.

8.8.1922   Coast Lines Ltd, Liverpool, and used as a barge at Falmouth, renamed *Truro Trader*.

1936   Stephen Portus, Liverpool Wadsworth Lighterage & Coaling Company Ltd, Liverpool, and used as a barge at Liverpool.

63. *Denbigh Coast* (1891) O.N. 98646

386 grt   178 nrt   53.46 × 8.53 × 3.62 m

B. Caird & Company Ltd, Greenock. Yard No. 263.

Single screw, triple expansion, steam engine, inverted direct acting, 85 rhp, 3 cylinder. By builder.

27.5.1891   Launched as *Grouse* for G. & J. Burns Ltd, Glasgow, for the Greenock–Larne service.

1922   Grahamston Shipping Company (W. T. Mitchell Ltd as managers), Glasgow. Renamed *Kelvindale*.

1923   Owners acquired by Burns & Laird Lines Ltd, Glasgow.

30.6.1924   Coast Lines Ltd, Liverpool. Renamed *Denbigh Coast*.

18.5.1929   To David MacBrayne (1928) Ltd, Glasgow. Renamed *Lochdunvegan*.

1931   New boilers fitted.

27.7.1948   Arrived at Faslane and broken up by Metal Industries Ltd.

64. *Dorset Coast* (2) (1924) O.N. 147272

483 grt   45.90 × 7.74 × 3.38 m

B. James Towers Shipbuilding Company Ltd, Bristol. Yard No. 180.

Single screw, triple expansion, steam, 72 rhp, 105 nhp. By J. G. Kincaid & Company Ltd, Greenock.

1924   Laid down as *Reedham* for Walford Lines Ltd, London.

24.5.1924   Launched as *Dorset Coast* for Coast Lines Ltd, Liverpool.

8.6.1929   Transferred to the Belfast Steamship Company Ltd. Renamed *Logic*.

1935   Renamed *Ulster Hero*.

1941   Sold to J. & A. Gardner & Company Ltd, Glasgow.

1945   Renamed *Saint Conan*.

1958   Broken up at Dublin.

65. *Allegiance* (1917) O.N. 140548

171 grt   27.9 × 6.5 m

B. W. J. Yarwood & Sons Ltd, Northwich. Yard No. 240.

Single screw, compound steam engine.

1917   Delivered to John Cockburn & Gunn Ltd, Newcastle.

7.1925   Coast Lines Ltd, Liverpool.

1961   Sold and renamed *Wharfedale*.

4.1966   Broken up at Preston.

66. *Cumberland Coast/Cambrian Coast* (1922) O.N. 146282

773 grt   61.02 × 9.47 × 3.62 m

B. Harland & Wolff Ltd, Govan. Yard No. 626.

Single screw, triple expansion, steam engine, 123 rhp and nhp. By A. & J. Inglis Ltd, Glasgow.

28.12.1922   Launched as *Gorilla* for G. & J. Burns Ltd, Glasgow.

1922   Burns & Laird Lines Ltd.

30.8.1925   Coast Lines Ltd. Renamed *Cumberland Coast*.

1930   Transferred to the City of Cork Steam Packet Company Ltd. Became *Kinsale*.

1.1.1933   Coast Lines Ltd, renamed *Cambrian Coast*.

21.1.1947   Belfast Steamship Company Ltd. Renamed *Ulster Merchant*.

10.1954   Broken up at Newport, Mon.

67. *Sutherland Coast* (1920) O.N. 144238

772 grt   60.96 × 9.75 × 4.35 m

B. Harland & Wolff Ltd, Govan. Yard No. 602.

Single screw, triple expansion, steam engine, 123 nhp, 3 cylinder. By A. & J. Inglis Ltd, Glasgow.

1920   Ordered by M. Langlands & Company Ltd for the Glasgow–Liverpool–Manchester service and it was intended to name her *Princess Caroline*.

14.10.1920   Launched as Redbreast for G. & J. Burns Ltd, Glasgow.

21.12.1925   Coast Lines Ltd, Liverpool. Renamed *Sutherland Coast*.

16.5.1930   Burns & Laird Lines Ltd, Glasgow. Renamed *Lairdsbrook* (to replace *Lairdselm*, which was lost in 1929).

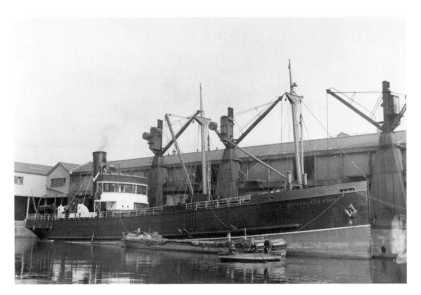

Sutherland Coast.

Scottish Coast.

5.9.1945   Holed alongside East India Wharf, Greenock, by the *City of Lincoln*.
11.3.1960   Arrived at Passage West and broken up by Haulbowline Industries Ltd.

68. *Scottish Coast* (1922) O.N. 146318
774 grt   333 nrt   61.11 × 9.47 × 3.74 m
B. A. & J. Inglis Ltd, Pointhouse. Yard No. 657.
Single screw, triple expansion, steam engine, 123 nhp, 3 cylinder. By builder.
20.9.1922   Launched as *Lurcher* for Burns & Laird Lines Ltd.

1925   Coast Lines Ltd, Liverpool. Renamed *Scottish Coast*.
1938   Belfast steamship Company Ltd. Renamed *Ulster Coast*.
1954   Sold to Ahern Shipping Ltd, Belfast. Renamed *Ahern Trader*.
10.1.1960   Broke her moorings and wrecked in a snowstorm at Muddy Hole, south of Fog Island on the north coast of Newfoundland.

69. *Antrim Coast* (1905) O.N. 119711
1,001 grt   66.53 × 10.08 × 4.32 m
B. Ramage & Ferguson Ltd, Leith. Yard No. 199.
Single screw, triple expansion, steam engine, 155 nhp, 3 cylinder. By builder.

6.4.1905	Launched as *Ploussa*.
1916	Antrim Iron Ore Company, renamed *Glentaise*.
1.8.1929	Coast Lines Ltd, renamed *Antrim Coast*.
1.4.1933	*Regina Pacis*.
1937	*Prado*.
1943	*Netzleger XI*.
29.8.1944	Scuttled by Germany at Marseilles. Later raised and broken up.

70. *Aberdeen Coast* (1903) O.N. 116003

1,013 grt   68.88 × 10.08 × 4.23 m

B. North of Ireland Shipbuilding Company Ltd, Londonderry. Yard No. 54.

Single screw, triple expansion, steam engine, 177 nhp, 3 cylinder. By McColl Ltd, Belfast.

1903	Delivered as *Glendun* to the Antrim Iron Ore Company Ltd.
1.4.1929	Coast Lines Ltd, Liverpool. Renamed *Aberdeen Coast*.
4.6.1934	Efesar Ltd, Estonia. Renamed *Efesar* and later *Ray*.
27.6.1935	Arrived at Briton Ferry and broken up by T. W. Ward Ltd.

71. *Cardigan Coast* (2) (1913) O.N. 132894

781 grt   58.73 × 9.32 × 3.81 m

B. Dublin Dockyard Company. Yard No. 82.

Single screw, compound steam engine, 87 nhp, 2 cylinder. By Ross & Duncan Ltd.

4.9.1913	Launched as *Patricia* for Michael Murphy Ltd.
1929	Coast Lines Ltd, Liverpool. Renamed *Cardigan Coast*.
12.1937	Sold to W. Thomas & Sons Ltd, Liverpool, and renamed *Eilian Hill*.
6.3.1941	Damaged by a mine off Barry.
19.6.1955	Arrived at Hendrik-Ido-Ambacht and broken up.

72. *Anglesey Coast* (1911) O.N. 132859

863 grt   61.02 × 9.32 × 3.81 m

B. Dublin Dockyard Company. Yard No. 74.

Single screw, compound steam engine, 87 nhp, 2 cylinder. By Ross & Duncan Ltd.

26.10.1911	Launched as *Enda* for Michael Murphy Ltd.
6.6.1929	Coast Lines Ltd, Liverpool. Renamed *Anglesey Coast*.
1937	Transferred to British Channel Islands Shipping Ltd. Renamed *Norman Queen*.
1937	Sold and renamed *Kylecroft*.
8.6.1955	Arrived at Llanelli and broken up.

73. *Pentland Coast*, 423 grt – See *Wexford Coast* (1915).

74. *Killarney* (1893), 2,081 grt – See *Magic* (1893). Belfast Steamship Company Ltd.

75. *Monmouth Coast* (2) (1924) O.N. 146413

878 grt   396 nrt   61.08 × 9.32 × 4.02 m

Single screw, triple expansion engine, 155 nhp, 3 cylinder. By Ross & Duncan, Govan. 9 knots.

B. Ayrshire Shipbuilders Ltd, Irvine. Yard No. 493.

7.2.1924	Launched as *Grania*.
1924	Delivered to Michael Murphy Ltd (J. O'Dowd Ltd as managers), Dublin.
1926	Michael Murphy Ltd acquired by the British & Irish Steam Packet Company Ltd.
1933	Coast Lines Ltd, Liverpool. Renamed *Monmouth Coast*.
24.4.1945	On a voyage from Sligo to Liverpool, with a cargo of 841 tons of pyrites, she was torpedoed and sunk 80 miles off Sligo by the

Twin-screw S/Y "KILLARNEY" (2150 tons)

YACHTING CRUISES FROM LIVERPOOL TO THE SCOTTISH FIRTHS AND FJORDS.
COAST LINES, LTD., ROYAL LIVER BUILDING, LIVERPOOL.

Killarney.

German submarine *U-1305* (later Russian *S-84*). Sixteen of the crew of seventeen were lost. It has also been reported that *U-956* or *U-293* were responsible for her loss.

76. *Fife Coast* (2) (1933) O.N. 162394

367 grt   188 nrt   41.30 × 7.68 × 2.86 m
B. Ardrossan Dockyard Company. Yard No. 352.
Single screw motor, 98 nhp, 4 cylinder. By J. G. Kincaid & Company Ltd.
13.10.1933   Launched as *Fife Coast*.
8.8.1940   On a voyage from London to Falmouth and Plymouth, with a cargo of refined sugar, she was sunk by a torpedo from German MTBs *S-21* and *S-27*, 15 miles west of Beachy Head.

77. *Carrick Coast* (1934) O.N. 162409

369 grt   193 nrt   41.30 × 7.65 × 2.86 m
B. Ardrossan Dockyard Company. Yard No. 354.
Single screw motor, 125 nhp, 4 cylinder by Atlas-Diesel A/B.
3.7.1934   Launched.
1934   Delivered as *Carrick Coast* to Coast Lines Ltd, Liverpool.
1951   Renamed *Zulu Coast* for Coast Lines Africa (Pty) Ltd.
7.4.1953   On a voyage from Cape Town to Port Nolloth, with a cargo of oil in drums and general cargo, she was stranded in fog 2 miles north of Groene River, South Africa.

78. *British Coast* (2) (1934) O.N. 162399

889 grt   70.6 × 10.7 × 6.6 m
Twin screw, 5 cylinder, British Polar oil engines. 12 knots.
B. Henry Robb & Company Ltd, Leith. Yard No. 198.
1934   Delivered as *British Coast*.
1964   Renamed *Newfoundland Coast*.
1979   To Coast Line Ltd, Canada.
14.7.1981   Wrecked 16 miles west of Providenciales, Turks & Caicos Islands. Declared a total loss.

79. *Atlantic Coast* (1934) O.N. 162405

890 grt   70.6 × 10.7 × 6.6 m
Twin screw, 5 cylinder, British Polar oil engines. 12 knots.
B. Henry Robb & Company Ltd, Leith. Yard No. 204.
16.5.1934   Launched as *Atlantic Coast*.
10.1939–5.1940   Made six voyages with cased petrol to supply the British Expeditionary Force in France.
23.12.1940   Detonated an acoustic mine, which severely damaged her engine room. She managed to get back to harbour and was repaired.

British Coast (2).

1940–45   Service on the west coast of Africa and took part in the invasion of North Africa at Oran. Participated in the Normandy landings and served the United States Army beaches of 'Omaha' and 'Utah', delivering cased petrol.

1962   Renamed *Pondo Coast*.

1967   Became *Pondo*.

1971   *Dona Gracia*.

3.1973   Broken up at Vado Ligure by G. Riccardi.

80. *Pacific Coast* (1935) O.N. 164258
1,210 grt   664 nrt   76.71 × 11.61 × 3.99 m
B. Ardrossan Dockyard Ltd, Ardrossan. Yard No. 357.
Twin screws, oil engine, 312 nhp, 10 cylinder. By British Auxiliaries Ltd.
4.4.1935   Launched as *Pacific Coast* for Coast Lines Ltd, Liverpool.

9.11.1939   Suffered an explosion and sank following a fire at Brest while carrying cased petrol.

3.5.1940   Arrived at Falmouth in tow and broken up.

81. *Ocean Coast* (1935) O.N. 164266
1,173 grt   76.8 × 11.6 × 7.0 m
B. Henry Robb & Company Ltd, Leith. Yard No. 215.
Twin screw, 5 cylinder, British Polar Engines Ltd. 12 knots.

1935   Delivered as *Ocean Coast* to Coast Lines Ltd, Liverpool.

1964   Sold and renamed *Effy*.

1967   *Anna Maria*.

8.2.1969   On a voyage from Hamburg to Conastantza with bagged cocoa beans, she grounded 10 miles north of Constantza. The wreck was abandoned and later broke up.

82. *Anglian Coast* (1935) O.N. 164270
594 grt   59.8 × 9.8 m
B. S. P. Austin & Son Ltd, Wear Dock. Yard No. 335.
Twin screw, oil engine 2SCSA, 10 cylinder. By British Auxiliaries Ltd.
9½ knots.

1.8.1935   Launched as *Anglian Coast* for Coast Lines Ltd, Liverpool.

1955   Coast Lines Africa (Pty) Ltd, renamed *Griqua Coast*.

5.3.1968   Scuttled off Saldanha Bay.

83. *Devon Coast* (2) (1936) O.N. 164297
646 grt   244 nrt   60.77 × 10.08 × 3.38 m
B. Ardrossan Dockyard Company. Yard No. 362.
Single screw, oil engine, 224 nhp, 4 cylinder. By J. G. Kincaid & Company Ltd.
9.5.1936   Launched as *Devon Coast* for Coast Lines Ltd, Liverpool.

2.12.1943   With a cargo of high octane gasoline in drums, she was bombed and destroyed by fire during an air raid by German aircraft at Bari. It was reported that she was refloated in 1948 but there is no confirmation of this and it is likely that she was broken up.

84. *Dorset Coast* (3) (1936) O.N. 164303

646 grt   244 nrt   60.77 × 10.08 × 3.38 m
B. Ardrossan Dockyard Company. Yard No. 363.
Single screw, oil engine, 224 nhp, 4 cylinder. By J. G. Kincaid & Company Ltd.

9.9.1936   Launched as *Dorset Coast* for Coast Lines Ltd, Liverpool.
12.5.1943   Bombed and sank at Algiers.
29.4.1946   Refloated and repaired.
1947   Sold to Soc. Algérienne de Sauvetage, Algiers. Renamed *Galatee.*
1949   Soc. Algérienne d'Armement Zagame et Cie, Algiers.
1953   Cie Maritime des Chargeurs Réunis, Le Havre. Renamed *Kaa.*
1955   Isabel Navigation Company S. A. (John Manners & Company Ltd), Panama. Renamed *Isabel.*
1965   Cia Naviera Viento del Sur S. A., Panama.
1974   Sold to Panamanian interests.
1974   Straits Chartering Agency Pte. Ltd, Singapore. Renamed *Terang.*
5.8.1976   Wrecked off Pasni, Pakistan.

85. *Pembroke Coast* (2) (1936) O.N. 164296

625 grt   61.5 × 10.4 × 6.4 m
B. Henry Robb Ltd, Leith. Yard No. 227.
Twin screw, 250 nhp, British Polar oil engines, 5 cylinder. By British Auxiliaries Ltd, Glasgow. 12 knots.

18.6.1936   Launched as *Pembroke Coast* for Coast Lines Ltd.

20.5.1940   On a voyage from Avonmouth carrying petrol and stores she was attacked and bombed by German aircraft.
21.5.1940   Scuttled off Harstad, Norway.

86. *Welsh Coast* (2) (1937) O.N. 165464

481 grt   49.89 × 8.04 × 3.04 m
B. N. V. Indust. Maats De Noord, Alblasserdam, Netherlands. Yard No. 566.
Single screw, 4SCSA oil engine, 94 nhp, 8 cylinder. By Humboldt-Deutz motoren AG.

1937   Ordered as *Mimija.*
1.1937   Delivered as Welsh Coast to Coast Lines Ltd, Liverpool.
5.1937   Transferred to the British Channel Islands Shipping Company Ltd, renamed *Emerald Queen.*
1947   Transferred to the Tyne Tees Shipping Company Ltd, renamed *Grampian Coast.*
1963   Sold to Italian interests, renamed *Gilda.*
1977   Floating restaurant at Porto Garibaldi, Italy.

87. *Antrim Coast* (2) (1936) O.N. 164314

646 grt   234 nrt   61.14 × 10.08 × 3.38 m
B. Ardrossan Dockyard Ltd, Ardrossan. Yard No. 364.
Single screw, oil engine, 224 nhp, 4 cylinder. By J. G. Kincaid & Company Ltd.

17.12.1936 Launched as *Antrim Coast* for Coast Lines Ltd, Liverpool.
31.8.1964   Transferred to the British Channel Islands Shipping Company Ltd.
30.12.1964 Renamed *Sark Coast.* Port of registry changed to London.
1967   Sold to L. Raissis, Beirut, and renamed *Miltiadis.*
15.1.1973   Breaking commenced at Perama.

88. *Palmston* (1907) O.N. 140428

430 grt   195 nrt   48.76 × 9.47 × 2.77 m

B. Fullerton & Company Ltd, Paisley. Yard No. 199.

Single screw, compound steam engine, 130 lbs, 59 rhp, 2 cylinder. By Colin Houston & Company Ltd.

26.7.1907   Launched as *La Plata* for La Fluvial-Antonio Carbone, Buenos Aires (Henry Burden & Company Ltd).

1917   Instone Transport & Trading Company Ltd (S. Instone & Company Ltd, London). Allocated O.N. 140428.

1922   S. Instone & Company Ltd, London.

1923   Invicta Coal & Shipping Company Ltd (C. E. Hallett Ltd, London and Sandwich).

1926   Henry Burden Jr & Company Ltd, London and Poole.

1937   Coast Lines Ltd.

5.1937   James Mitchell & Company Ltd, Leith.

1940   Risdon Beazley Ltd, Leith and Southampton.

1946   T. & W. Colassi Ltd, London.

1947   A/S Rederi Anholt, R. L. Albertsen, Copenhagen.

1949   Converted to a motor ship 2SA, 5 cylinder, by Alpha Frederikshavns MV.

8.1962   Broken up at Randers by Logstrup & Company Ltd.

89. *Burdenna IV* (1920) O.N. 145163

146 grt   38.31 × 5.00 × 2.28 m

B. Kings Lynn Shipbuilding Company Ltd.

Single screw, 2SCSA, 2 cylinder, oil engine. By Petters Ltd.

1920   Sailing barge *Anglomex No. 1*.

1933   Engined and purchased from Henry Burden & Company Ltd as *Burdenna IV*.

1.1938   Sold to T. W. Dawson Ltd.

1939   Sold to Stevinson, Hardy & Company Ltd.

1940   Comben Longstaff & Company Ltd.

1949   John Harker Ltd, Knottingley, renamed *Bardale H.*

22.3.1971   Broken up.

90. *Norfolk Coast* (3) (1937) O.N. 164344

646 grt   234 nrt   61.14 × 10.08 × 3.38 m

B. Ardrossan Dockyard Company. Yard No. 367.

Single screw, 6 cylinder, 4SCSA, diesel engine, 224 nhp. By John Kincaid & Company Ltd, Greenock.

29.9.1937   Launched as *Norfolk Coast*.

28.2.1945   On a voyage from Cardiff to Liverpool she was torpedoed and sank 20 miles west of Fishguard by the German submarine *U-1302*.

Norfolk Coast (3).

91. *Cornish Coast* (3) (1936) O.N. 164313

219 grt   127 nrt   36.57 × 8.26 × 2.40 m

B. Ardrossan Dockyard Ltd, Ardrossan. Yard No. 365.

Single screw, oil engine, 98 nhp, 4 cylinder. By J. G. Kincaid & Company Ltd.

16.12.1936   Launched for Coast Lines Ltd, Liverpool, for use as a lighter at Falmouth.

1949   Sold to M. H. Bland, Gibraltar. Renamed *Gibel Musa*.

12.1954   Owned by Leon Farouche, Tangiers.

1959   Deleted from Lloyd's Register.

92. *Hampshire Coast* (2) (1937) O.N. 164317

485 grt   51.5 × 8.5 × 3.4 m

B. N. V. Indust. Maats De Noord, Alblasserdam, Netherlands. Yard No. 564.

Single screw, oil engine, 4SCSA, 94 nhp, 8 cylinder. By Humboldt Deutz-motoren AG. 8½ knots.

1937   Delivered as *Hampshire Coast* for Coast Lines Ltd, Liverpool.

9.1946   Sold to Springwell Shipping Ltd. Renamed *Springhaven*.

12.1947   To the Dundee, Perth & London Shipping Company Ltd. Renamed *Gannochy*.

25.2.1958   On a voyage from Penmaenmawr to Liverpool, she foundered in the Mersey Channel.

93. *Denbigh Coast* (2) (1937) O.N. 164312

484 grt   49.9 × 7.5 × 3 m

B. Scheeps de Noord Alblasserdam, Netherlands. Yard No. 562.

Single screw, oil engine, 94 nhp. By Deutz-Humboldt Klöckner, Humboldt Deutz A. G., Köln, Germany.

1937   Delivered as *Denbigh Coast*.

1951   Transferred to Burns & Laird Lines, renamed *Lairdsfern*.

1959   Reverted to *Denbigh Coast*.

18.7.1960   On a voyage from Manchester to Belfast, she sank in collision with *Irish Maple* in the Crosby Channel, Liverpool.

94. *Kentish Coast* (2) (1938) O.N. 166237

459 grt   50.50 × 8.04 × 2.92 m

B. J. Smit, Foxhol, Netherlands. Yard No. 523.

Single screw, oil engine, 4SCSA, 94 nhp, 8 cylinder. By Humboldt Deutz-motoren AG. 9 knots.

7.1938   Delivered as *Kentish Coast* to Coast Lines Ltd, Liverpool.

1962   Sold to Luigi C. Melloni, Savona, and renamed *Melisenda*.

1971   Renamed *Monte Carmo*.

1973   Renamed *Vanna*.

1974   Renamed *Alekekos*.

Renamed *Aboude*.

1992   Deleted from Lloyd's Register.

95. *Welsh Coast* (3) (1937) O.N. 164349

646 grt   234 nrt   61.14 × 10.08 × 3.38 m

B. Ardrossan Dockyard Ltd, Ardrossan. Yard No. 368.

Single screw, oil engine, 224 nhp, 6 cylinder. By J. G. Kincaid & Company Ltd.

4.12.1937   Launched as *Welsh Coast* for Coast Lines Ltd, Liverpool.

1955   Transferred to the British Channel Islands Shipping Company Ltd, renamed *Guernsey Coast*.

6.8.1964   On a voyage from St Peter Port to Shoreham, with a cargo of tomatoes, she was in collision with the Liberian *Catcher* in fog and sank 38 miles north-east of Cap de la Hague.

96. *Mersey Coast* (1938) O.N. 166234

509 grt   61.6 × 9.8 × 5.8 m

Mersey Coast.

Normandy Coast.

B. Scheeps de Noord, Alblasserdam, Netherlands. Yard No. 569.
Single screw, 4SCSA, oil engine, 144 nhp, 750 bhp, 6 cylinder. By
Humboldt Deutz-motoren AG.

6.1938	Delivered as *Mersey Coast*.
1955	Re-engined with new Humboldt-Deutz oil engine.
6.11.1958	Transferred to British Channel Islands Shipping Company Ltd.
5.10.1962	Coast Lines Ltd.
4.1967	Sold to Greek interests and renamed *Agios Artemios*.

31.5.1971–1.6.1971 On a voyage from Karachi to the Persian Gulf, it was discovered that she was leaking and was grounded 9 miles south-east of Ormara, Pakistan.

97. *Normandy Coast* (1916) O.N. 139129
1,428 grt   79.2 × 11.6 × 4.6 m
B. Sir Raylton Dixon & Company Ltd, Middlesbrough. Yard No. 592.
Single screw, triple expansion, steam engine, 162 nhp. By Richardsons, Westgarth & Company Ltd, Middlesbrough.

17.4.1916	Launched as *Lady Cloe* for the British & Irish Steam Packet Company Ltd.
7.1938	Coast Lines Ltd. Renamed *Normandy Coast*.
11.1.1945	On a voyage from London to Liverpool, with steel plates, she was torpedoed and sunk off Port Lynas, Anglesey, by the German submarine *U-1055*.

98. *Clyde Coast* (2) (1938) O.N. 166243

511 grt   59.61 × 9.63 × 2.95 m

B. Scheeps de Noord, Alblasserdam, Netherlands. Yard No. 570.

Single screw, oil engine, 144 nhp, 750 bhp. By Humboldt Deutz-motoren, Köln-Deutz, Germany. 10½ knots.

21.5.1938	Launched as *Clyde Coast* for Coast Lines Ltd, Liverpool.
3.1956	Owned by the Belfast Steamship Company, renamed *Ulster Senator*.
1958	New engines by Humboldt Deutz-motoren, Köln-Deutz, Germany. 915 bhp.
1959	Transferred to William Sloan & Company Ltd, became *Deveron*.
1963	Sold to E. C. Georgopoulos & A. N. Athanassiades & Company, Piraeus, Greece and renamed *Nissos Delos*.
1966	Sold to Dimitrios Argyreas, Piraeus, Greece and renamed *Dora Maria*.
1968	Renamed *Maria*.
1969	Renamed *Ismini L.*
1972	Sold to Ismini L. Shipping Company Ltd, Piraeus, Greece.
1973	Sold to D. Papadimitriou & V. Dalabiras, Thessaloniki, Greece.
1974	Sold to E. Papadimitriou, Piraeus, Greece, and renamed *Makedonia*.
1979	Sold to N. Palaeopoulos, Piraeus, Greece.
28.9.1979	On a voyage from Larnaca to Jounieh, Lebanon, she sank 7 miles off Cape Kiti, Cyprus.

99. *Brittany Coast* (1918) O.N. 143218

1,389 grt   85.2 × 11.6 m

B. Caledon Shipbuilding & Engineering Company Ltd. Yard No. 267.

Single screw, triple expansion, steam engine, 277.5 rhp, 196 nhp. By builder. 12 knots.

1918	Ordered by the British Government as a war standard ship.
18.3.1919	Launched as *War Garry*.
21.5.1919	Delivered as *Lady Emerald* to the British & Irish Steam Packet Company Ltd, London.
1921	Registered in Dublin.
1936	Owners became the British & Irish Steam Packet Company (1936) Ltd, Dublin.
1938	Renamed *Carlow*.
	Owner renamed the British & Irish Steam Packet Company Ltd.
1939	To Coast Lines Ltd, Liverpool, renamed *Brittany Coast*.
1946	Transferred to Burns & Laird Lines Ltd, renamed *Kildare*.
1948	Registered under the British & Irish Steam Packet Company Ltd, Liverpool.
1952	To Burns & Laird Lines Ltd, renamed *Lairdsford*.
5.4.1960	Arrived at Troon and broken up.

100. *Galway Coast* (1915) O.N. 139074

1,542 grt   79.24 × 11.58 × 4.57 m

B. Clyde Shipbuilding & Engineering Company Ltd, Port Glasgow. Yard No. 314.

Single screw, triple expansion, steam engine, 134 rhp, 216 nhp, 3 cylinder. By builder. 11 knots.

27.5.1915	Launched.
1915	Delivered to the British & Irish Steam Packet Company Ltd.
1936	Owned by the British & Irish Steam Packet Company (1936) Ltd (Dublin).
1938	Renamed *Galway*.

1938   Owners renamed British & Irish Steam Packet Company Ltd.

5.1939   Transferred to Coast Lines Ltd, Liverpool, renamed *Galway Coast*.

1945   Sold to Virtu Steamship Company Ltd (Anthony & Bainbridge Ltd), Liverpool.

1946   Renamed *Virtu*.

1947   Registered at *Malta*.

27.2.1948   On a voyage from Port Said to Tobruk she grounded off Raz Azzaz lighthouse, between Bardia and Tobruk, Libya.

19.5.1948   Refloated, towed to Tobruk and laid up.

11.1950   Broken up at Tobruk.

101. *Avon Coast* (1922) O.N. 147391

1,036 grt   70.28 × 10.66 × 4.54 m

B. W. Dobson & Company, Walker on Tyne. Yard No. 220.

Single screw, triple expansion, steam, 193 rhp and nhp, 3 cylinder by North East Marine Engineering Company Ltd, Newcastle. 10¾ knots.

20.11.1922   Launched as *Sapper* for Fisher, Renwick Steamers Ltd, Manchester.

1923   Delivered.

4.1939   Sold to Coast Lines Ltd, Liverpool, renamed *Avon Coast*.

9.1949   To the Belfast Steamship Company Ltd, renamed *Ulster Star*.

9.1954   Broken up at Briton Ferry.

102. *Medway Coast* (1924) O.N. 147403

1,014 grt   70.25 × 10.66 × 4.57 m

B. Tyne Iron Shipbuilding Company, Willington Quay. Yard No. 228. 10 knots.

Single screw, triple expansion, steam engine, 193 nhp, 3 cylinder. By North East Marine Engineering Company Ltd.

17.6.1924   Launched as *Sentry* for Fisher, Renwick Steamers Ltd, Manchester.

4.1939   Sold to Coast Lines Ltd, Liverpool, renamed *Medway Coast*.

9.1949   Transferred to the Belfast Steamship Company Ltd, renamed *Ulster Duchess*.

9.1955   Broken up at Port Glasgow.

103. *Thames Coast* (1914) O.N. 135360

1,045 grt   70.3 × 10.7 × 4.54 m

B. W. Dobson & Company Ltd, Newcastle. Yard No. 189.

Single screw, triple expansion, steam engine, 170 nhp, 3 cylinder. By North Eastern Marine Ltd, Sunderland.

1914   Delivered as *Cuirassier* to Fisher Renwick & Company Ltd, Newcastle.

4.1939   Coast Lines Ltd, Liverpool (Powell, Bacon & Hough Ltd). Renamed *Thames Coast*.

11.1946   Sold to Malabar Steamship Company Ltd, Bombay (Mumbai), India. Renamed *Jagdamba*.

30.12.1948   On a voyage from Calicut to Tuticorin with a cargo of baled cotton she was stranded 30 miles south of Tuticorin and later broken up.

104. *Kerry Coast* (1918) O.N. 143158

1,391 grt   82.47 × 11.61 × 4.93 m

B. Caledon Shipbuilding & Engineering Company Ltd. Yard No. 266.

Single screw, triple expansion, steam, 280 rhp, 196 nhp. By builder. 12 knots.

1918   Ordered by the British Government as a war standard ship.

18.2.1919   Launched as *War Spey*, delivered as *Lady Patricia* to the British & Irish Steam Packet Company Ltd, London.

1921   Registered in Dublin.

1936   Owned by the British & Irish Steam Packet Company (1936) Ltd (Dublin).

1938   Renamed *Kerry*.
Owner became the British & Irish Steam Packet Company Ltd.

5.1939   To Coast Lines Ltd, Liverpool, renamed *Kerry Coast*.

1941   To Burns & Laird Lines Ltd, Liverpool.

11.3.1944   Sunk following a collision with *Mosdale* in the Mersey.

20.5.1945   Raised and salvaged.

1945   Sold to Henry P. Lenaghan & Sons Ltd, Belfast, renamed *Bangor Bay*.

1946   Purchased by the Burns & Laird Lines Ltd, Liverpool, renamed *Kerry*.

1947   Transferred to the British & Irish Steam Navigation Company Ltd.

6.1959   Broken up at Passage West.

105. *Glamorgan Coast* (2) (1920) O.N. 143533

879 grt   60.96 × 9.44 × 3.96 m
B. Dublin Dockyard Company Ltd, Dublin. Yard No. 105.
Single screw, triple expansion, steam, 120 rhp, 155 nhp, 3 cylinder. By Ross & Duncan Ltd, Glasgow.

27.11.1920   Launched as *Finola* for Michael Murphy Ltd, Dublin.

1921   Registered in Cardiff.

1926   Michael Murphy Ltd acquired by the British & Irish Steam Packet Company Ltd.

1936   British & Irish Steam Packet Company (1936) Ltd.

5.1939   Transferred to Coast Lines Ltd, Liverpool. Renamed *Glamorgan Coast*.

5.1947   Transferred to British Channel Traders Ltd, London. Renamed *Stuart Queen*.
To Queenship Navigation Ltd, London.

1952   To Zillah Shipping Company Ltd (W. A. Savage Ltd), Liverpool. Renamed *Caldyfield*.

1955   Broken up at Preston.

106. *Suffolk Coast* (3) (1938) O.N. 166362

535 grt   53.3 × 8.5 × 3.4 m
B. Scheeps E. J. Smit, Westerbroek. Yard No. 653.
Single screw, oil engine, 94 nhp. By Deutz-Humboldt, Klöckner Humboldt Deutz, Köln, Germany.

1938   Delivered as *Marali* to M. Porn & Company Ltd, London.

11.1939   Coast Lines Ltd, Liverpool. Renamed *Suffolk Coast*.

1963   Sold to L. G. Melloni and renamed *Melania*.

9.2.1970   Sank 10 miles south of Leghorn.

107. *Moray Coast* (2) (1940) O.N. 166307

687 grt   251 nrt   990 dwt 61.50 × 10.11 × 3.41 m
B. Ardrossan Dockyard Company. Yard No. 379.
Single screw, oil engine, 218 nhp, 7 cylinder. By British Auxiliaries Ltd.

6.7.1940   Launched as *Moray Coast* for Coast Lines Ltd.

9.1954   Transferred to the British Channel islands Shipping Company Ltd. Renamed *Jersey Coast*.

1967   Sold to Orri Navigation Lines, Jeddah, and renamed *Star of Ibrahim*.

1973   Purchased by Ahmed Mohamed Baaboud & Hussan Mohamed Fayez & Sons, Jeddah. Renamed *Blue Sky*.

9.1980   Machinery damaged.

9.2.1982   Scuttled off Shaab al Musmary, Jeddah.

108. *Southern Coast* (2) (1943) O.N. 168858

883 grt   424 nrt   1,415 dwt   71.47 × 10.72 × 3.56 m
B. Ardrossan Dockyard Company. Yard No. 391.

Moray Coast (2).

Single screw, oil engine, 2SCSA, 1,280 bhp, 8 cylinder. By British Auxiliaries Ltd.

28.1.1943   Launched as *Southern Coast* for Coast Lines Ltd, Liverpool.

1955   Belfast, Mersey & Manchester Steamship Company Ltd. Renamed *Colebrooke*.

1959   William Sloan & Company Ltd, Glasgow.

1962   Transferred to the British Channel Islands Shipping Company Ltd. Renamed *Forth*.

1962   Reverted to *Southern Coast*.

1967   Varverakis & Hadjigeorgiou, Piraeus. Renamed *Eleistria*.

1979   Naviglory Ship Corporation Ltd, Panama. Renamed *Al Rubaiya*.

27.6.1985   Sprang a leak and sank at Bombay (Mumbai) while waiting to be broken up.

1986   Broken up.

109. *Orkney Coast* (2) (1921) O.N. 145595

650 grt   250 nrt   48.76 × 8.99 × 3.41 m

B. Ailsa Shipbuilding Company Ltd, Troon. Yard No. 381.

Single screw, triple expansion, steam engine, 81 nhp, 3 cylinder. By builder.

20.5.1921   Launched as *Arclight* for Light Shipping Company Ltd (Ross & Marshall Ltd), Greenock.

1933   Gilchrist Traders (Steamships) Ltd (F. B. Johnston Ltd), Liverpool. Renamed *Fire Queen*.

11.1945   Coast Lines Ltd, Liverpool. Renamed *Orkney Coast*.

1949   Zillah Shipping Company Ltd. Renamed *Dransfield*.

10.11.1955   Arrived at Troon and broken up by the West of Scotland Shipbreaking Company Ltd.

110. *Perdita* (1910) O.N. 131309

543 grt   53.3 × 8 m

B. Mackay Brothers Ltd, Alloa. Yard No. 14.

Single screw, triple expansion, steam engine, 97 nhp, 3 cylinder. By McColl, Pollock & Company.

15.11.1910   Launched.

1943   Purchased from R. Gilchrist & Company Ltd.

1945   Sold to Mersey Ports Stevedoring Company Ltd.

5.1951   Sold to Giovanni Fornara, Italy.

1952   Re-engined and renamed *Sedula*.

1953   Renamed *Susanna*.

12.2.1953   Wrecked on Abu Faramish reef, 30 miles south of Jeddah.

111. *Victor* (1907) O.N. 124200

437 grt   165 nrt   45.72 × 7.65 × 2.83 m

B. John Shearer & Sons Ltd, Glasgow. Yard No. 46.

Single screw, compound steam engine, 68 nhp, 2 cylinder. By Hutson & Son Ltd.

17.6.1907   Launched as *Victor* for Glasgow Steam Coasters Company Ltd (Paton & Hendry, Peter D. Hendry, Glasgow, as managers).

1911   Hendry, McCallum & Company, Glasgow, as managers.

1914   North Eastern Shipping Company Ltd (G. Elmslie & Son, Aberdeen, as managers).

             Registered in Aberdeen.

1918   South Wales & Liverpool Steamship Company Ltd (R. Gilchrist & Company, Liverpool, as managers).

1942   Coast Lines Ltd, Liverpool.

1944   Ribble Shipping Company Ltd (William J. Ireland, Liverpool).

1947   H. Harrison (Shipping) Ltd (S. W. Coe & Company Ltd, Liverpool).

1948   Glynwood Navigation Company Ltd (W. G. Thomas, Liverpool).

28.4.1953   Arrived at Llanelli and broken up by the Rees Shipbreaking Company.

112. *Shetland Coast* (1925) O.N. 147311

801 grt   58.06 × 9.50 × 3.56 m

B. J. Duthie & Sons Ltd, Aberdeen. Yard No. 464.

Single screw, triple expansion, steam engine, 186 nhp, 3 cylinder. By A. Hall & Company Ltd.

24.2.1925   Launched as *Portia* to R. Gilchrist & Company Ltd.

1943   Coast Lines Ltd, Liverpool. Renamed *Shetland Coast*.

1946   Michael Murphy Ltd, became *Portia* again.

1950   Zillah Shipping Company Ltd. Renamed *Fairfield*.

13.11.1955   Arrived at Troon and broken up by the West of Scotland Shipbreaking Company Ltd.

113. *Robina* (1914) O.N. 135726

306 grt   121 nrt   48.64 × 7.95 × 2.71 m

B. Ardrossan Dockyard Company, Ardrossan. Yard No. 259.

Twin screw, triple expansion, steam engine, 79 nhp, 6 cylinder. By McKie & Baxter Ltd.

24.4.1914   Launched for a service across Morecambe Bay by the New Morecambe Bay Central Pier Company Ltd (William A. Turner as managers).

1915–1919   Requisitioned as an auxiliary patrol vessel.

1920   Chartered to W. H. Tucker & Company Ltd, Cardiff, for services to Bristol and Weston-super-Mare.

1921   Laid up.

1922   William & Pratt Cordingley, Pudsey, for the Barrow–Fleetwood service for the Furness Railway Company.

1923–1925   Chartered to the Blackpool Steam Shipping Company Ltd and H. D. Bickerstaffe.

1925   William McCalla, Belfast, to operate from Belfast.

1927   William Trevor McCalla (Ulster Steam Tender Company), Belfast.

1929   Registered in Belfast.

6.1940   Requisitioned by the Admiralty as an examination vessel in Belfast Lough.

3.1941   Ulster Steam Tender Company Ltd, Belfast.

1942   Troop tender on the River Clyde.

1942   Caledonian Steam Packet Company Ltd, Glasgow, as managers.

1946   Purchased by Coast Lines Ltd but her draught was too large for her to operate Falmouth excursion sailings.

1946–1947   Chartered to David MacBrayne Ltd.

1948   Chartered to the Island Shipping Company Ltd and operated on the Guernsey–Sark service.

5.6.1949   On a voyage from Guernsey to Sark, she collided with and sank *Herm Coast* of the Island Shipping Company Ltd.

1949   Sold to the Southampton, Isle of Wight & South of England Royal Mail Steam Packet Company Ltd, Southampton.

8.1953   Towed to Rotterdam by the tug *Noord Holland* and broken up by Hendrik-Ido-Ambacht.

Hadrian Coast.

114. *Hadrian Coast* (194) O.N. 168807

692 grt   247 nrt   1,010 dwt   61.35 × 10.11 × 3.38 m

B. Ardrossan Dockyard Company. Yard No. 385.

Single screw, oil engine, 218 nhp, 7 cylinder. By British Auxiliaries Ltd.

12.7.194   Launched as *Empire Atoll* for the Ministry of War Transport (Coast Lines Ltd, Liverpool, as managers).

12.1946   Tyne Tees Steam Shipping Company Ltd, Newcastle. Renamed *Hadrian Coast*.

9.1948   Aberdeen Steam Navigation Company Ltd, Aberdeen.

1.1964   Coast Lines Ltd, Liverpool.

10.3.1967 Following the failure of her engines, she drifted within yards of rocks near the Smalls Lighthouse off the Pembrokeshire coast. Most of the crew were ordered to abandon ship with the master and five officers remaining on board while the ship drifted. A tug later arrived and took her to Milford Haven.

9.1967   Sold to Daviou Agoudimos & Kissiounis, Piraeus, Greece, and renamed *Elda*.

10.1.1970 On a voyage from Ravenna to Kenitra, with a cargo of fertilizer, she was grounded 2 miles east of Mehdiya, Morocco. Declared a total loss.

115. *Hampshire Coast* (3) (1940) O.N. 168075

1,224 grt   625 nrt   72.69 × 10.42 × 4.32 m

B. Ardrossan Dockyard Company. Yard No. 378.

Single screw, triple expansion, steam engine, 850 ihp, 129 nhp, 3 cylinder. By J. G. Kincaid & Company Ltd.

14.11.1940 Launched as *Stuart Queen*.

6.1946   Coast Lines Ltd, Liverpool. Renamed *Hampshire Coast*.

5.1952   Transferred to the Tyne Tees Steam Shipping Company Ltd, Newcastle.

3.1959   Broken up at Hendrik-Ido-Ambacht.

116. *Hibernian Coast* (1946) O.N. 182013

1,258 grt   1,529 dwt   79.24 × 12.19 × 4.72 m

B. Hall Russell & Company Ltd, Aberdeen. Yard No. 800.

Twin screw, oil engine, 2SCSA, 8 cylinder. By builder. 14 knots.

27.9.1946   Launched as *Aberdonian Coast* for the Aberdeen Steam Navigation Company Ltd.

1948   Coast Lines Ltd, Liverpool. Renamed *Hibernian Coast*.

25.9.1968   Renamed *Port Said Coast*.

5.1974   Arrived at Spain.

5.1974   Broken up at Murcia.

117. *Devon Coast* (3) (1937) O.N. 145577

972 grt   62.48 × 10.05 m

B. Burntisland Shipbuilders Ltd. Yard No. 211.

Single screw, 2SCSA, oil engine, 81 rhp, 5 cylinder. By British Auxiliaries Ltd.

23.8.1937   Launched as *Lottie R.* for Stone & Rolfe Steamships Ltd, Llanelly.

1946   Renamed *Yewbranch*.

4.1947   Coast Lines Ltd, became *Devon Coast*.

8.1963   *Windsor Queen*.

1965   *Elca*.

1967   *Eleni R.*

9.1973   Broken up at Perama.

118. *Dorset Coast* (4) (1938) O.N. 166365

482 grt   49.43 × 8.04 × 2.98 m

B. Boeles Werf, Bolnes. Yard No. 868.

Single screw, oil engine, 4SCSA, 400 bhp, 8 cylinder. By Humboldt Deutz-motoren AG.

1938   Delivered to British Channel Islands Shipping Company Ltd as *Saxon Queen*.

3.1947   Coast Lines Ltd, renamed *Dorset Coast*.

19.2.1951   Transferred to Coast Lines Africa and renamed *Matabele Coast*.

22.11.1961   Sold to the Union Steam Ship Company, South Africa.

Devon Coast (3).

27.5.1965   *Matabele Coast* was immobile at the anchorage in Luderitz Harbour following the loss of her propeller. *Zulu Coast* came aside and commenced towing her to Cape Town.

28.5.1965   Wind increased for the next thirty-six hours.

30.5.1965   Wind reached Force 7.

31.5.1965   Weather improved and speed was increased to 6 knots.

1.6. 1965   *Zulu Coast* and *Matabele Coast* arrived at No. 6 Quay, Cape Town.

1966   Owned by Unicorn Shipping Lines, South Africa.

4.1967   Broken up at Durban.

119. *Lady Killarney* (1911) O.N. 132019

2,284 grt   99.18 × 12.71 × 4.93 m

B. Harland & Wolff Ltd, Belfast. Yard No. 424.

Twin screw, triple expansion, steam engine, 840 rhp, 840 nhp, 6,400 bhp. By builder. 18 knots.

Lady Killarney.

7.9.1911   Launched as *Patriotic* for the Belfast Steamship Company Ltd, Belfast.

1912   Delivered.

1919   Belfast Steamship Company Ltd acquired by Coast Lines Ltd.

1930   Transferred to the British & Irish Steam Packet Company Ltd, renamed *Lady Leinster*.

1936   British & Irish Steam Packet Company (1936) Ltd.

1938   Renamed *Lady Connaught*.

1940   Registered in Liverpool.

26.12.1940   On a voyage from Liverpool to Belfast she was damaged by mines. Laid up.

1941   Abandoned by insurance underwriters.

1942   Purchased from underwriters and converted to a cattle carrier. Engines 500 rhp, 792 nhp, 2,700 bhp, 3,000 ihp. 14 knots.

1944   Converted to a hospital carrier ship, No. 55, by Barclay, Curle & Company Ltd, Glasgow.

1946   Converted to a cruise ship by builders at Belfast.

1947   Managed by Coast Lines Ltd, Liverpool. Renamed *Lady Killarney*.

1956   Broken up at Port Glasgow.

120. *Pacific Coast* (2) (1947) O.N. 181092
1,188 grt   608 nrt   1,703 dwt
B. Ardrossan Dockyard Ltd, Ardrossan. Yard No. 403.
Twin screw, oil engine, 2SCSA, 375 nhp, 2 × 6 cylinder. By J. G. Kincaid Ltd.

9.1.1947   Launched as *Pacific Coast* for Coast Lines Ltd, Liverpool.

1964   On short term charter to the Mossgiel Shipping Company, a wholly owned subsidiary of the Ellerman Papayanni Line, for a voyage from Liverpool to Lisbon, Oporto, Cadiz and Gibraltar. She returned via London to Liverpool. She carried the funnel markings of the Ellerman Line and was commanded by Captain Leask, Chief Officer was J. Dougan and Second Officer, H. Cunliffe; all possessed foreign-going masters' tickets.

26.7.1968   Sold to Alomar Mechanical Engineering Company, Kuwait. Renamed *Kuwait Coast*.

1970   Kuwait Coast Line, Kuwait.

1974   Musseib Arjumand Zayarti, Abadan. Renamed *Nassar*.

29.11.1976   On a voyage from Abadan to Bombay in ballast she broke her moorings and stranded on Port Rashid breakwater, Dubai.

121. *Baltic Coast/Cape Coast* (1947) O.N. 182434
1,722 grt   753 nrt   85.19 × 13.16 × 5.39 m
B. Ardrossan Dockyard Ltd, Ardrossan. Yard No. 404.
Twin screw, oil engine, 2SCSA, 2 × 8 cylinder. By British Polar Engines Ltd.

27.11.1947   Launched as *Baltic Coast* for Coast Lines Ltd, Liverpool.

1951   Renamed *Cape Coast* for a joint venture with Thesen's of Durban.

13.3.1952   On a voyage from Matadi to Boma she suffered a serious fire and was abandoned, 8 miles from Boma.

1953   Sold to Henry P. Lenaghan & Sons Ltd, Belfast. Renamed *Browns Bay*.

1955   Ceylon Shipping Lines Ltd, Colombo. Renamed *Chilaw*.

1961   Combined Navigation Company (Panama) Ltd, Panama (United China Shipping, Hong Kong).

8.12.1961   Foundered 700 miles north-east of Singapore, near Ladd Reef, during a typhoon. Twenty-eight of her crew lost their lives.

122. *Caledonian Coast* (1948) O.N. 182018
1,265 grt   1,529 dwt   80.77 × 12.25 × 3.81 m
B. Hall Russell & Company Ltd, Aberdeen. Yard No. 803.
Twin screw, oil engine, 2SCSA, 258 nhp, 8 cylinder. By builder.

1948   Delivered as *Caledonian Coast*.

1967   On charter to the Brocklebank Line, renamed *Makalla*.

19.11.1968   Renamed *Ahmadi Coast*.

8.4.1974   Arrived at Cartagena and broken up by Navarro Frances Ltd.

123. *Adriatic Coast* (1949) O.N. 182490
1,050 grt   1,553 dwt   72.51 × 11.64 × 4.11 m
B. Hall Russell & Company Ltd, Aberdeen. Yard No. 811.
Single screw, oil engine, 2SCSA, 8 cylinder by builder.

1.3.1949   Launched as *Adriatic Coast*.

3.10.1968   Sold to Greek interests and renamed *Trader*.

1972   *Ermis*.

1973   *Potamia*.

Cape Coast. (Courtesy of Dave Crolly)

Adriatic Coast.

1975   *Stella III.*
1980   Broken up.

124. *Baltic Queen* (1943) O.N. 169665

1,791 grt   78.9 × 12.8 × 6.4 m

B. Butler Shipbuilding Incorporated (Walter Butler), Wisconsin, USA. Yard No. 17.

Single screw, triple expansion, steam engine, 188 nhp, 3 cylinder. By Prescott & Company, Menominee, Michigan, USA. 10 knots.

9.5.1943   Launched as a Standard Type as *Gurden Gates* (originally registered to A. Coker & Company Ltd). Ministry of War Transport, London.

1949   Coast Lines Ltd, Liverpool, as *Baltic Queen.*

4.1950   Sold to Italian interests and renamed *Cesare Corsini.*

1953   Renamed *Arno.*

1964   *Irida.*

1965   *O Kalos Samaritis.*

1965   *Three Stars.*

17.2.1967   On a voyage from Tripoli (Lebanon) to Tripoli (Libya), with a cargo of cement and lime, she caught fire and was abandoned near Cape Gata, Cyprus. She was beached at Episkopi Bay and later towed to the Akrotiri peninsula and beached. She was later declared a total loss.

125. *Damara* (1942) O.N. 169577

1,791 grt   76.38 × 12.83 × 5.60 m

B. Butler Shipbuilding Incorporated (Walter Butler), Wisconsin, USA. Yard No. 5.

Single screw, triple expansion, steam engine, 3 cylinder. By Prescott Company, Menominee, Michigan.

9.8.1942   Launched as a Standard Type as *William Bursley*, with work carried out at Belfast for trading to South African ports (Queenship Navigation Ltd). Ministry of War Transport, London. (A. Coker & Company).

11.1950   Sold to Italian interests. Renamed *Pietro Conali.*

1954   *Lake Charles.*

1962   *Rimandi Mibaja.*

9.5.1964   On a voyage from Paramaribo to Mobile with bauxite she grounded off Gorling Bluff in the Grand Cayman Islands.

126. *Sark Coast* (1945) O.N. ??

318 grt   45.78 × 6.73 × 3.04 m

B. Teeside Bridge & Engineering Company Ltd, South Bank.

Single screw, oil engine, 4SCSA. By Davey Paxman & Company Ltd.

1945   Delivered as *LCG (M) 156* to Island Shipping Company Ltd.

1949   Coast Lines Ltd, Liverpool. Renamed *Sark Coast.*

1952   Sold to the French Government. Renamed *Madinina.*

1957   To St Vincent interests.

13.12.1963   On a voyage from Trinidad to Martinique she sank 12 miles north of St Vincent.

127. *Herero Coast* (1950) O.N. 185474

493 grt

B. Bodewes Scheeps, Martenshoek, Netherlands. Yard No. 123.

Single screw, oil engine, 4SCSA, 6 cylinder. By builder.

1950   Delivered as *Poseidon.*

24.11.1953   Coast Lines Africa (Pty) Ltd. Renamed *Herero Coast.*

31.8.1959   To the Union Steam Ship Company, South Africa.

1966   Unicorn Shipping Lines, South Africa.

6.1968   Broken up at Durban, South Africa by K. Nathan Pty Ltd.

128. *Irish Coast* (3) (1952) O.N. 185446

3,824 grt   99.88 × 15.72 × 4.45 m

B. Harland & Wolff Ltd, Belfast. Yard No. 1461.

Twin Screw, oil engine, 2SCSA, 1,300 nhp, 6,500 bhp, 8,150 ihp, 20 cylinder. By builder. 17½ knots.

8.5.1952   Launched as *Irish Coast* for Coast Lines Ltd, Liverpool.

16.8.1968   Sold to Epirotiki Steamship Navigation Company, George Potamianos S. A., Piraeus, Greece. Renamed *Orpheus*.

1969   Renamed *Semiramis II* and later *Achilleus*.

1970   Renamed *Apollon 11*.

1982   Sold to Corporation Naviera International de Panama S. A., Panama. Renamed *Regency*.

1983   Purchased by Triton Holding Corporation (Passman Shipping Agency S. A., Miami, Florida).

1989   Wrecked in hurricane in the Philippines.

1990   Broken up at Manila.

129. *Western Coast* (5) (1951) O.N. 183821

782 grt   68.51 × 10.75 × 3.41 m

B. Goole Shipbuilding & Engineering Company Ltd, Goole. Yard No. 476. Single screw, oil engine, 2SCSA, 7 cylinder. By builder.

19.6.1951   Launched as *Western Coast* to Coast Lines Ltd, Liverpool.

12.7.1958   Transferred to William Sloan & Company Ltd, Glasgow, and renamed *Tay*.

12.1967   Sold and renamed *Charalambos*.

1973   *Erika*.

14.5.1973   On a voyage from Galati to Hull with timber she struck a rock near Ayios Eustratios and sank.

Right: Irish Coast (3).

130. *Cheshire Coast* (2) (1954) O.N. 185481

1,202 grt   75.22 × 11.76 × 3.59 m

B. Cammell Laird & Company Ltd, Birkenhead. Yard No. 1251.

Single screw, oil engine, 2SCSA, Sulzer, 290 nhp, 5 cylinder. By George Clark (1938) Ltd.

6.1.1954   Launched as *Cheshire Coast* for Coast Line Ltd, Liverpool.

23.9.1965   Belfast Steamship Company Ltd, Belfast. Port of registry continued to be Liverpool.

1967   Chartered to the Brocklebank Line, renamed *Malabar*.

19.10.1967   Chartered to Prince Line, renamed *Spartan Prince*.

1967   Coast Lines Ltd, Liverpool.

1971   Reverted to *Cheshire Coast* at the termination of the charter. Coast Lines (Service) Ltd, Liverpool.

Cheshire Coast (2).

Coast Lines acquired by P&O (P&O Short Sea Shipping Ltd).

Sold to Amanda Shipping Company Ltd, Piraeus. Renamed *Venture*.

1974   Purchased by Skiros Shipping Company Ltd (Dinami Shipping Agency Ltd, Surrey). Renamed *Azelia*.

7.1980   Broken up at Cartagena.

131. *Lancashire Coast* (3) (1953) O.N. 185482

1,020 grt   1,027 dwt   407 nrt   78.02 × 11.91 × 6.52 m

B. Charles Hill & Sons Ltd, Bristol. Yard No. 389.

Single screw, oil engine, 2SCSA, 1,625 bhp, Sulzer, 161 nhp, 5 cylinder. By George Clark (1938) Ltd, Sunderland.

18.11.1953   Launched.

4.1954   Delivered as *Lancashire Coast* to Coast Lines Ltd, Liverpool.

29.9.1965   Transferred to the Belfast Steamship Company Ltd, Belfast. Port of registry continued to be Liverpool.

5.1967   Converted into a cattle/car carrier by Harland & Wolff Ltd at Belfast for the Belfast–Liverpool route.

12.1967   Transferred to Coast Lines Ltd, Liverpool.

2.4.1968   Chartered to Prince Line Ltd, renamed *Trojan Prince*.

4.1969   Managed by the Belfast Steamship Company Ltd, reverted back to *Lancashire Coast*.

26.2.1971   Coast Lines Ltd acquired by the P&O Steam Navigation Company Ltd.

6.1971   Registered under Coast Lines (Services) Ltd.

1.10.1971   Managed by P&O Short Sea Shipping Ltd.

1.11.1972   Registered under the Belfast Steamship Company Ltd.

31.3.1975   Managed by P&O Ferries.

21.9.1978   Registered under P&O Ferries Ltd.

26.6.1980   Sold to United West Desert for Development de Honduras S de RL, renamed *Paolino*.

24.12.1981   Laid up at Piraeus, Greece.

5.1982   Transferred to Chalkis, Greece.

9.1983   Sold to Marine Construction of Salamis, Greece, for demolition.

3.1984   Demolition commenced at Salamis.

132. *Fife Coast* (3) (1954) O.N. 185507

906 grt   1,057 dwt   344 nrt   69 × 10.85 × 6.33 m

B. George Brown & Company Ltd, Greenock. Yard No. 260.

Single screw, 1,440 bhp, 4SCSA, Sulzer, diesel engine, 8 cylinder. By builder at Sunderland. 12 knots.

20.9.1954   Launched by Mrs Gordon Beazley.

12.1954   Delivered as *Fife Coast* to Coast Lines Ltd, Liverpool.

20.6.1958   Transferred to William Sloan & Company Ltd, Glasgow, renamed *Fruin*.

24.12.1963   Operated by the Belfast Steamship Company Ltd, Belfast, renamed *Stormont*.

29.9.1965   Transferred to Coast Lines Ltd, Liverpool. Port of registry continued to be Belfast.

13.12.1966   Transferred to Tyne Tees Shipping Company Ltd, Newcastle.

26.2.1971   Tyne Tees Shipping Company Ltd acquired by P&O Steam Navigation Company Ltd.

1.10.1971   Managed by P&O Short Sea Shipping Ltd.

31.3.1975   Operated by P&O Ferries.

16.7.1976   Owned by P&O Ferries (General European) Ltd (P&O Ferries as managers).

14.10.1976   Sold to Farouk Rassem, W. Moukahal and Ahmed Hassan Zeido (Union Commercial Company as managers), Lebanon, renamed *Rabunion VII*.

1992   Purchased by Baraa Z. Shipping Company SARL (Zeido Hassan Zeido as managers), Beirut, renamed *Baraa Z.*

6.1994   Broken up at Tripoli, Lebanon.

133. *Essex Coast* (1955) O.N. 187106

892 grt   65.98 × 10.72 × 3.56 m

B. Ardrossan Dockyard Ltd, Ardrossan. Yard No. 417.

Single screw, oil engine, 257 rhp, 1,440 bhp. By George Clark (1938) Ltd, Sunderland.

24.3.1955   Launched as *Essex Coast* for Coast Lines Ltd, Liverpool.

1957   Transferred to the Belfast, Mersey & Manchester Steamship Company Ltd (John J. Mack & Sons Ltd, Belfast, as managers). Renamed *Mountstewart*.

1960   Managed by the Belfast Steamship Company Ltd, retained previous colours.

1965   Transferred to Coast Lines Ltd.

1967   Operated for British Channel Islands Shipping Company Ltd, London.

1968   Transferred back to Coast Lines Ltd.

1969   Sold to Greek Currant Producers Line of Panama. Renamed *Evdelos*.

1970   Arrested by Admiralty Marshal at Shoreham.

1971   Sold to Pounds Shipowners & Shipbreakers Ltd, Portsmouth.

1972   Purchased by Pothitos Shipping Cia. S. A., Piraeus, Greece. Renamed *Michalis*. Owners later became Pothitos Shipping Company, Piraeus.

1975   Sold to Mossel Bay Shipping Company Ltd, Piraeus.

1976   Sold to Proodos Shipping Company Ltd (Prodromos Cia.) (Financiera y Marittima S. A., Piraeus as managers). Renamed *Poodos*.

1971   Sold to Amanda Shipping Company Ltd, Piraeus. Renamed *Venture*.

1974   Purchased by Skiros Shipping Company Ltd (Dinami Shipping Agency Ltd as managers). Renamed *Azelia*.

1975   Registered in Limassol.

1980   Broken up at Cartagena, Colombia.

Mountstewart (2).

Scottish Coast (2) at Liverpool on the Belfast–Liverpool service, showing the car lift that had been installed for the Ardrossan–Belfast service.

134. *Scottish Coast* (2) (1956) O.N.187159

2,817 grt   100.55 × 15.72 × 4.66 m

B. Harland & Wolff Ltd, Belfast. Yard No. 1547.

Twin screw, oil engine, 2SA each 1,160 rhp, 6,500 bhp, 10 cylinder. By builder. 17½ knots.

21.8.1956   Launched as *Scottish Coast* for Coast Lines Ltd, Liverpool.

1958   Managed by Burns & Laird Lines Ltd.

1.1.1968   To Coast Lines Ltd, Liverpool.

11.1969   Sold to Kavounides Shipping Company, S. A. Ltd, Piraeus, Greece. Renamed *Galaxias*.

Hellenic Cruises S. A. (Kavounides Shipping Company, S. A. Ltd, Piraeus, Greece, as managers).

1986   Based at Vancouver on charter.

1987   Sold to Global Cruises S. A., San Antonio, Texas, USA.

1989   Sold to Princesa Amorosa Company Ltd (Louis Shipping Ltd, Limassol, Cyprus, as managers). Renamed *Princesa Amorosa* and operating to Rhodes, Patmos, Mykonos, Santorini, Heraklion, Port Said and Ashdod.

1996–1997   Louis Ship Management Ltd (Louis Cruise Lines) as managers.

2000   Laid up.

2002   Arrived at Mumbai.

2003   Broken up at Mumbai.

135. *Cambrian Coast* (2) (1957) O.N. 187173

560 grt   850 dwt   270 nrt   56.96 × 9.11 × 3.99 m

B. Scheeps Ijsselwerf, Rotterdam, Netherlands. Yard No. 111.

Single screw, 4SA, 620 bhp, D. & J. Boot 'De Industrie', Alphen 8 cylinder engine.

11.1957   Delivered as *Jan T.*, renamed *Cambrian Coast*.

26.2.1971   Coast Lines Ltd acquired by the P&O Steam Navigation Company Ltd.

14.6.1971   Sold to W. E. Dowds, Newport, Monmouthshire, renamed *Lorraine D.*

1982   Renamed *Glenhaven*.

24.6.1988   Arrived at Milford Haven and broken up.

136. *Somerset Coast* (3) O.N. 187194

1,376 grt   1,734 dwt   68.39 × 10.85 × 4.02 m

B. Clelands Shipbuilding Company Ltd, Wallsend. Yard No. 223.

Single screw, oil engine, 2SA, 7 cylinder. By George Clark (1938) Ltd. 11 knots.

20.3.1958   Launched as *Somerset Coast* (she had been purchased on the stocks).

19.5.1959   Renamed *Richmond Queen*.

1974   *Gomba Enterprise*.

1976   *Atlantic Enterprise*.

2.10.1978   Arrived at Brake and broken up by Eckhardt & Company.

137. *Spaniel* (2) (1955) O.N. 187114

1,262 grt   65.07 × 11.00 × 5.51 m

B. George Brown & Company Ltd, Greenock. Yard No. 262.

Single screw, oil engine, 2SA, Sulzer, 126 nhp, 7 cylinder. By builder. 11 knots.

21.6.1955   Launched as *Brentfield*.

1959   Renamed *Spaniel*.

1.1.1965   Transferred to Burns & Laird Line. Port of registry changed to Glasgow.

9.9.1968   To Coast Lines Ltd, Liverpool.

Conister at Douglas, Isle of Man.

1970   Coast Lines (Services) Ltd.

1971   Managed by P&O Short Sea Shipping Ltd.

8.1972   To the Belfast Steamship Company Ltd.

11.1973   Sold to the Isle of Man Steam Packet Company Ltd, renamed *Conister*.

29.9.1981   Arrived at Aviles and broken up.

138. *Pointer* (2) (1956) O.N. 187140

907 grt   1,151 dwt   442 nrt 71.26 × 11.39 × 4.66 m

B. Ardrossan Dockyard Ltd, Ardrossan. Yard No. 422.

Single screw, 1,260 bhp, 2SCSA, Sulzer, diesel engine, 7 cylinder. By G. Clark & NE Marine (Sunderland) Ltd, Sunderland. 10½ knots.

2.2.1956   Launched.

7.1956	Delivered as *Birchfield* to the Zillah Shipping Company Ltd (W. A. Savage Ltd as managers), Liverpool.
4.12.1958	Transferred to Coast Lines Ltd, Liverpool.
1.1959	Renamed *Pointer*.
1.1.1965	Transferred to Burns & Laird Lines Ltd, Glasgow. Port of registry changed to Glasgow.
9.8.1968	Transferred to Coast Lines Ltd, Liverpool.
1970	Registered under Coast Lines (Services) Ltd, Liverpool.
26.2.1971	Coast Lines Ltd acquired by the P&O Steam Navigation Company Ltd.
1.10.1971	Managed by P&O Short Sea Shipping Ltd.
1.6.1972	Transferred to the Belfast Steamship Company Ltd, Belfast.
31.3.1975	Managed by P&O Ferries.
6.8.1975	Sold to Isthmian Navigation Company Ltd (Hellenic Mediterranean Lines Company Ltd as managers), Greece, renamed *Taurus III*.
1976	Management transferred to Compania Armadora de Sudamerica S. A., Limassol.
1981	Sold to Thomas Bourtsalas, Greece, to be demolished.
11.11.1981	Delivered at Eleusis but not broken up.
1984	Sold to Phalarope Shipping Ltd, Valetta, Malta. Later resold to Larnaca Project S de RL (S. Ch. Jeropoulous & Company Ltd as managers), San Lorenzo, Honduras, renamed *Larnaca Town*.
1985	Renamed *Mina*.
16.5.1986	Arrived at Perama and broken up.

139. *Dorset Coast* (5) (1959) O.N. 301304

1,206 grt   1,297 dwt   626 nrt   67.08 × 10.94 × 4.48 m
B. Ardrossan Dockyard Ltd, Ardrossan. Yard No. 427.
Single screw, oil engine, 2SCSA, Sulzer, 1,260 bhp, 7 cylinder. By G. Clark & NE Marine (Sunderland) Ltd, Sunderland. 11½ knots.

13.1.1959	Launched as *Dorset Coast*.
5.1959	Delivered as *Dorset Coast* to Coast Lines Ltd, Liverpool.
1966	Converted to a container ship.
1971	Registered under Coast Lines (Services) Ltd.
26.2.1971	Coast Lines Ltd acquired by the P&O Steam Navigation Company Ltd.
1.10.1971	Managed by P&O Short Sea Shipping Ltd.
1.8.1972	Registered under the Belfast Steamship Company Ltd.
1.10.1973	Registered under the General Steam Navigation (Trading) Ltd.
31.3.1975	Managed by P&O Ferries.
30.4.1976	Registered under P&O Ferries (General European) Ltd.
14.7.1978	Registered under P&O Ferries Ltd.
22.2.1979	Sold to James Stewart Tyrrell and resold to Delta Marine & Trading Company, Egypt, renamed *El Hussein*.
1981	Sold to Omar Ibrahim, Saudi Arabia. Resold to Sayed Mohamed Sadaka Hitfa, Egypt, renamed *El Kheer*. Sold to Naviera Denton Venture S de R L, San Lorenzo, Honduras, renamed *Denton Venture*.
1984	Sold to Isabella Maritime Company, Piraeus, renamed *Ourania*.
1985	Purchased by Brugse Scheepssloperij S.A., Belgium, for demolition.
24.6.1985	Arrived at Bruges and broken up.

140. *Lurcher* (2) (1938) O.N. 165957

859 grt   455 nrt   61.81 × 10.11 × 3.47 m
B. Scott & Sons Ltd, Bowling. Yard No. 349.
Single screw, oil engine, 2SA, 81 nhp, 5 cylinder. By British Auxilliaries Ltd.

25.10.1938	Launched as *Yewmount* for John Stewart & Company Shipping Ltd, Glasgow.
1947	Renamed *Saxon Queen* for Queenship Navigation Ltd.
5.1959	Coast Lines Ltd, Liverpool. Renamed *Lurcher*.

Dorset Coast (5).

Lurcher (2) at Birkenhead following her collision on the River Mersey in 1961.

21.1.1961   On a voyage from Liverpool to Glasgow she was in collision with the *Stamatios G. Embiricos* off the North Tower Buoy in the River Mersey.

30.3.1961   Refloated.

31.3.1964   Arrived at Preston and broken up by T. W. Ward Ltd.

141. *Buffalo* (1961) O.N. 303187

2,163 grt   1,845 dwt   1,072 nrt   78.63 × 12.98 × 7.62 m

B. Ardrossan Dockyard Ltd, Ardrossan. Yard No. 430.

Single screw, oil engine, 2SCSA, 2,800 bhp, 7 cylinder by British Polar Engines Ltd, Glasgow. 3,857 cubic metres (136,220 cubic feet). 14 knots.

2.5.1961   Launched.

1.1962   Delivered to Coast Lines Ltd, Liverpool (Link Line Ltd).

26.2.1971   Coast Lines Ltd acquired by the P&O Steam Navigation Company Ltd.

1.10.1971   Managed by P&O Short Sea Shipping Ltd.

12.1971   Registered under Coast Lines (Services) Ltd.

Converted to carry 91 × 20-foot equivalent containers. Remeasured as 1,482 grt, 575 nrt, 1,760 deadweight tonnage.

24.2.1972   Renamed *Norbrae* for the Hull–Rotterdam service of North Sea Ferries.

5.1972   Deadweight 1,775 tons, 1,482 grt.

1.8.1972   Registered under Tyne Tees Steam Shipping Company Ltd.

14.1.1974   Renamed *Roe Deer* for the Tilbury–Zeebrugge service.

31.3.1975   Managed by P&O Ferries.

30.4.1976   Registered under P&O Ferries (General European) Ltd.

22.12.1976   Sold to A. Harvey & Company Ltd, Newfoundland, Canada.

1977   Renamed *Newfoundland Container*.
Registered under Newfoundland Container Lines Ltd.

1978   Registered under Harvey Containership Ltd.

1985   Sold to Victory Seaways Enterprises Ltd, Cayman Islands, renamed *Caribbean Victory*.

1986   Sold to Renaissance Maritime Incorporated, Honduras, renamed *Lefkimmi*.

1988   Renamed *St George*, same owners.

1992   Sold to the International Shipping Corporation, Brazil, renamed *Container Express*.

12.1.1999   Scuttled.

Bison leaves Waterloo Dock on a voyage from Liverpool to Belfast.

142. *Bison* (1961) O.N. 303189

2,144 grt   1,993 dwt   1,070 nrt   78.63 × 12.86 × 7.62 m

B. Charles Hill & Sons Ltd, Bristol. Yard No. 435.

Single screw, oil engine, 2SCSA, 2,800 bhp, 7 cylinder. By British Polar Engines Ltd, Glasgow. 3,426 cubic metres (121,000 cubic feet). 13 knots.

11.7.1961   Launched.

1.1962   Delivered to Coast Lines Ltd (Link Lines Ltd), Liverpool.

26.2.1971   Coast Lines Ltd acquired by the P&O Steam Navigation Company Ltd.

1.10.1971   Managed by P&O Short Sea Shipping Ltd.

18.11.1971   Renamed Norbank for the Hull–Rotterdam service of North Sea Ferries.

12.1971   Registered under Coast Lines (Services) Ltd.
Converted to carry eighty-four 20-foot equivalent containers.

1.8.1972   Registered under Tyne Tees Steam Shipping Company Ltd.

31.3.1975   Managed by P&O Ferries.

30.4.1976   Registered under P&O Ferries (General European) Ltd.

28.7.1978   Registered under P&O Ferries Ltd.

6.10.1978   Sold to Suriname National Shipping Company, Suriname, renamed *Flamingo*.

1990   Broken up.

143. *Wirral Coast* (2) (1962) O.N. 303863

881 grt   1,112 dwt   384 nrt   62 × 10.9 × 4.93 m

B. Cammell Laird & Company Ltd, Birkenhead. Yard No. 1308.

Single screw, oil engine, 2SCSA, 1,200 bhp at 235 rpm, 6 cylinder. By Sulzer Brothers Ltd. 12½ knots.

Wirral Coast in the East Float, Birkenhead, on 8 November 1969. (Courtesy of Dave Crolly)

17.7.1962   Launched by Mrs Hill, wife of the secretary of the Liverpool Steamship Owners' Association.

9.1962   Delivered to Coast Lines Ltd.

8.11.1969   On a voyage from Ireland to Liverpool, she lost two containers in gale force winds and was guided by tugs into the Mersey where the *Vigilant* stood by. She was towed into Birkenhead Docks where part of her cargo was discharged at the West Float, prior to moving to Waterloo Dock.

1971   Owners restyled as Coast Lines (Services) Ltd.

1.10.1971   Management transferred to P&O Short Sea Shipping Ltd.

14.9.1972   Sold to James Tyrrell Ltd, renamed *Shevrell*.

1973   Purchased by Usborne & Son (London) Ltd (Buries Markes Ltd, London, as managers), renamed *Portmarnock*.

1978   Owned by Fulpass Ltd (G. T. Gillie & Blair Ltd, Newcastle, as managers). It was announced that she would be renamed *Brookline* but this did not occur and she remained as *Portmarnock*.

1979   Sold to Khodor Itani, Lebanon, renamed *Nadia 1*. Resold to Mrs Nadia Hussein Mekkaoui, Lebanon, renamed *Nadia*.

27.11.1985   Wrecked off the coast of Lebanon in a storm.

144. *Terrier* (1957) O.N. 303875

1,127 grt   1,483 dwt   616 nrt   67.05 × 10.63 × 5.73 m

B. N. V. Scheepswerf Gebr van der Werf, Deest, Netherland. Yard No. 269. Single screw, oil engine, 4SCSA, 1,150 bhp, 6 cylinder. By Mak. Maschinenbau Kiel AG., Kiel, West Germany. 11¾ knots.

17.5.1957   Launched.

7.1957   Delivered as *Ebba Robbert* to Det Dansk-Norske Dampskibsselskab (R. A. Robbert as managers), Denmark.

1959   Purchased by Rederiet Seaway (R. Fischer-Nielsen as managers), Copenhagen, Denmark, renamed *Stege*.

3.1963   Sold to Coast Lines Ltd, Liverpool, renamed *Terrier*.

6.1965   Fitted with a new hinged arms system at Greenock which resulted in a 20 per cent improvement in her carrying capacity. This enabled her to take an extra six units on the arms in the hold, giving a total capacity of thirty-seven units.

1971   Operated by Coast Lines (Services) Ltd, Liverpool.

26.2.1971   Coast Lines Ltd was acquired by the P&O Steam Navigation Company Ltd.

1.10.1971   Managed by P&O Short Sea Shipping Ltd.

7.4.1972   Sold to James Tyrrell Ltd, renamed *Murell*.

7.1973	Acquired by Nobleza Naviera S. A., Uruguay, renamed *Quijote*.
1994	Renamed *Omar G.*, registered in Paraguay.
2005	*Asunción.*
31.10.2009	Lost.

145. *Kentish Coast* (3)/*Ulster Duchess*/*Ulster Weaver* (1946) O.N. 168544

498 grt   59.13 × 9.20 × 3.27 m

B. Ardrossan Dockyard Company. Yard No. 406.

Single screw, oil engine, 187 rhp, 960 bhp, 6 cylinder. By British Polar Engines Ltd, Glasgow.

16.5.1946   Launched as *Ulster Duchess* for the Belfast Steamship Company Ltd.

Delivered to British Channel Islands Shipping Company Ltd.

1947   Renamed *Jersey Coast.*

1954   Transferred to the Belfast Steamship Company Ltd, became *Ulster Weaver.*

1964   To Coast Lines Ltd, Liverpool, renamed *Kentish Coast.*

1968   Sold to Alomar Mechanical Engineering Company (F. H. Hamza & A. M. Kulaib, Kuwait, as managers). Renamed *Salmiah Coast.*

1970   Sold to Kuwait Coast Line Company W. L. (F. H. Hamza & A. M. Kulaib, Kuwait, as managers).

1975   Sold to Abdul H. G. Zaddah, Abadan, Iran.

1999   Deleted from Lloyd's Register.

146. *Irish Coast* (4) (1970) O.N. 400920

763 grt   71.23 × 11.58 × 6.24 m

B. Bodewes Scheeps, Martenshoek, Netherlands. Yard No. 156.

Single screw, oil engine, 4SA, 1,500,bhp, 8 cylinder. By Atlas-Mak, Masch.

1970   Delivered as *Owenglas* for Greenore Ferry Services Ltd.

1971   Coast Lines Ltd. Renamed *Irish Coast.*

1975	*Owenglas.*
1991	*Safad.*
1997	*Al Nasser 1.*
1999	*Arwa II.*
2000	*Al Muhaisni.*
2003	*Ahmad N.*
2009	*Abu Yasser 1.*
2013	*Makkah II.*

British Channel Islands Shipping Company Ltd.

147. *Channel Queen* (1921) O.N. 146138

710 grt   55 × 8.5 m

B. C. Rennoldson & Company Ltd, South Shields. Yard No. 195.

Single screw, triple expansion, steam engine. 9 knots.

4.8.1921   Launched as *Channel Queen* for the London & Channel Islands Shipping Company Ltd (Cheeswright & Ford Ltd).

1937   Coast Lines Ltd, Liverpool.

1939   Comben, Longstaff & Company Ltd. Renamed *Westown.*

1940   Sold to George W. Grace & Company Ltd.

1946   Sold to Holderness Steam Ship Company Ltd.

1947   Renamed *Holdernook.*

1956   Glynwood Navigation Company Ltd, renamed *Logholder.*

27.12.1956   Arrived at Dover and broken up by Dover Industries Ltd.

148. *Foam Queen* (1922) O.N. 145716

811 grt   57.7 × 9.2 m

B. London & Montrose Shipbuilding & Repair Company Ltd, Montrose. Yard No. 93.

Single screw, triple expansion, steam engine. 8 knots.

1922   Delivered as *River Exe*.

1925   Renamed *Foam Queen*.

2.11.1943   On a voyage from Goole to Poole, with a cargo of coal, she was torpedoed between Dungeness and Beachy Head. Her stern was destroyed and she was towed to Dover and the cargo was discharged.

149. *London Queen* (1933) O.N. 163319

781 grt   59.4 × 9.4 m

B. Burntisland Shipbuilding Company Ltd, Burntisland. Yard No. 174. Single screw, triple expansion, steam engine. 10 knots.

1933   Delivered to the London & Channel Islands Shipping Company Ltd (Cheeswright & Ford Ltd).

1937   Coast Lines Ltd, Liverpool.

1947   British Channel Islands Traders Ltd.

Queenship Navigation Ltd.

1948   Belfast, Mersey & Manchester Steamship Company Ltd, renamed *Stormont*.

1950   Renamed *Cavan*.

1953   Zillah Shipping Company Ltd. Renamed *Northfield*.

31.3.1956   Arrived at Preston and broken up by T. W. Ward Ltd.

150. *Island Queen* (1934) O.N. 163464

779 grt   59.43 × 9.44 m

B. Burntisland Shipbuilding Company Ltd, Burntisland. Yard No. 180. Single screw, triple expansion, steam engine, 3 cylinder. By D. Rowan Ltd, Glasgow.

13.4.1934   Launched for the London & Channel Islands Shipping Company Ltd (Cheeswright & Ford Ltd).

1937   Coast Lines Ltd, Liverpool.

Stormont.

14.7.1940   On a voyage from Blyth to Cowes with a cargo of coal she was bombed and sunk off Folkestone. Three crew lost their lives.

151. *Jersey Queen* (1936) O.N. 165361

910 grt   60.1 × 9.8 × 4 m

B. Burntisland Shipbuilding Company Ltd, Burntisland. Yard No. 201. Single screw, triple expansion, steam engine. By builder.

31.10.1936   Launched.

1936   Delivered to the London & Channel Islands Shipping Company Ltd (Cheeswright & Ford Ltd).

1937   Coast Lines Ltd, Liverpool.

6.10.1940   On a voyage from Blyth to Plymouth with a cargo of coal she was mined and sunk near St Anthony Point, Falmouth.

152. *Norman Queen* (1911) O.N. 132859
863 grt   61 × 9.3 m
B. Dublin Dockyard Company. Yard No. 74.
Single screw, compound steam engine. 10 knots.
26.10.1911   Launched as *Enda* to Michael Murphy Ltd.
1929   Coast Lines Ltd, Liverpool. Renamed *Anglesey Coast*.
1937   Transferred to British Channel Islands Shipping Ltd. Renamed *Norman Queen*.
1937   Sold and renamed *Kylecroft*.
8.6.1955   Arrived at Llanelli and broken up by T. B. Rees Ltd.

153. *Emerald Queen* (1936) O.N. 165464
481 grt   49.9 × 8 m
B. N. V. Indust. Maats De Noord, Alblasserdam, Netherlands. Yard No. 566.
Single screw, oil engine. 9 knots.
1936   Laid down as *Mimija*.
1.1937   Delivered as *Welsh Coast*.
5.1937   Transferred to British Channel Islands Shipping Ltd. Renamed *Emerald Queen*.
1947   Transferred to the Tyne Tees Steam Shipping Company Ltd, renamed *Grampian Coast*.
1963   Sold and became *Gilda*.
1975   Floating restaurant at Porto Garibaldi, Italy.

154. *Norman Queen* (2) (1937) O.N. 166353
957 grt   60.2 × 9.8 × 4 m
B. Burntisland Shipbuilding Company Ltd, Burntisland. Yard No. 216.
Single screw, triple expansion, steam engine, 129 nhp. By D. Rowan & Company Ltd, Glasgow.

31.12.1937   Launched.
1938   Delivered as *Norman Queen*.
8.3.1941   On a voyage from London to Boston (Lincs), with a cargo of timber, she was torpedoed and sunk by a German submarine off South Haisbro buoy, east of Cromer.

155. *Saxon Queen* (1940) O.N. 166365
482 grt   49.4 × 8 m
B. Bodewes Scheeps, Martenshoek, Netherlands. Yard No. 868.
Single screw oil engine. 9 knots.
11.12.1940   Bombed and damaged in the Thames Estuary.
1947   Coast Lines Ltd, renamed *Dorset Coast*.
1951   Transferred to Coast Lines Africa and renamed *Matabele Coast*.
1961   Sold to the Union Steam Ship Company, South Africa.
1966   Owned by Unicorn Shipping Lines, South Africa.
4.1967   Broken up at Durban, South Africa.

156. *Guernsey Queen* (1939) O.N. 167240
565 grt   51.7 × 8.6 m
B. Burntisland Shipbuilding Company Ltd, Burntisland. Yard No. 228.
Single screw, oil engine, 2SCSA, 5 cylinder. By Atlas. 11 knots.
5.4.1939   Launched.
1939   Delivered as *Guernsey Queen*.
21.10.1944   Mined at Boulogne. Beached and later refloated and salvaged.
1947   Repaired and sold to George Gibson Ltd, renamed *Traquair*.
19.8.1956   On a voyage from Leith to Terneuzen she foundered east of Aldeburgh.

157. *Channel Queen* (2) (1940) O.N. 167630

567 grt   275 nrt   700 dwt 51.75 × 8.56 × 2.95 m

B. Burntisland Shipbuilding Company Ltd, Burntisland, Fife. Yard No. 245.

Single screw, oil engine, 2SCSA, 800 bhp, 5 cylinder. By British Auxiliaries Ltd.

10.6.1940	Launched.
1940	Delivered as *Channel Queen*.
1947	Renamed *Channel Coast*.
1959	Renamed *Glenfield*.
1960	Became *Alderney Coast*.
1966	Sold and renamed *Astronaftis*.
1975	Renamed *Sea Horse* and later *Mastro Costas*.
21.2.1976	On a voyage to Lagos, with a cargo of steel pipes and tomato paste, she developed a leak and was beached in Monrovia, Liberia.

158. *Alderney Queen* (1940) O.N. 165336

633 grt   53.9 × 8.7 m

B. Henry Robb Ltd, Leith. Yard No. 236.

Single screw, oil engine.

1940	Delivered as Lockwood for France, Fenwick & Company Ltd.
9.10.1940	On a voyage from Blyth to Plymouth she was bombed and sunk west of Skomer Island, Pembroke.

159. *Coral Queen* (1940) O.N. 168060

303 grt   148 nrt   380 dwt 40.23 × 7.49 × 2.25 m

B. Burntisland Shipbuilding Company Ltd, Burntisland. Yard No. 246.

Single screw, oil engine, 2SCSA, 330 bhp, 6 cylinder. By Crossley Ltd, Manchester.

25.6.1940	Launched.
1941	Delivered as *Coral Queen*.
1947	Transferred to Queenship Navigation Ltd.
1948	Renamed *Coral Coast*.
1950	Sold to Gambian interests and renamed *Fulladu*.
1.1965	Arrived Las Palmas and broken up.

160. *Tudor Queen* (1940) O.N. 168071

1,029 grt   582 nrt   1,400 dwt   62.24 × 10 × 4.02 m

B. Burntisland Shipbuilding Company Ltd, Burntisland. Yard No. 247.

Single screw, triple expansion, steam engine, 600 ihp, 3 cylinder. By D. Rowan Ltd.

31.12 1940	Launched.
1941	Delivered as *Tudor Queen*.
1947	Transferred to Queenship Navigation Ltd.
25.9.1959	Arrived at Troon and broken up by the West of Scotland Shipbreaking Company Ltd.

161. *Stuart Queen* (1940) O.N.168075

1,224 grt   625 nrt   72.69 × 10.42 × 4.32 m

B. Ardrossan Dockyard Company, Ardrossan. Yard No. 378.

Single screw, triple expansion, steam engine, 850 ihp, 3 cylinder. By J. G. Kincaid & Company Ltd.

14.11.1940	Launched as *Stuart Queen*.
1946	Coast Lines Ltd, Liverpool. Renamed *Hampshire Coast*.
1952	Transferred to Tyne Tees Steam Shipping Company Ltd.
1959	Broken up in Holland.

162. *Silver Coast* (1937) O.N.165124

606 grt   49.5 × 8.8 m

B. N. V. van Duivendijk, Netherlands. Yard No. 25.

Single screw, oil engine. 9 knots.

14.10.1937	Launched as *Ngarua*.
1940	Purchased by Merchants Ltd. Renamed *Silver Coast*.
1943	To British Channel Traders Ltd.
1946	To Burns & Laird Lines Ltd, renamed *Lairdsoak*.
1960	Zillah Shipping Company Ltd, renamed *Garthfield*.
1962	Sold to Greek interests, renamed *Krios*.
1968	*Kyriakoula K.*
1974	*Dimitrios II.*
1992	Deleted from Lloyd's Register.

163. *Jersey Coast* O.N. 168544

498 grt   214 nrt   671 dwt   61.44 × 9.20 × 3.27 m

B. Ardrossan Dockyard Company Ltd. Yard No. 406.

Single screw, oil engine, 187 rhp, 960 bhp, 6 cylinder. By British Polar Engines Ltd, Glasgow.

16.5.1946	Launched as *Ulster Duchess* for the Belfast Steamship Company Ltd.

Delivered to British Channel Islands Shipping Company Ltd.

1947	Renamed *Jersey Coast*.
1954	Transferred to the Belfast Steamship Company Ltd, became *Ulster Weaver*.
1964	To Coast Lines Ltd, Liverpool, renamed *Kentish Coast*.
1968	Sold to Alomar Mechanical Engineering Company (F. H. Hamza & A. M. Kulaib, Kuwait, as managers). Renamed *Salmiah Coast*.
1970	Sold to Kuwait Coast Line Company W. L. (F. H. Hamza & A. M. Kulaib, Kuwait, as managers).
1975	Sold to Abdul H. G. Zaddah, Abadan, Iran.
1999	Deleted from Lloyd's Register.

164. *Silver Coast* (2) (1938)

50 grt

B. Amsterdam Shipbuilders Ltd, Amsterdam, Netherlands.

1938	Delivered as a Fort William cruising launch.
1947	Purchased to provide excursions around Poole Harbour.
1950	Sold and converted to a private yacht.

165. *Guernsey Coast* (1942) O.N. 168513

507 grt   59.25 × 9.20 × 2.62 m

B. Ardrossan Dockyard Ltd, Ardrossan. Yard No. 380.

Single screw, oil engine, 156 nhp, 800 bhp, 6 cylinder. By British Auxiliaries Ltd.

19.2.1942	Launched as *Ulster Duke* for the Belfast Steamship Company Ltd.
1946	British Channel Islands Shipping Company Ltd. Renamed *Guernsey Coast*.
1955	Belfast Steamship Company Ltd. Renamed *Ulster Spinner*.
1968	Sold to Michael A. Araktingi, Beirut. Renamed *Al-Amin*.
1972	Wafik Begdache, Beirut. Renamed *Hamid*.
1980	Ayat Bakhirat Company Ltd, Limassol. Renamed *Elvira*.
4.1997	Laid up at Mina Raysut, Oman.

166. *Brittany Coast* (2) (1948) O.N.182867

584 grt   675 dwt   51.81 × 8.53 × 3.04 m

B. Burntisland Shipbuilding Company Ltd. Burntisland, Fife. Yard No. 310. Single screw, oil engine, 184 nhp, 800 bhp. By British Polar Engines Ltd, Glasgow.

20.5.1948	Launched for British Channel Islands Shipping Company Ltd, London.
1948	Delivered as *Brittany Coast*.

1950   Transferred to the British & Irish Steam Packet Company Ltd, renamed *Inniscarra*.

1952   Registered in Dublin.

1969   Sold to Oldham Brothers, Liverpool, to be broken up.

1970   Sold to Kassos Maritime Enterprises Ltd, Greece, and renamed *Elni*.

1971   Purchased by Vassilios and Gerassimos Zavitsanos, Piraeus, Greece.
Sold to Theodoros and Vassilios Zavitsanos and Theodoros Argiris, Piraeus, Greece.

1972   Sold to Mrs Kyriaki D. Kallimassia and Mrs Evangelia B. Dimopoulou, Piraeus, Greece. Renamed *Ria*.

2.1982   Broken up at Naples.

167. *Kentish Coast* (2) (1938) O.N. 166237
459 grt   50.5 × 8 m
B. J. Smit, Foxhol, Netherlands. Yard No. 523.
Single screw, oil engine. 9 knots.

1938   Delivered as *Kentish Coast* to Coast Lines Ltd, Liverpool.
1962   *Melisenda*.
1971   *Monte Carmo*.
1973   *Vanna*.
1974   *Alekekos*.
            Aboude.
1992   Deleted from Lloyd's Register.

168. *Jersey Coast* (2) (1940) O.N. 166307
687 grt   251 nrt   990 dwt 61.50 × 10.11 × 3.41 m
B. Ardrossan Dockyard Company Ltd. Yard No. 379.
Single screw, oil engine, 218 bhp, 7 cylinder. By British Auxiliaries Ltd.
6.7.1940   Launched as *Moray Coast* for Coast Lines Ltd, Liverpool.

1954   British Channel Islands Shipping Ltd. Renamed *Jersey Coast*.
1967   Sold to Orri Navigation Lines, Jeddah. Renamed *Star of Ibrahim*.
1973   Ahmed Mohamed Baaboud & Hussan Mohamed Fayez & Sons, Jeddah. Renamed *Blue Sky*.
9.1980   Machinery damaged.
9.2.1982   Scuttled south of Shaab al Musmary, off Jeddah.

169. *Guernsey Coast* (2) – See *Welsh Coast* (1938) Coast Lines Ltd.

170. *Alderney Coast* – See *Channel Queen* (1940).

171. *Mersey Coast* – See Coast Lines Ltd (1940).

172. *Southern Coast* (2) – See Coast Lines Ltd (1943).

173. *Sark Coast* (2) – See *Antrim Coast* (2) Coast Lines Ltd.

174. *Olivian Coast* – See Tyne Tees Steam Shipping Company.

175. *Cyprian Coast* – See Tyne Tees Steam Shipping Company.

Queenship Navigation Ltd.

176. *Coral Queen* (1947–48) See British Channel Islands Shipping Company Ltd.

177. *Tudor Queen* (1947–59) See British Channel Islands Shipping Company Ltd.

178. *London Queen* (1947–48) See British Channel Islands Shipping Company Ltd.

179. *Stuart Queen* (2) (1920) O.N. 143533
879 grt   60.96 × 9.44 × 3.96 m
B. Dublin Dockyard Company Ltd, Dublin. Yard No. 105.
Single screw, triple expansion, steam engine, 120 rhp, 155 nhp. By Ross & Duncan Ltd, Glasgow.
27.11.1920   Launched as *Finola* for Michael Murphy Ltd, Dublin.
1921   Registered in Cardiff.
1926   Michael Murphy Ltd acquired by the British & Irish Steam Packet Company Ltd.
1936   British & Irish Steam Packet Company (1936) Ltd.
1939   Transferred to Coast Lines Ltd, Liverpool. Renamed *Glamorgan Coast*.
1947   Transferred to British Channel Traders Ltd, London. Renamed *Stuart Queen*.
              To Queenship Navigation Ltd, London.
1952   To Zillah Shipping Company Ltd (W. A. Savage Ltd), Liverpool. Renamed *Caldyfield*.
14.9.1955   Arrived at Preston and broken up.

180. *Windsor Queen* (1942) O.N. 168400
1,033 grt   62.17 × 10.05 m
B. Burntisland Shipbuilding Company Ltd, Burntisland. Yard No. 365.
Single screw, triple expansion, steam engine, 3 cylinder. By D. Rowan & Company Ltd, Glasgow.
17.12.1942   Launched as *Windsor Queen* for British Channel Traders Ltd.
1947   Transferred to Queenship Navigation Ltd.
3.10.1959   Arrived at Broom, Belgium, and broken up.

181. *Norman Queen* (3) (1944) O.N. 169965
1,047 grt   570 nrt   1,435 dwt   62.33 × 9.96 × 3.99 m
B. Ardrossan Dockyard Company Ltd. Yard No. 397.
Single screw, triple expansion, steam engine, 650 ihp, 3 cylinder. By J. G. Kincaid & Company Ltd.
25.5.1944   Launched for British Channel Traders Ltd.
1947   Transferred to Queenship Navigation Ltd.
3.6.1961   Arrived at Hendrik-Ido-Ambacht and broken up.

182. *Highland Queen* (1945) O.N. 180684
1,043 grt   570 nrt   1,435 dwt   62.33 × 9.96 × 3.99 m
B. Ardrossan Dockyard Company Ltd. Yard No. 399.
Single screw, triple expansion, steam engine, 650 ihp, 3 cylinder. By J. G. Kincaid & Company Ltd.
24.5.1945   Launched for British Channel Traders Ltd.
1947   Transferred to Queenship Navigation Ltd.
18.6.1959   Arrived at Hendrik-Ido-Ambacht and broken up.

183. *Balmoral Queen* (1945) O.N. 180791
1,043 grt   574 nrt   1,435 dwt   62.33 × 9.96 × 3.99 m
B. Ardrossan Dockyard Company. Yard No. 400.
Single screw, triple expansion, steam engine, 650 ihp. By J. G. Kincaid & Company Ltd.
22.10.1945   Launched for British Channel Traders Ltd.
1947   Transferred to Queenship Navigation Ltd.
15.6.1959   Arrived at Hendrik-Ido-Ambacht and broken up.

184. *Roman Queen* (1944) O.N. 163850
1,047 grt   574 nrt   1,435 dwt   62.33 × 9.96 × 3.99 m
B. Ardrossan Dockyard Company. Yard No. 398.
Single screw, triple expansion, steam engine, 650 ihp, 3 cylinder. By J. G. Kincaid & Company Ltd.
30.10.1944   Launched as *Empire Drover* for the Ministry of War Transport.

1946   Purchased by Queenship Navigation Ltd. Renamed *Roman Queen.*

6.1961   Broken up at Hendrik-Ido-Ambacht.

185. Saxon Queen (2) (1938) O.N. 165957

859 grt   455 nrt   61.81 × 10.11 × 3.47 m

B. Scott & Sons Ltd, Bowling. Yard No. 349.

Single screw, oil engine. By Atlas-Diesel A/B.

25.10.1938   Launched as *Yewmount* for John Stewart & Company Shipping Ltd, Glasgow.

1947   Renamed *Saxon Queen* for Queenship Navigation Ltd.

1959   Coast Lines Ltd, Liverpool. Renamed *Lurcher.*

21.1.1961   On a voyage from Liverpool to Glasgow she was in collision with the *Stamatios G. Embiricos* off the North Tower Buoy in the River Mersey.

30.3.1961   Refloated.

31.3.1964   Arrived at Preston and broken up by T. W. Ward Ltd.

186. Celtic Queen (1937) O.N. 162144

849 grt   60.3 × 9.4 m

B. John Lewis & Company Ltd, Aberdeen. Yard No. 142.

Single screw, oil engine. 9½ knots.

1937   Delivered as *Gwenthills.*

1945   Purchased by Queenship Navigation Ltd. Renamed *Celtic Queen.*

6.1959   Arrived at Hendrik-Ido-Ambacht and broken up.

187. Nordic Queen (1944) O.N. 169522

1,063 grt   582 nrt   1,400 dwt   62.42 × 10 × 4.17 m

B. George Brown & Company Ltd, Greenock. Yard No. 232.

Single screw, triple expansion, steam engine, 3 cylinders. By Rankin & Blackmore Ltd.

18.12.1944   Launched as *Empire Balham* for the Ministry of War Transport.

1946   British Channel Traders Ltd. Renamed *Nordic Queen.*

1946   Purchased by Queenship Navigation Ltd.

1958   Sold to Maldavian Nationals Trading Corporation (Ceylon) Ltd. Renamed *Maldive Star.*

12.1972   Broken up at Gadani Beach.

188. Richmond Queen (1930) O.N. 162326

1,600 grt   76.20 × 11.27 × 5.66 m

B. D. & W. Henderson & Company Ltd, Meadowside. Yard No. 906.

Single screw, triple expansion, steam engine, 180 lbs, 232 nhp, 3 cylinder. By builder.

25.9.1930   Launched as *Maurice Rose* for Richard Hughes & Company Ltd, Liverpool.

1934   Richard Hughes & Company (Liverpool) Ltd, Liverpool.

1947   Transferred to the Tyne Tees Steam Shipping Company Ltd. Renamed *Baltic King.*

A. Coker & Company Ltd, Liverpool.

1949   Purchased by Queenship Navigation Ltd, renamed *Richmond Queen.*

4.10.1957   Arrived at Dunston and broken up by Clayton & Davie Ltd.

189. Sandringham Queen (1949) O.N. 169224

1,220 grt   1,503 dwt   66.99 × 10.69 × 4.57 m

B. George Brown & Company Ltd, Greenock. Yard No. 250.

Single screw, oil engine, 2SA, 1190 hp, 7 cylinder. By British Polar Engines Ltd. 11 knots.

21.12.1949   Launched as *Sandringham Queen* for Queenship Navigation Ltd and completed as *Iberian Coast* for the Tyne Tees Steam Shipping Company Ltd.

1966   Spiridione Lucchi, Venice. Renamed *Pupi*.

1976   Annivasamar Hellas Ltd, Piraeus. Renamed *Agios Nicolaos*.

26.8.1978   On a voyage from Barletta to Mozambique with a cargo of wheat she suffered an engine room fire and sank west of Crete.

190. *Sandringham Queen* (2) (1955) O.N. 186298

1,308 grt   1,640 dwt   70.9 × 11 m

B. Goole Shipbuilders Ltd, Yard No. 499.

Single screw, oil engine.

21.7.1955   Launched as *Sandringham Queen*.

1972   Sold and renamed *Bright Sky*.

1976   *Greek Sky*.

1.1983   Broken up at Ravenna, Italy, by Placuzzi Sp. A.

191. *Osborne Queen* (1956) O.N. 187581

1,424 grt   685 nrt   1,730 dwt   73.21 × 11 × 4.63 m

B. Ardrossan Dockyard Company. Yard No. 423.

Single screw, oil engine, 8 cylinder. By George Clark & North Eastern Marine (Sunderland) Ltd.

18.12.1956   Launched as *Osborne Queen* for the Queenship Navigation Ltd.

15.10.1965   Sold to Watts, Watts & Company Ltd, Britain Steam Ship Company Ltd, London (Comben Longstaff Ltd as managers).

1968   Eskgarth Shipping Company Ltd, London

1972   Sold to Nefeli Shipping Company Ltd, Famagusta, Cyprus, and renamed *Nefeli*.

5.11.1972   On a voyage from Garston to Antwerp in ballast, she went aground near Land's End after striking Longships Rocks in thick fog. Declared a total loss.

192. *Richmond Queen* (2) (1958) O.N. 187194

1,376 grt   1,734 dwt   71.6 × 10.8 m

B. Clelands Shipbuilders Ltd, Wallsend. Yard No. 223.

Single screw, oil engine.

20.3.1958   Launched as *Somerset Coast*.

1959   Renamed *Richmond Queen*.

20.10.1965   Sold to the Britain Steamship Company Ltd.

1974   Sold and renamed *Gomba Enterprise*.

1976   *Atlantic Enterprise*.

2.10.1978   Arrived at Brake and broken up by Eckhardt & Company.

193. *Windsor Queen* (2) (1937) O.N. 145577

972 grt   62.48 × 10 m

B. Burntisland Shipbuilders Ltd. Yard No. 211.

Single screw, oil engine, 2SCSA, 5 cylinder. By British Auxiliaries Ltd.

1937   Delivered as *Lottie R* to the Stone & Rolfe Steam Ship Company Ltd.

1946   Renamed *Yewbranch*.

1947   Coast Lines Ltd, became *Devon Coast*.

1963   To Queenship Navigation Ltd, renamed *Windsor Queen*.

1965   *Elca*.

1967   *Eleni R*.

9.1973   Broken up at Perama.

Belfast Steamship Company Ltd.

194. *Magic/Classic* (1893) O.N. 99966

1,640 grt   94.79 × 11.58 × 4.57 m

B. Harland & Wolff Ltd, Belfast. Yard No. 271.

Magic.

Twin screw, triple expansion, steam, 493.5 hp, 507 nhp, 3,500 ihp. By builder.

20.4.1893   Launched as *Magic* for the Belfast Steamship Company Ltd, Belfast.

1914   Requisitioned by the Admiralty as hospital ship HMHS *Magician.*

1916   Renamed HMHS *Magic II.*

1918   Renamed HMHS *Classic.*

1919   Returned to owners for commercial service as *Classic.* Belfast Steamship Company acquired by Coast Lines Ltd.

1924   Transferred to the City of Cork Steam Packet Company Ltd, Cork. Renamed *Killarney.*

1927   Registered in Liverpool.

1931   Coast Lines Ltd, Liverpool.

1940   Requisitioned by the Admiralty as HMS *Killarney.*

1946   Returned to owner's service.

1947   Sold to Bury Court Shipping Company Ltd, London. Renamed *Attiki.*

1948   Sold to Epirotiki Steamship Navigation Company (George Potamianos, Piraeus, Greece as managers). Renamed *Adrias.*

6.10.1951   On a voyage from Rhodes to Piraeus she was wrecked on Falconera Island, Greece.

195. *Comic* (1896) O.N. 104466

935 grt   71.93 × 9.44 × 4.57 m

B. Harland & Wolff Ltd, Belfast. Yard No. 306.

Twin screw, triple expansion, steam engine, 263 rhp & nhp, 6 cylinder. By builder. 13 knots.

8.6.1896   Launched as *Comic* for the Belfast Steamship Company Ltd, Belfast.

1919   Belfast Steamship Company Ltd acquired by Coast Lines Ltd.

1921   Transferred to Laird Line Ltd, Glasgow. Renamed *Cairnsmore.*

1922   Transferred to Burns & Laird Lines Ltd, Glasgow.

1929   Transferred to the British & Irish Steam Packet Company Ltd, Dublin. Renamed *Lady Kerry.*

1934   Broken up at Preston.

196. *Logic* (1902) O.N. 108619

959 grt   71.93 × 9.44 × 4.57 m

B. Harland & Wolff Ltd, Belfast. Yard No. 306.

Twin screw, triple expansion, steam engine, 263 rhp & nhp. By builder. 13 knots.

26.10.1897   Launched as *Logic* for Thomas Gallaher & Company Ltd, Belfast. Chartered to the Belfast Steamship Company Ltd.

26.6.1902   In collision with *Princess May* in Larne Harbour.

1904   Purchased by the Belfast Steamship Company Ltd, Belfast.

1919   Belfast Steamship Company Ltd acquired by Coast Lines Ltd.

1921   Transferred to Laird Line Ltd, Glasgow. Renamed *Culzean*.

1922   Transferred to Burns & Laird Lines Ltd, Glasgow.

5.6.1923   Grounded in the Victoria Channel, Belfast, refloated later that day.

1929   Transferred to the British & Irish Steam Packet Company Ltd, Dublin. Renamed *Lady Carlow*.

1936   Sold to Smith & Company Ltd for demolition.

1937   Sold to the West of Scotland Shipbreaking Company Ltd and broken up at Troon.

197. *Graphic/Ulster Duke* (2) (1906) O.N. 120714
1,871 grt   97.53 × 12.49 × 5.18 m
B. Harland & Wolff Ltd, Belfast. Yard No. 379.
Twin screw, quadruple expansion, steam engine, 824 rhp, 788 nhp. By builder. 18 knots.

27.2.1906   Launched as *Graphic* for the Belfast steamship Company Ltd.

1919   Belfast Steamship Company Ltd acquired by Coast Lines Ltd.

3.6.1923   In collision with the *Balsam* in the Victoria Channel, Belfast, and sank.

24.6.1923   Raised and repaired with new engines, 660 nhp.

1929   Transferred to the British & Irish steam Packet Company Ltd, Dublin. Renamed *Lady Munster*.

1936   British & Irish Steam Packet Company (1936) Ltd.

1938   Renamed *Louth*.

1939   Registered in Liverpool.

1948   Transferred to the Belfast Steamship Company Ltd, renamed *Ulster Duke*.

1951   Sold to shipbreakers in Italy.

14.5.1951   On her tow to La Spezia she broke away and sank in Finisterre Bay.

198. *Heroic* (1906) O.N. 120712
1,869 grt   97.53 × 12.49 × 5.18 m
B. Harland & Wolff Ltd, Belfast. Yard No. 378.
Twin screw, quadruple expansion, steam engine, 824 rhp, 804 nhp. By builder. 18 knots.

13.1.1906   Launched as *Heroic* for the Belfast Steamship Company Ltd, Belfast.

1914   Requisitioned by the Admiralty as an armed boarding vessel as HMS *Heroic*.

1915   Operated as a fleet messenger ship.

1919   Returned to owners' commercial service.
Belfast Steamship Company Ltd acquired by Coast Lines Ltd.

1924   New engines fitted, 651 rhp 649 nhp.

1930   Transferred to the British & Irish Steam Packet Company Ltd, renamed *Lady Connaught*.

1936   British & Irish Steam Packet Company (1936) Ltd.

1938   Renamed *Longford*.

1940   Registered in Liverpool.

1953   Broken up at Barrow.

199. *Patriotic* (1911) O.N. 132019
2,254 grt   99.18 × 12.71 × 4.93 m
B. Harland & Wolff Ltd, Belfast. Yard No. 424.

Heroic.

Twin screw, triple expansion, steam engine, 840 rhp, 840 nhp, 6,400 bhp. By builder. 18 knots.

7.9.1911   Launched as *Patriotic* for the Belfast Steamship Company Ltd, Belfast.

1912   Delivered.

1919   Belfast Steamship Company Ltd acquired by Coast Lines Ltd.

1930   Transferred to the British & Irish Steam Packet Company Ltd, renamed *Lady Leinster*.

1936   British & Irish Steam Packet Company (1936) Ltd.

1938   Renamed *Lady Connaught*.

1940   Registered in Liverpool.

26.12.1940   On a voyage from Liverpool to Belfast she was damaged by mines. Laid up.

1941   Abandoned by insurance underwriters.

1942   Purchased from underwriters and converted to a cattle carrier.

Engines 500 rhp, 792 nhp, 2,700 bhp, 3,000 ihp, 14 knots.

1944   Converted to a hospital carrier ship, No. 55, by Barclay, Curle & Company Ltd, Glasgow.

1946   Converted to a cruise ship by builders at Belfast.

1947   Managed by Coast Lines Ltd, Liverpool. Renamed *Lady Killarney*.

1956   Broken up at Port Glasgow.

200. *Optic* (1921) O.N. 145416
496 grt   49.07 × 7.65 × 2.80 m
B. Ardrossan Dockyard Ltd, Ardrossan. Yard No. 325.
Single screw, triple expansion, steam engine, 57 rhp. By Hall, Russell & Company Ltd, Aberdeen.

15.3.1921   Launched as *Optic* for the Belfast Steamship Company Ltd, Belfast.

1929   Sold to A. F. Henry & MacGregor Ltd, Leith. Renamed *Rattray Head*.

5.4.1941   On a voyage from Leith and Methil Roads to Stromness with a cargo of bricks and general goods she was sunk by aircraft 8 miles east-north-east of Aberdeen.

201. *Caloric* (1895) O.N. 104611
1,174 grt   76.20 × 10.24 × 4.87 m
B. A. & J. Inglis Ltd, Pointhouse, Glasgow. Yard No. 234.
Single screw, triple expansion, steam engine, 260 rhp, 265 nhp. By builder.

5.2.1895	Launched as *Spaniel* for G. & J. Burns Ltd, Glasgow.
1920	G. & J. Burns Ltd, Glasgow, acquired by Coast Lines Ltd.
1921	Transferred to the Belfast Steamship Company Ltd, renamed *Caloric*.

Operated as a cattle carrier.

23.1.1932	Arrived at Sunderland and broken up.

202. *Dynamic*/*Ulster Star* (1904) O.N. 118188

576 grt   56.81 × 8.56 × 4.20 m

B. Ramage & Ferguson Ltd, Leith. Yard No. 197.

Single screw, triple expansion, steam engine, 135 rhp, 135 nhp. By builder. 11 knots.

14.9.1904	Launched as *James Crombie* for the Aberdeen, Leith & Moray Firth Steam Shipping Company Ltd, Aberdeen.
1909	Managed by J. Crombie & Sons Ltd.
1914	Aberdeen, Leith & Moray Firth Steam Shipping Company Ltd, Aberdeen, acquired by M. Langlands & Sons.
1915	Sold to George S. MacLellan, Thomas W. McIntyre and Sir Archibald M. Shaw (Laird Line Ltd as managers). Renamed *Broom*.
1919	Laird Line Ltd acquired by Coast Lines Ltd.

Purchased by Laird Line Ltd, Glasgow.

1922	Transferred to the City of Cork Steam Packet Company Ltd, Cork. Renamed *Lismore*.

Later transferred to the Belfast Steamship Company Ltd, Belfast. Renamed *Dynamic*.

1931	Renamed *Ulster Star*.
1940	Chartered to David MacBrayne Ltd.
1949	Returned to owner and broken up at Troon.

203. *Logic*/*Ulster Hero* (1924) O.N. 147272

483 grt   45.90 × 7.74 × 3.38 m

B. James Towers Shipbuilding Company Ltd, Bristol. Yard No. 180.

Single screw, triple expansion, steam engine, 72 rhp, 105 nhp. By J. G. Kincaid & Company Ltd, Greenock.

1924	Laid down as *Reedham* for Walford Lines Ltd, London.
24.5.1924	Launched as *Dorset Coast* for Coast Lines Ltd, Liverpool.
1929	Transferred to the Belfast Steamship Company Ltd. Renamed *Logic*.
1935	Renamed *Ulster Hero*.
1941	Sold to J. & A. Gardner & Company Ltd, Glasgow.
1945	Renamed *Saint Conan*.
1958	Broken up at Dublin.

204. *Ulster Monarch* (1929) O.N. 148163

3,735 grt   105.46 × 14.08 × 4.63 m

B. Harland & Wolff Ltd, Belfast. Yard No. 635.

Twin screw, oil engine, 1,192 rhp, 1,193 nhp, 6,150 bhp. By builder. 18 knots.

24.1.1929	Launched as *Ulster Monarch* for the Belfast Steamship Company Ltd.
25.4.1929	Trials.
11.6.1929	Maiden voyage from Belfast to Liverpool.
14.2.1930	On the day of *Ulster Queen*'s maiden voyage from Belfast to Liverpool, Stanley Baldwin travelled on *Ulster Monarch* from Liverpool to Belfast.
5.10.1940	Requisitioned by the Admiralty as HMS *Ulster Monarch*.
1940	Served in the Norway campaign and the evacuation of France after Dunkirk. Commissioned under the White Ensign and joined the fleet of Combined Operations, becoming involved with training of commando troops, followed by trooping voyages to Iceland and Gibraltar.

1944   Took part in the Normandy invasion, followed by trooping between South Coast ports and the Continent.

1945   Returned to owner's commercial service.

30.11.1950 Returned to service after the funnels were cut down and reduced in height. Forward mast shortened and the rear mast replaced by a shorter lighter one, mounted on the superstructure. Open rails replaced the solid bulwarks on the boat deck.

1957   Withdrawn from service for five months.

2.10.1966   Final sailing Liverpool–Belfast.

2.10.1966   Sailed light Belfast–Birkenhead and laid up.

1966   Broken up at Ghent.

Ulster Monarch embarking passengers at Princes Landing Stage, Liverpool.

205. *Ulster Queen* (1929) O.N. 161857

3,735 grt   105.46 × 14.08 × 4.63 m

B. Harland & Wolff Ltd, Belfast. Yard No. 696.

Twin screw, oil engine, 1,192 rhp, 1,193 nhp, 6,150 bhp. By builder. 18 knots.

28.3.1929   Launched as *Ulster Queen* for the Belfast Steamship Company Ltd.

14.2.1930   Maiden voyage Belfast–Liverpool.

28.2.1940   Ran aground at Maughold Head in Ramsey Bay, Isle of Man, at 0235 hours. The ninety-three passengers were transferred to the *Duke of Lancaster* by lifeboat. The vessel later swung into a position almost parallel to the coast and the crew members on board were taken off by breeches buoy.

25.3.1940   Refloated.

15.8.1940   Requisitioned by the Admiralty and converted to an auxiliary anti-aircraft cruiser. Renamed HMS *Ulster Queen*.

1943   Became a fighter direction ship.

1946   Completed service for the Royal Navy.

Sold to the General Steam Navigation Company Ltd.

1950   Broken up at Antwerp.

206. *Ulster Prince* (1929) O.N. 161858

3,735 grt   105.46 × 14.08 × 4.63 m

B. Harland & Wolff Ltd, Belfast. Yard No. 697.

Twin screw, oil engine, 1,192 rhp, 1,193 nhp, 6,150 bhp. By builder. 18 knots.

25.4.1929   Launched as *Ulster Prince* for the Belfast Steamship Company Ltd, Belfast.

4.3.1930   Handed over to the Belfast Steamship Company on the same day that *Innisfallen* was launched for the City of Cork Steam Packet's service from Fishguard to Cork.

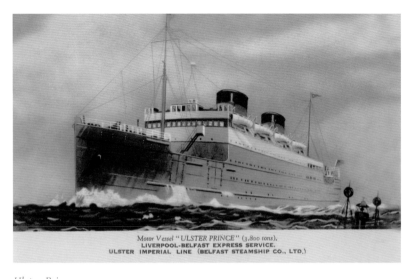

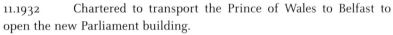

Ulster Prince.

Ulster Castle. (Courtesy of A. Duncan)

11.1932   Chartered to transport the Prince of Wales to Belfast to open the new Parliament building.

28.8.1940   Requisitioned by the Admiralty as HMS *Ulster Prince*.

25.4.1941   On a voyage from Suda Bay, Crete, to Nauplia, she grounded at Nauplia, was bombed and destroyed by fire.

207. *Ulster Castle* 1,217 grt – See *Lady Kildare*, British & Irish Steam Packet Company Ltd.

208. *Ulster Coast* (1922) O.N. 146318
774 grt   61.11 × 9.47 × 3.74 m
B. A. & J. Inglis Ltd, Pointhouse, Glasgow. Yard No. 657.

Single screw, triple expansion, steam engine, 123 rhp and nhp. By builder. Ordered by G. & J. Burns Ltd.

20.9.1922   Launched as *Lurcher* for Burns & Laird Lines Ltd.

1925   Transferred to Coast Lines, Liverpool. Renamed *Scottish Coast*.

1938   To the Belfast Steamship Company Ltd, Belfast. Renamed *Ulster Coast*.

1954   Sold to Ahern Shipping Ltd, Montreal. Renamed *Ahern Trader*.

10.1.1960   Broke her moorings at Muddy Hole, Gander Bay, Newfoundland, and wrecked in a snowstorm.

209. *Ulster Duke/Ulster Spinner* (1942) O.N. 168513
532 grt   748 dwt   59.25 × 9.20 × 2.62 m

Ulster Spinner.

Single screw, oil engine, 156 nhp, 800 bhp. By British Auxiliaries Ltd, Glasgow. 10½ knots.
B. Ardrossan Dockyard Company. Yard No. 380.

18.2.1942	Launched.
1942	Delivered as *Ulster Duke* for the Belfast Steamship Company Ltd, Belfast.
1946	Transferred to British Channel Islands Shipping Company Ltd.
1947	Renamed *Guernsey Coast*.
1955	Transferred to the Belfast Steamship Company Ltd, became *Ulster Spinner*.
1968	Sold to Michael A. Araktingi, Beirut, Lebanon, and renamed *Al-Amin*.
1971	Sold to Wafik Begdaykhe, Beirut, Lebanon.
1972	Renamed *Hamid*.

1980	Sold to Ayat Bakhirat Company Ltd, Limassol, Cyprus. Became *Elvina*.
4.1997	Laid up at Mina Raysut, Oman, following employment in the Somali/Oman livestock trade.
12.1997	Grounded near Salalah.

210. *Ulster Duchess/Ulster Weaver* (1946) O.N. 168544
498 grt   59.13 × 9.20 × 3.27 m
B. Ardrossan Dockyard Company. Yard No. 406.
Single screw, oil engine, 187 rhp, 960 bhp, 6 cylinder. By British Polar Engines Ltd, Glasgow.

16.5.1946	Launched as *Ulster Duchess* for the Belfast Steamship Company Ltd.
	Delivered to British Channel Islands Shipping Company Ltd.
1947	Renamed *Jersey Coast*.
1954	Transferred to the Belfast Steamship Company Ltd, became *Ulster Weaver*.
1964	To Coast Lines Ltd, Liverpool, renamed *Kentish Coast*.
1968	Sold to Alomar Mechanical Engineering Company (F. H. Hamza & A. M. Kulaib, Kuwait, as managers). Renamed *Salmiah Coast*.
1970	Sold to Kuwait Coast Line Company W. L. (F. H. Hamza & A. M. Kulaib, Kuwait, as managers).
1975	Sold to Abdul H. G. Zaddah, Abadan, Iran.
1999	Deleted from Lloyd's Register.

211. *Ulster Prince* (2) (1937) O.N. 164343
4,303 grt   107.59 × 15.30 × 4.45 m
B. Harland & Wolff Ltd, Belfast. Yard No. 995.
Twin screw, oil engine, 1,348 rhp, 1,347 nhp, 5,100 bhp. By builder.

Ulster Prince (2).

24.6.1937   Launched as *Leinster* for Coast Lines Ltd, Liverpool.

1938   Registered in Dublin and transferred to the British & Irish Steam Packet (1936) Ltd.

Later the British & Irish Steam Packet Company Ltd.

1940   Charter ended and she was registered in Liverpool.

1946   Managed by the Belfast Steamship Company Ltd, renamed *Ulster Prince*.

1966   Renamed *Ulster Prince I*.

1967   Sold to Van Heyghen Frères, Belgium, to be broken up.

Sold to Epirotiki Lines (George Potamianos Ltd), Greece, and renamed *Adria*.

1969   To Epirotiki Steamship Company Ltd, Famagusta, Cyprus. Renamed *Adria*.

1969   Renamed *Odysseus*.

1979–1980   Broken up at Faslane.

212. *Ulster Mariner* (1922) O.N. 145979

773 grt   332 nrt   61.26 × 9.47 × 3.74 m

B. A. & J. Inglis Ltd, Pointhouse. Yard No. 607.

Single screw, triple expansion, steam engine, 123 rhp and nhp, 3 cylinder. By builder. 10 ½ knots.

1922   Ordered by G. & J. Burns Ltd, taken over by the British & Irish Steam Packet Company Ltd (as *Lady Olive*), then by G. & J. Burns Ltd.

22.8.1922   Launched as *Ayrshire Coast* for Coast Lines Ltd, Liverpool.

1923   Transferred to Burns & Laird Lines Ltd, Glasgow. Renamed *Spaniel*.

1925   Coast Lines Ltd, reverted to *Ayrshire Coast*.

1947   To the Belfast Steamship Company Ltd, renamed *Ulster Mariner*.

22.7.1955   Arrived at Passage West and broken up.

213. *Ulster Merchant* (1920) O.N. 146282

763 grt   60.96 × 9.47 × 3.62 m

B. Harland & Wolff Ltd, Govan. Yard No. 626.

Single screw, triple expansion, steam engine, 123 rhp and nhp. By A. & J. Inglis Ltd, Pointhouse. 9½ knots.

1920   Ordered as *Princess Dagmar*.

28.12.1920   Launched as *Gorilla* for G. & J. Burns Ltd.

1922   Registered in Glasgow.

1922   Owned by Burns & Laird Lines Ltd.

1925   Transferred to Coast Lines Ltd, Liverpool. Renamed *Cumberland Coast*.

1929   Transferred to the City of Cork Steam Packet Company Ltd, Cork. Renamed *Kinsale*.

1933   Returned to Coast Lines Ltd, renamed *Cambrian Coast*.

1947   Transferred to the Belfast Steamship Company Ltd, renamed *Ulster Merchant*.

1954   Broken up at Newport, Mon.

214. *Ulster Hero* (2) (1920) O.N. 143635

1,104 grt   73.18 × 10.63 × 4.35 m

B. Sir Raylton Dixon & Company Ltd, Middlesbrough. Yard No. 611.

Single screw, triple expansion, steam engine, 177 rhp, 162 nhp. By Richardsons, Westgarth & Company Ltd, Middlesbrough. 11½ knots.

23.3.1920   Launched as *Princess Olga* for M. Langlands & Sons Ltd.

1920   Completed for Coast Lines Ltd, Liverpool, renamed *Lancashire Coast*.

1948   Managed by the Belfast Steamship Company Ltd, renamed *Ulster Hero*.

12.1954   Broken up at Barrow.

215. *Ulster Star* (2) (1922) O.N. 147391

1,036 grt   70.28 × 10.66 × 4.54 m

B. W. Dobson & Company, Walker on Tyne. Yard No. 220.

Single screw, triple expansion, steam engine, 193 rhp and nhp. By North East Marine Engineering Company Ltd, Newcastle. 10¾ knots.

20.11.1922   Launched as *Sapper* for Fisher, Renwick Steamers Ltd, Manchester.

1923   Delivered.

1939   Sold to Coast Lines Ltd, Liverpool, renamed *Avon Coast*.

1949   To the Belfast Steamship Company Ltd, renamed *Ulster Star*.

9.1954   Broken up at Briton Ferry.

216. *Ulster Duchess* (2) (1924) O.N. 147403

1,014 grt   70.25 × 10.66 × 4.57 m

B. Tyne Iron Shipbuilding Company, Willington Quay. Yard No. 228. 10 knots.

Single screw, triple expansion, steam engine, 193 rhp & nhp. By North East Marine Engineering Company Ltd, Newcastle.

17.6.1924   Launched as *Sentry* for Fisher, Renwick Steamers Ltd, Manchester.

1939   Sold to Coast Lines Ltd, Liverpool, renamed *Medway Coast*.

1949   Transferred to the Belfast Steamship Company Ltd, renamed *Ulster Duchess*.

9.1955   Broken up at Port Glasgow.

217. *Ulster Chieftain* (1937) O.N. 165759

586 grt   57.79 × 9.63 × 3.32 m

B. J. Koster Hzn Scheepswerf 'Gideon', Groningen, Netherlands. Yard No. 158.

Single screw, oil engine, 144 nhp, 825 bhp. By Humboldt Deutz-motoren A. G., Köln-Deutz, Germany.

18.11.1937   Launched as *Sandhill*.

1938   Delivered to the Tyne Tees Steam Shipping Company Ltd, Newcastle.

1943   Tyne Tees Steam Shipping Company Ltd acquired by Coast Lines Ltd.

1946   Renamed *Valerian Coast*.

1948   Transferred to the Aberdeen Steam Navigation Company Ltd, Aberdeen, renamed *Hebridean Coast*.

1951   To the Tyne Tees Steam Shipping Company Ltd.

1953   Transferred to the Belfast steamship Company Ltd, renamed *Ulster Chieftain*.

1956   To the Tyne Tees Steam Shipping Company Ltd, renamed *Durham Coast*.

1960   Managed by the British & Irish Steam Packet Company Ltd, renamed *Wicklow*.

1961   New engines fitted by Humboldt Deutz-motoren A. G., Köln-Deutz, Germany. 870 bhp, 10 ½ knots.

1970   Sold to Sistallic Shipping Company Ltd, Famagusta, Cyprus, and renamed *Sinergasia*.

1973   Sold to Aghios Sostis Maritime Company Ltd, Cyprus. Renamed *Sonia*.

1974   Purchased by the Fortitude Maritime Company, Greece, became *Margarita P.*

1976   Sold to Cia de Nav. Scotia S. A., Panama.

1980   Broken up at Baia, Italy.

218. *Ulster Drover* (1930) O.N. 152236
891 grt   67.45 × 10.75 × 4.60 m
B. Vickers Shipyard, Dublin. Yard No. 146.
Twin screw, triple expansion, steam engine, 196 rhp, 249 nhp. By McKie & Baxter Ltd, Glasgow.

28.7.1930   Launched as *Sligo* for the Sligo Steam Navigation Company Ltd, Sligo.

1936   Burns & Laird Lines Ltd, Glasgow. Renamed *Lairdsdale*.

1954   Transferred to the Belfast Steamship Company Ltd, renamed *Ulster Drover*.

11.1959   Broken up at Troon.

219. *Ulster Herdsman* (1923) O.N. 147874
1,526 grt   82.29 × 11.33 × 5.30 m
B. Caledon Shipbuilding & Engineering Company Ltd, Dundee. Yard No. 284.

Single screw, triple expansion, steam engine, 212 rhp, 196 nhp. By builder. 13½ knots.

18.6.1923   Launched as *Copeland*.

1923   Delivered to the Clyde Shipping Company Ltd, Glasgow.

1940   Requisitioned as a convoy rescue ship.

1945   Returned to owner.

1946   Sold to the North Continental Shipping Company Ltd (G. Heyn & Sons Ltd, Belfast, as managers). Renamed *North Down*.

1947   Sold to Mountain Steamship Company Ltd (G. Heyn & Sons Ltd as managers).

1954   Sold to Union International Company Ltd (Blue Star Line Ltd, Liverpool, as managers). Renamed *Drover*.

Sold to the Belfast steamship Company Ltd, renamed *Ulster Herdsman*.

1963   Broken up at Passage West.

220. *Ulster Pioneer* (1955) O.N. 185555
1,016 grt   72.63 × 11.06 × 3.32 m
B. George Brown & Company, Greenock. Yard No. 261.
Single screw, oil engine, 257 rhp, 1,440 bhp. By George Clark & Company (1938) Ltd, Sunderland.

24.2.1955   Launched.

1955   Delivered as *Ulster Pioneer* to the Belfast Steamship Company Ltd.

1963   Transferred to William Sloan & Company Ltd, renamed *Talisker*.

1965   Managed by Burns & Laird Lines Ltd, Glasgow.

1967   Transferred to Coast Line Ltd, Liverpool.

1970   Sold to Bat Snapir Mediterranean Lines Ltd, Israel (Mediterranean Lines Ltd, Haifa, as managers), and renamed *Bat Snapir*.

1974   Sold to Woodbine Shipping Corporation Incorporated, Hong Kong, renamed *Woodbine*.

1975   Sold to Asia Baru Navigation Pte Ltd, Singapore, became *Hong Shen*.

1976   Sold to Leong Mee Sendirian Berhad, Sarawak.

7.11.1988   On a voyage with a cargo of tyres and steel from Port Keland to Kota Kinabalu, she sank 40 miles south-west of Kota Kinabalu.

221. *Ulster Premier* (1955) O.N. 185563

979 grt   416 nrt   72.84 × 11.03 × 3.35 m

B. A. & J. Inglis Ltd, Pointhouse, Glasgow. Yard No. 1537.

Single screw, oil engine, 280 rhp, 1,440 bhp, 8 cylinder. By George Clark & Company (1938) Ltd, Sunderland.

26.4.1955   Launched as *Ulster Premier* for the Belfast Steamship Company Ltd, Belfast.

1963   Transferred to William Sloan & Company Ltd, Glasgow. Renamed *Kelvin*.

1965   Managed by Burns & Laird Lines Ltd, Glasgow.

1967   Transferred to Coast Lines Ltd.

1968   Sold to Albaran Bay Corporation of Panama, London. Renamed *Vasilia*.

1972   Sold to H. K. Tannis, Kingstown, St Vincent. Renamed *Alftan*.

1976   Purchased by Tacamar Panamena S. A., Panama. Renamed *Tacamar III*.

1982   Sold to Flota Mercante de Quimicos Flomerquim C. A., Caracas. Renamed *Canaima*.

3.1983   Laid up in Venezuela and broken up at Cartagena.

222. *Ulster Senator* (1938) O.N. 166243

511 grt   59.61 × 9.63 × 2.95 m

B. Scheeps de Noord, Alblasserdam, Netherlands. Yard No. 570.

Single screw, oil engine, 144 nhp, 750 bhp. By Humboldt Deutz-motoren, Köln-Deutz, Germany. 10½ knots.

21.5.1938   Launched as *Clyde Coast* for Coast Lines Ltd, Liverpool.

1956   Owned by the Belfast Steamship Company, renamed *Ulster Senator*.

1958   New engines by Humboldt Deutz-motoren, Köln-Deutz, Germany. 915 bhp.

1959   Transferred to William Sloan & Company Ltd, became *Deveron*.

1963   Sold to E. C. Georgopoulos & A. N. Athanassiades & Company, Piraeus, Greece and renamed *Nissos Delos*.

1966   Sold to Dimitrios Argyreas, Piraeus, Greece, and renamed *Dora Maria*.

1968   Renamed *Maria*.

1969   Renamed *Ismini L.*

1972   Sold to Ismini L. Shipping Company Ltd, Piraeus, Greece.

1973   Sold to D. Papadimitriou & V. Dalabiras, Thessaloniki, Greece.

1974   Sold to E. Papadimitriou, Piraeus, Greece, and renamed *Makedonia*.

1979   Sold to N. Palaeopoulos, Piraeus, Greece.

28.9.1979   On a voyage from Larnaca to Jounieh, Lebanon, she sank 7 miles off Cape Kiti, Cyprus.

223. *Ulster Sportsman* (1936) O.N. 187106

789 grt   69.79 × 11.33 × 3.50 m

B. Harland & Wolff Ltd, Belfast. Yard No. 976.

Twin screw, oil engine, 330 rhp, 332 nhp, 1,400 bhp. By builder.

21.7.1936   Launched as *Lairdswood* for Burns & Laird Lines Ltd, Glasgow.

Ulster Sportsman.

1959   Transferred to the Belfast Steamship Company Ltd, renamed *Ulster Sportsman.*
1966   Sold to Transrodopi S. A., Burundi, and renamed *Transrodopi IV.*
1968   Sold to Navigation Maritime Bulgare, Bulgaria, and renamed *Alnilam.*
8.1970   Broken up at La Felguera.

224. *Mountstewart* – See *Essex Coast,* Coast Lines Ltd.

225. *Brookmount* – See *Lairds Ben,* Burns & Laird Lines Ltd.

226. *Colebrooke* – See *Lairds Moor,* Burns & Laird Lines Ltd.

227. *Stormont* (2) – See *Fife Coast* (3), Coast Lines Ltd.

228. *Ulster Prince* (3) (1966) O.N. 305572
4,270 grt   1,367 dwt   2,115 nrt   114.92 × 16.48 × 9.06 m
B. Harland & Wolff Ltd, Belfast. Yard No. 1667.
Two controllable pitch propellers, 7,200 bhp, 2 × 12 cylinder, 4SCSA, Pielstick Vee diesel engine. By Crossley Premier Engines Ltd, Manchester. Passengers: 1,022 (428 berths).
13.10.1966   Launched by Lady Erskine of Rerrick, wife of the Governor of Northern Ireland.
6.4.1967   Delivered to the Belfast Steamship Company Ltd, Belfast.
19.4.1967   Maiden voyage Liverpool–Belfast.
26.2.1971   Coast Lines Ltd acquired by the P&O Steam Navigation Company Ltd.
1.10.1971   Managed by P&O Short Sea Shipping Ltd.
31.3.1975   Managed by P&O Ferries.
21.9.1978   Owned by P&O Ferries Ltd.
10.12.1981   Sailed from Liverpool and laid up at Ostend.
27.8.1982   Sold to Panmar Ferries Services Ltd (Sidra Shipping Enterprises S. A. as managers), Cyprus, renamed *Lady M.*
1984   Purchased by Varsity S. A., Panama, renamed *Tangpakorn* for service from Hong Kong to China.
1988   Sold to the China Ocean Shipping Company, China, renamed *Long Hu.*
Purchased by Shun Tak Enterprises, Bahamas, renamed *Macmosa* for the Macau–Taiwan service.
1989   Sold to Chin Hing Ltd, Bahamas.
1995   Sold to Aquila Maritime Services, Panama, renamed *Neptunia II* and then *Neptunia.*
Chartered to Neckar Reisen for the Bari–Cesme service.

Ulster Prince (3).

1996   Acquired by Panther Marine Corporation, Panama, renamed *Panther*.

1998   Managed by Hellenic Mediterranean Lines Company Ltd.

2000   Chartered to Superferries, renamed *Vatan* for the Cesme–Brindisi route.
Sold to Manar Marine Services Incorporated, Panama, renamed *Manar*.

2001   Sold to Al Thuraya Marine Service Company, Dubai, for the Port Rashid–Umm Qasr service.

3.2004   Sold to be broken up in India.

24.3.2004   Arrived at Alang.

229. *Ulster Queen* (2) (1966) O.N. 305575

4,270 grt   1,390 dwt   2,115 nrt   114.87 × 16.45 × 9.06 m

B. Cammell Laird & Company Ltd, Birkenhead. Yard No. 1823.

Two controllable pitch propellers, 7,200 bhp, 2 × 12 cylinder, 4SCSA, Pielstick Vee diesel engine. By Crossley Premier Engines Ltd, Manchester.

Passengers: 1,022 (428 berths).

29.3.1966   Keel laid at Birkenhead.

1.12.1966   Launched by Lady Robinson, wife of the Chairman of Coast Lines Ltd, Sir Arnet Robinson.

31.5.1967   Delivered to the Belfast Steamship Company Ltd, Belfast.

6.6.1967   Maiden voyage Liverpool–Belfast.

26.2.1971   Coast Lines Ltd was acquired by the P&O Steam Navigation Company Ltd.

1.10.1971   Managed by P&O Short Sea Shipping Ltd.

20.7.1974   A bomb exploded in the First Class lounge 45 minutes after she had arrived at Belfast but caused only superficial damage and no injuries. The ship had been cleared after a telephone warning.

31.3.1975   Managed by P&O Ferries.

21.9.1978   Owned by P&O Ferries Ltd.

10.12.1981 Sailed from Liverpool to Ostend to lay up awaiting sale.

22.4.1982   Sold to the Pangloss Navigation Company Ltd, Cyprus.

1986   Renamed *Al Kahera*.

1987   Renamed *Ala-Eddin*.

1988   Sold to the Sinbad Navigation Company Ltd (Hellenic Mediterranean Lines, Limassol, as managers), renamed *Poseidonia*. Transferred to Silkwave Maritime Company Ltd.

2000   Renamed *La Patria*.

2002   Renamed *Poseidonia*.

2005   Renamed *Al-Kafain* to carry pilgrims to/from Saudi Arabia.

2.11.2005   Suffered a serious engine room fire off Hurghada. Attempts were made to take her in tow, but she was swept southwards until she struck the reef at Sha'ab Sheer and sank. There were no passengers on board and the crew were rescued by a passing vessel.

230. *Donautal/Ulster Sportsman* (2)/*St Magnus* (3) (1970) O.N. 360886
1,000 grt   1,219 dwt   411 nrt   96.81 × 15.83 × 10.32 m
B. Rickmars Werft, Bremerhaven, West Germany. Yard No. 362.
Twin controllable pitch screws 4,000 bhp, 2 × 9 cylinder, 2SCSA, diesel engines. By Atlas-MaK Masch. Kiel. Twelve drivers, 25 × 40-foot units or equivalent. 16 knots.
14.3.1970   Launched.
23.5.1970   Delivered as *Donautal* to Partenreederei, West Germany (J. A. Reinecke as managers).
1.6.1974   Sold to the Belfast Steamship Company Ltd (P&O Short Sea Shipping Ltd as managers), renamed *Ulster Sportsman*.
31.3.1975   Managed by P&O Ferries.
10.1975   Chartered to Truckline Ferries Ltd for the Poole–Cherbourg service.
12.1.1976   Renamed *Dorset*.
1.1978   Charter ended.
2.4.1978   Registered at London.
12.5.1978   Renamed *St Magnus* and placed on the Aberdeen/Orkney and Shetland service.
6.1978   Relieved on the Normandy Ferries service from Dover.
14.7.1978   Owned by P&O Ferries Ltd.
6.2.1979   Relieved on the Normandy ferries service from Dover to Boulogne.
5.1985   Managed by POETS Fleet Management Ltd, operated by P&O Ferries Ltd.

1.1.1989   Owned by P&O Scottish Ferries Ltd.
4.6.1990   In P&O service on the Portsmouth–Le Havre route.
8.1990   At Weymouth for repairs.
27.9.1990   Laid up at Southampton.
1990   Sold to Blaesbjerg Marine, Aarhus, Denmark (Bahamas flag), renamed *Codan Marine.*
1991   Sold to Scan-Pol Marine S. A., Port Vila, Panama, renamed *Parseta.*
1992   Bareboat charter to Polferries for the Swinoujscie–Ystead route.
1995   Purchased by the Polish Baltic Shipping Company, Port Vila, Panama.

Ulster Prince (3) at her berth in Princes Dock, Liverpool.

1996	Operated on the Swinoujscie–Aabenraa route.
1997	Sold to Consalidada de Ferrys C. A., Pampatar, Venezuela, renamed *Dona Juana* for service on the mainland to Margarita Island.
20.6.2010	Reported sunk, after lying at anchor for three years.

231. *Saaletal* (1969) IMO 6925707

994 grt   1,184 dwt   96.8 × 88 m

B. Rickmars Werft, Bremerhaven, West Germany. Yard No. 359.

Twin controllable pitch screws, 4,000 bhp, 2 × 9 cylinder, 2SCSA, diesel engines by Atlas-MaK Masch. Kiel. Twelve drivers, 25 × 40-foot units or equivalent. 16 knots.

26.7.1969	Launched as *Thule* for J. A. Reinecke, Lubeck.
6.1971	Chartered to the Belfast Steamship Company Ltd as *Saaletal*.
1974	Renamed *Cotentin*.
1981	*Miranda 1*.
1986	*Caribe Merchant*.
1996	*Romana 1*.
2005	*El Capitain*.
2006	*Angel Pearl*.
2007	*Princess Carol*.
6.6.2012	Deleted from register.

232. *Ulster Merchant* (2) (1971) O.N. 362473

499 grt   1,208 dwt   325 nrt   70.10 × 12.03 × 6.00 m

B. Schiffs C. Cassens Schiffswerft, Emden. Yard No. 101.

Single screw, 1,000 bhp, 6 cylinder, 4SCSA, diesel engine. By Atlas-MaK Maschinenfabrik, Kiel, West Germany. 129 TEUs. 12½ knots.

16.1.1971	Launched.
1971	Delivered as *Embdena* for 'Embdena', Emder Küstenschiffahrt GmbH & Company K. G., West Germany.
1972	Renamed *British Unit*. Renamed *Embdena*.
28.11.1973	Purchased by the Belfast Steamship Company Ltd (P&O Short Sea Shipping Ltd as managers), Belfast, renamed *Ulster Merchant*.
31.3.1975	Managed by P&O Ferries.
4.7.1977	Renamed *Eland*.
21.9.1978	Transferred to P&O Ferries Ltd.
17.11.1978	Sold to Sun Shipping Ltd, Cayman Islands.
1979	Renamed *Hybur Sun*.
1992	Sold to Pioneer Sun Ltd (Pioneer Shipping Incorporated as managers, Nassau, Bahamas), renamed *Pioneer Sun*.
2009	Renamed *El Principe Andres*.

233. *Pointer* (3) (1970) O.N. 363274

1,206 grt   1,200 dwt   561 nrt   97.01 × 15.85 × 10.32 m

B. Kroegerwerft GmbH, Rendsburg, West Germany. Yard No. 1356.

Twin screw, 4,000 bhp, 2 × 9 cylinder, 2SCSA, diesel engines. By Atlas-Mak Masch. Kiel, West Germany. 34 × 40-foot trailers. 16 knots.

17.7.1970	Launched.
10.1970	Delivered as *Isartal* to Transanglia Schiffahrts GmbH & Company (J. A. Reinecke as managers), West Germany.
1973	Renamed *Antwerpen*.
1974	Registered under Rollonoff Shipping Ltd, London, renamed *Preseli*.
6.11.1974	Purchased by the P&O Steam Navigation Company Ltd, bareboat chartered to British Rail for the Fishguard–Rosslare service.
31.3.1975	Managed by P&O Ferries.
31.12.1976	Owned by the Belfast Steamship Company Ltd.
6.4.1977	Charter to British Rail completed.
9.6.1977	Renamed *Pointer*.

14.7.1978   Owned by P&O Ferries Ltd.

31.12.1984   Transferred to POETS Fleet Management Ltd.

18.12.1985   Sold to Sea Malta Company Ltd, Malta, renamed *Zebbug*.

2006   *Fehim Bey.*

2013   *Al Astair.*

234. *ASD Meteor* (1971) O.N. 362507

1,975 grt   106.28 × 16.03 × 6 m

B. Kristiansands M/V A/S, Kristiansand, Norway. Yard No. 216.

Twin screw, Pielstick oil engine, 8,000 bhp, 2 × 8 cylinder. By Lindholmen Motor A/B, Gothenburg, Sweden. 19 knots.

8.1.1971   Launched as *Holmia* for A/B Siljarederiet, Finland.

1973   Sold to the International Chartering Corporation, Singapore. Renamed *ASD Meteor.*

1973   Chartered by P&O for the Belfast Steamship Company Ltd/ British Rail.

1975   Sold to P&O, Belfast. Renamed *Penda.*

1975   To Hain-Norse Ltd, Belfast.

1978   Owned by P&O Ferries Ltd.

1980   Renamed *N. F. Jaguar.*

1981   Chartered to the Isle of Man Steam Packet Company Ltd.

1982   Sold to James Fisher & Sons PLC, Barrow. Managed by the Isle of Man Steam Packet Company Ltd. Renamed *Peveril.*

1993   Sold to the Isle of Man Steam Packet Company Ltd.

2000   Owned by Marine Express Incorporated, K. Arnesan Shipping A/S, Panama. Renamed *Caribbean Express.*

2001   Sold to Cadre S. A., Phnom-Penh, Cambodia. Renamed *Express.*

30.1.2004   Lost.

Burns & Laird Lines Ltd.

235. *Pointer/Lairdsvale* (1896) O.N. 106001

1,183 grt   534 nrt   76.20 × 10.85 × 4.84 m

B. A. & J. Inglis Ltd, Pointhouse. Yard No. 240.

Single screw, triple expansion, steam engine, 3 cylinder, 265 nhp. By builder.

Passengers: 400 saloon and 639 steerage passengers. Sixty-two berths, 230 cattle and two horses.

21.3.1896   Launched as *Pointer* for G. & J. Burns Ltd, Glasgow.

1922   Burns & Laird Lines Ltd.

30.5.1929   Renamed *Lairdsvale.*

4.3.1933   Arrived at Blyth and broken up by Hughes Bolckow Ltd.

236. *Magpie/Lairdsgrove* (1898) O.N. 108749

1,280 grt   400 nrt   80.77 × 10.94 × 5.05 m

B. A. & J. Inglis Ltd, Pointhouse. Yard No. 246.

Single screw, triple expansion, steam engine, 3 cylinder, 367 nhp. By builder.

8.2.1898   Launched as *Magpie* for G. & J. Burns Ltd.

1922   Burns & Laird Lines Ltd.

1923   Oil fired boilers fitted by D. & W. Henderson Ltd.

30.5.1929   Renamed *Lairdsgrove.*

1939   Became a freight only vessel.

5.1948   Sold to be broken up but used as an accommodation ship.

1950   Broken up at Faslane.

237. *Vulture/Lairdsrock* (1898) O.N. 108764

1,280 grt   399 nrt   80.77 × 10.94 × 5.05 m

B. A. & J. Inglis Ltd, Pointhouse. Yard No. 246.

Single screw, triple expansion, steam engine, 367 nhp, 3 cylinder. By builder.

14.6.1898   Launched as *Vulture* for G. & J. Burns Ltd, Glasgow. Operated on the Glasgow–Belfast and Ardrossan–Belfast routes.

1914–1918   Operated Aberdeen–Bergen sailings.

1922   Burns & Laird Lines Ltd.

1924   Oil fired boilers fitted by D. & W. Henderson Ltd.

30.5.1929   Renamed *Lairdsrock*.

1.1937   David MacBrayne Ltd. Renamed *Lochgarry*.

1939–1945   Requisitioned by the Admiralty and operated between Scotland and Iceland and assisted in the evacuation of Dunkirk.

1942   1,669 grt.

21.1.1942   On a voyage from Glasgow to Oban in ballast she was wrecked off Rathlin Island with forty-nine crew and one passenger on board. Twenty-three people lost their lives.

238. *Coney/Lairdsferry* (1918) O.N. 141880

697 grt   280 nrt   59.43 × 9.75 × 3.96 m

B. Harland & Wolff Ltd, Govan. Yard No. 510.

Single screw, triple expansion, steam engine, 175 lbs, 97 nhp, 3 cylinder. By A. & J. Inglis Ltd.

14.2.1918   Launched as *Coney* for G. & J. Burns Ltd, Glasgow. Heavy lift capacity.

1922   Burns & Laird Lines Ltd.

30.5.1929   Renamed *Lairdsferry*.

18.1.1952   Arrived at Port Glasgow and broken up by Smith & Houston Ltd.

239. *Grouse/Kelvindale* (1891) O.N. 98646

386 grt   178 nrt   53.46 × 8.53 × 3.62 m

B. Caird & Company Ltd, Greenock. Yard No. 263.

Single screw, triple expansion, steam engine, 3 cylinder, inverted direct acting, 86 hp. By builder.

27.5.1891   Launched as *Grouse* for G. & J. Burns Ltd, Glasgow, to operate on the Greenock–Larne route.

1922   Grahamston Shipping Company (W. T. Mitchell Ltd), Glasgow. Renamed *Kelvindale* for the Glasgow and Greenock to Campbeltown, Stranraer and Preston route.

1923   Burns & Laird Lines Ltd.

1924   Coast Lines Ltd. Renamed *Denbigh Coast*.

1929   To David MacBrayne (1928) Ltd, Glasgow. Renamed *Lochdunvegan*.

1931   New boilers fitted.

27.7.1948   Arrived at Faslane and broken up by Metal Industries Ltd.

240. *Hound* (1893) O.N. 99892

1,061 grt   332 nrt   76.29 × 9.78 × 4.72 m

B. Fairfield Shipbuilding & Engineering Company Ltd, Govan. Yard No. 370.

Single screw, triple expansion, steam engine, 165 lbs, 359 nhp, 3 cylinder. By builder.

1.3.1893   Launched as *Hound* for G. & J. Burns Ltd, Glasgow.

1922   Burns & Laird Lines Ltd.

1926   M. G. A. Manuelides Brothers, Piraeus, Greece. Renamed *Mary M.*

1929   Hellenic Coast Lines, Greece.

1933   Renamed *Lesbos*.

1942   *Korytza*.

1945   Ministry of War Transport, London.

1946   Hellenic Coast Lines, Greece.

1950   Broken up.

241. *Moorfowl/Lairdsmoor* (1919) O.N. 143335
1,578 grt   80.77 × 11.64 × 5.12 m
B. A. & J. Inglis Ltd, Glasgow. Yard No. 311.
Single screw, triple expansion, steam engine, 165 lbs, 414 nhp, 3 cylinder. By builder.

1.4.1919	Ordered as *Moorfowl* for G. & J. Burns Ltd's Belfast route. Her construction was delayed, leading to the company refusing to accept her. She was then sold to the City of Cork Steam Packet Company Ltd and was launched as *Killarney*.
1920	Transferred to G. & J. Burns Ltd, renamed *Moorfowl*.
1922	Burns & Laird Lines Ltd.
1926	Upper deck extended and new observation lounge built.
30.5.1929	Renamed *Lairdsmoor*.
7.4.1937	On a voyage from Dublin to Glasgow with thirty-three crew, six passengers, four cattlemen and 321 cattle in fog, she was in collision at 0320 hours with *Taranaki* off Black Head, Wigtownshire. *Taranaki* struck her around the bridge area and *Lairdsmoor* sank within 30 minutes. All on board were rescued by *Taranaki* except Captain John Campbell and fireman Edward McBride. *Lairdcrest* stood by to assist.

242. *Partridge/Lairdsloch* (1906) O.N. 124121
1,523 grt   82.41 × 11.58 × 5.36 m
B. John Brown & Company Ltd, Clydebank. Yard No. 373.
Single screw, triple expansion, steam engine, 175 lbs, 460 nhp, 3 cylinder. By builder.

23.5.1906	Launched as *Partridge* for G. & J. Burns Ltd, Glasgow.
1914	Requisitioned by the Admiralty as an armed boarding vessel and later a transport between Malta and Marseilles.
1916	HMS *Partridge II*.
1919	Returned to owners.

113.11.1929	Renamed *Lairdsloch*.
2.11.1936	Arrived at Dalmuir and broken up by Arnott Young & Company Ltd.

243. *Woodcock/Lairdswood* (1906) O.N. 121346
1,619 grt   688 nrt   82.41 × 11 × 5.05 m
B. John Brown & Company Ltd, Clydebank. Yard No. 372.
Single screw, triple expansion, steam engine, 3 cylinder, 460 nhp. By builder.

10.4.1906	Launched as *Woodcock* for G. & J. Burns Ltd Ardrossan–Belfast night mail service.
11.1914	Requisitioned by the Admiralty as an armed boarding vessel. She was renamed HMS *Woodnut* as the General Steam Navigation Company owned a ship named *Woodcock*.
1920	Renamed *Woodcock*.
1922	Burns & Laird Lines Ltd.
7.11.1929	Renamed *Lairdswood*.
10.1930	To the Aberdeen Steam Navigation Company Ltd, Aberdeen. Renamed *Lochnagar*.
1940–1945	Requisitioned by the Admiralty and was engaged in the evacuation from Norway. She also sailed to Iceland and the Shetland Islands.
8.1946	Sold to Rena Cia de Nav. S. A. (P. Protopapas, Panama), becoming *Rena* to carry 360 emigrants between Europe and Australia.
1951	Renamed *Blue Star*.
26.4.1952	Arrived at La Spezia and broken up.

244. *Sable/Lairdselm* (1911) O.N. 129571
687 grt   280 nrt   59.49 × 9.78 × 4.69 m
B. A. & J. Inglis Ltd, Glasgow. Yard No. 294.

Single screw, triple expansion, steam engine, 124 nhp, 3 cylinder. By builder.

29.3.1911	Launched as *Sable* for G. & J. Burns Ltd, Glasgow.
1922	Burns & Laird Lines Ltd, Glasgow.
30.6.1929	Renamed *Lairdselm*.
21.12.1929	She sailed from Glasgow at 1700 hours for a voyage to Harland & Wolff at Belfast with 200 tons of diesel engine sections and the cargo shifted.
22.12.1929	She anchored in Loch Ryan at 0200 hours and rolled over at 0930 hours. The crew managed to row to Cairnryan Lighthouse and *Lairdselm* sank east of Milleur Point.

245. *Puma/Lairdsford* (1899) O.N. 111025

1,226 grt   80.77 × 10.72 × 4.72 m

B. Caledon Shipbuilding & Engineering Company Ltd, Dundee. Yard No. 149.

Single screw, triple expansion, steam engine, 3 cylinder. By builder.

9.6.1899	Launched as *Duke of Rothesay* for the Dublin & Glasgow Sailing & Steam Packet Company (Duke Line) for the Glasgow–Dublin service. Cost £37,850.00.
1908	To G. & J. Burns Ltd, Glasgow. Renamed *Puma*.
1922	Burns & Laird Lines Ltd, Glasgow.
1929	Renamed *Lairdsford*.
7.2.1934	Arrived at Preston and broken up by T. W. Ward Ltd.

246. *Tiger/Lairdsforest* (1906) O.N. 123124

1,389 grt   83.82 × 11.18 × 4.72 m

B. Caledon Shipbuilding & Engineering Company Ltd, Dundee. Yard No. 187.

Single screw, quadruple expansion, steam engine, 4 cylinder. By builder.

Passengers: 164 saloon passengers, 996 steerage, 530 cattle and 3 horses.

10.4.1906	Launched as *Duke of Montrose*.
1906	Delivered to the Dublin & Glasgow Sailing & Steam Packet Company (Duke Line). Cost £45,000
1908	To G. & J. Burns Ltd, Glasgow. Renamed *Tiger*.
1922	Burns & Laird Lines Ltd, Glasgow.
1929	Renamed *Lairdsforest*.
1931	Transferred to the British & Irish Steam Packet Company Ltd, renamed *Lady Louth*. Her passenger accommodation was removed and she became a cattle carrier.
1934	On fire at Birkenhead.

Broken up at Port Glasgow by Smith & Houston Ltd.

247. *Gorilla* (1920) O.N. 146282

772 grt   351 nrt   61.02 × 9.47 × 3.62 m

B. Harland & Wolff Ltd, Govan. Yard No. 626.

Single screw, triple expansion, steam engine, 123 nhp, 660 ihp, 3 cylinder. By A. & J. Inglis Ltd.

29.12.1920	Launched as *Gorilla*. Ordered by M. Langlands as *Princess Dagmar*, completed for G. & J. Burns Ltd and delivered to Burns & Laird Lines Ltd.
10.8.1922	Sunk in Cork, refloated and repaired at Glasgow by her builders.
1925	Coast Lines Ltd, Liverpool. Renamed *Cumberland Coast*.
1929	To the City of Cork Steam Packet Company Ltd, Cork. Renamed *Kinsale*.
1933	Coast Lines Ltd, Liverpool. Renamed *Cambrian Coast*.
1947	Belfast Steamship Company Ltd, Belfast. Renamed *Ulster Merchant*.
8.10.1954	Arrived at Newport, Monmouthshire, and broken up by J. Cashmore Ltd.

248. *Lurcher* – See *Scottish Coast* (1922). Coast Lines Ltd.

249. *Redbreast/Lairdsbrook* (1920) O.N. 144238
772 grt   60.96 × 9.75 × 4.35 m
B. Harland & Wolff Ltd, Govan. Yard No. 602.
Single screw, triple expansion, steam engine, 123 nhp, 600 ihp, 3 cylinder.
By A. & J. Inlis Ltd.
14.10.1920   Launched as *Redbreast*. Ordered by M. Langlands for the Glasgow–Liverpool–Manchester service as *Princess Caroline*, completed for G. & J. Burns Ltd.
1922   Burns & Laird Lines Ltd.
1926   Coast Lines Ltd. Renamed *Sutherland Coast*.
16.5.1930   Transferred to Burns & Laird Lines Ltd, renamed *Lairdsbrook*. Replaced *Lairdselm*.
5.9.1945   Holed when *City of Lincoln* collided with her at the East India Wharf, Greenock.
1951   New boiler fitted.
11.3.1960   Arrived at Passage West and broken up by Haulbowline Industries Ltd.

250. *Brier/Lairdsoak* (1882) O.N. 86704
710 grt   256 nrt   64 × 9.81 × 4.60 m
B. D. & W. Henderson & Company Ltd, Glasgow. Yard No. 248.
Single screw, compound steam engine, 177 nhp, 2 cylinder. By builder.
14.9.1882   Launched as *Brier* for Alex A. Laird & Company for the Glasgow–Londonderry route.
1922   Burns & Laird Lines Ltd.
30.5.1929   Renamed *Lairdsoak*. Known as 'Laird soak' as a porthole on the bow split the name in two.
1931   Michael Murphy Ltd, Dublin. Renamed *Enda*.

27.2.1933   On a voyage from Londonderry to Heysham with twenty-three crew, two passengers and 150 cattle on board in storm conditions, she went ashore in Clanyard Bay, Mull of Galloway. Total loss but all were rescued. *Lairdsburn* was sailing between Glasgow and Dublin that night with the Scottish rugby team on board and arrived twelve hours late.

251. *Maple/Lairdsglen* (1914) O.N. 136293
1,294 grt   535 nrt   79.58 × 11.76 × 5.05 m
B. Ailsa Shipbuilding Company Ltd, Troon. Yard No. 283.
Single screw, triple expansion, steam engine, 180 lbs, 467 nhp, 3 cylinder. By builder.
26.2.1914   Launched as *Maple* for Laird Line Ltd, Glasgow, for the Glasgow–Londonderry service.
1914–1919   Requisitioned by the Admiralty and operated from Taranto–Marseilles–Malta–Port Said–Alexandria.
1922   Burns & Laird Lines Ltd.
30.8.1929   Renamed *Lairdsglen*.
1932   The 'Navy' top was removed from the funnel.
1933   Observation lounge forward fitted on the upper deck and new wheelhouse.
1.12.1939   In collision with *Findhorn* off Cumbraes/Holy Isle. *Findhorn* beached at Kilchattan Bay. The Board of Trade Inquiry found in favour of *Lairdsglen*.
6.1951   Broken up by Smith & Houston Ltd at Port Glasgow.

252. *Lily/Lairdspool* (1896) O.N. 106053
668 grt   229 nrt   58 × 8.93 × 4.05 m
B. Blackwood & Gordon Ltd, Port Glasgow. Yard No. 236.
Single screw, triple expansion, steam engine, 170 lbs, 126 nhp, 3 cylinder.
By builder.

7.11.1896   Launched as *Lily* for the Glasgow, Dublin & Londonderry Steam Packet Company Ltd (A. A. Laird & Company Ltd), Glasgow, to operate to Sligo, Westport and Ballina.

1907   Laird Line Ltd, Glasgow.

1922   Burns & Laird Lines Ltd.

30.6.1929   Renamed *Lairdspool* and chartered to the British & Irish Steam Packet Company Ltd for a time.

1937   To David MacBrayne Ltd. Renamed *Lochgorm*.

1942   Requisitioned by the Admiralty, managed by McCallum, Orme & Company Ltd.

1946   Returned to David McBrayne Ltd.

5.6.1951   Arrived at Port Glasgow and broken up by Smith & Houston Ltd.

253. *Olive/Lairdsbank* (1893) O.N. 102618

1,141 grt   381 nrt   79.24 × 10.08 × 4.81 m

B. D. & W. Henderson & Company Ltd, Glasgow. Yard No. 368.

Single screw, triple expansion, steam engine, 368 nhp, 3 cylinder. By builder.

26.7.1893   Launched as *Olive* for the Glasgow, Dublin & Londonderry Steam Packet Company Ltd (A. A. Laird & Company Ltd), Glasgow.

1907   Laird Line Ltd, Glasgow.

1922   Burns & Laird Lines Ltd, Glasgow.

30.5.1929   Renamed *Lairdsbank*.

1930   Transferred to the North of Scotland, Orkney & Shetland Steam Navigation Company Ltd, Aberdeen. Renamed *St Catherine* to replace *St Sunniva*.

16.6.1937   Arrived at Rosyth and broken up by Metal Industries Ltd.

254. *Rose/Lairdsrose* (1902) O.N. 115692

1,093 grt   458 nrt   76.35 × 11.64 × 4.87 m

B. A. & J. Inglis Ltd, Glasgow. Yard No. 271.

Single screw, triple expansion, steam engine, 150 lbs, 330 nhp, 3 cylinder. By builder.

1.5.1902   Launched as *Rose* for the Glasgow, Dublin & Londonderry Steam Packet Company Ltd (A. A. Laird & Company Ltd), Glasgow.

1907   William MacConnell, Laird Line Ltd, Glasgow.

1908   Laird Line Ltd, Glasgow.

1914–1918   Requisitioned by the Admiralty as a troopship. Operated in the Mediterranean: Taranto, Italy, Greece.

1922   Burns & Laird Lines Ltd, Glasgow.

30.5.1929   Renamed *Lairdsrose*.

1939–1945   Passenger certificate lapsed.

1949   Broken up by the British Steel Corporation Ltd at Bowness.

255. *Thistle* (1884) O.N.89935

803 grt   359 nrt   66.14 × 9.78 × 4.69 m

B. D. & W. Henderson & Company Ltd, Glasgow. Yard No. 317.

Single screw, compound, 100 lbs, 249 nhp, 2 cylinder. By builder.

29.5.1884   Launched as *Thistle* for the Glasgow, Dublin & Londonderry Steam Packet Company Ltd (A. A. Laird & Company Ltd), Glasgow. The company's first steel-built vessel.

Londonderry and Glasgow, Heysham or Fleetwood services.

1890   827 grt, 314 nrt.

1893   Lengthened to 70.40 metres.

1916   922 grt, 390 nrt.

12.1928   Arrived at Port Glasgow and broken up by Smith & Houston Ltd.

256. *Turnberry/Lairdsheather* (1889) O.N. 96657

515 grt   393 nrt   57.91 × 8.90 × 3.99 m

B. Archibald McMillan & Son, Dumbarton. Yard No. 294.

Single screw, triple expansion, steam engine, 160 lbs, 154 nhp, 3 cylinder by J. G. Kincaid & Company Ltd.

10.9.1889	Launched as *Spindrift* for Charles F. Leach, London.
1899	Ayr Steam Shipping Company Ltd (Rowan & Bain, Glasgow). Renamed *Turnberry*.
1908	Ayr Steam Shipping Company Ltd acquired by Laird Line Ltd.
1921	Laird Line Ltd, Glasgow.
1922	Burns & Laird Lines Ltd.
30.5.1929	Renamed *Lairdsheather*.
1930	New engine, 515 grt, 215 nrt, 154 nhp. By J. G. Kincaid & Company Ltd.
3.1937	Sold to T. W. Ward Ltd and broken up at Barrow-in-Furness.

257. *Dunure* (1878) O.N. 80430

748 grt   354 nrt   66.35 × 9.26 × 4.69 m

B. D. & W. Henderson & Company Ltd, Glasgow. Yard No. 189.

Single screw, compound steam engine, 2 cylinder. By builder.

27.11.1878	Launched as *Cedar* for the Glasgow, Dublin & Londonderry Steam Packet Company Ltd (A. A. Laird & Company Ltd), Glasgow.
1906	Ayr Steam Shipping Company Ltd. Renamed *Dunure*.
1921	Laird Line Ltd, Glasgow.
1922	Burns & Laird Lines Ltd.
1924	Sold to P. H. Kavounidos, Piraeus. Renamed *Nicolaos Kavounides* and later *Bosphoros*.
1926	Renamed *Express*.
1927	Alex A. Yannoulatos, Piraeus. Renamed *Zephiros*.
1931	Hellenic Coast Lines, Piraeus.
1933	Renamed *Spetsai*.
1937	Broken up at Savona, Italy.

258. *Cairnsmore* (1896) O.N. 104466

935 grt   71.93 × 9.44 × 4.57 m

B. Harland & Wolff Ltd, Belfast. Yard No. 306.

Twin screw, triple expansion, steam engine, 263 rhp & nhp. By builder. 13 knots.

8.6.1896	Launched as *Comic* for the Belfast Steamship Company Ltd, Belfast.
1919	Belfast Steamship Company Ltd acquired by Coast Lines Ltd.
1921	Transferred to Laird Line Ltd, Glasgow. Renamed *Cairnsmore*.
1922	Transferred to Burns & Laird Lines Ltd, Glasgow.
1929	Transferred to the British & Irish Steam Packet Company Ltd, Dublin. Renamed *Lady Kerry*.
1934	Broken up at Preston by T. W. Ward Ltd.

259. *Culzean* (1897) O.N. 108619

959 grt   71.93 × 9.44 × 4.57 m

B. Harland & Wolff Ltd, Belfast. Yard No. 306.

Twin screw, triple expansion, steam engine, 263 rhp & nhp. By builder. 13 knots.

26.10.1897	Launched as *Logic* for Thomas Gallaher & Company Ltd, Belfast. Chartered to the Belfast Steamship Company Ltd.
26.6.1902	In collision with *Princess May* in Larne Harbour.
1904	Purchased by the Belfast Steamship Company Ltd, Belfast.
1919	Belfast Steamship Company Ltd acquired by Coast Lines Ltd.
1921	Transferred to Laird Line Ltd, Glasgow. Renamed *Culzean*.
1922	Transferred to Burns & Laird Lines Ltd, Glasgow.
5.6.1923	Grounded in the Victoria Channel, Belfast, later refloated that day.

1929   Transferred to the British & Irish Steam Packet Company Ltd, Dublin. Renamed *Lady Carlow*.

5.1936   Sold to Smith & Company Ltd for demolition.

260. *Spaniel* – See *Ayrshire Coast*, Coast lines Ltd.

261. *Setter* – See *Clyde Coast*, Coast Lines Ltd.

262. *Lairdscastle* (1924) O.N. 146419

1,945 grt   1,031 nrt   84.30 × 11.46 × 4.66 m

B. Ardrossan Dockyard Company Ltd. Yard No. 329.

Single screw, quadruple steam engine, 336 nhp, 4 cylinder. By J. G. Kincaid & Company Ltd.

25.3.1924   Launched as *Lady Limerick* for the British & Irish Steam Packet Company Ltd.

1930   Transferred to Burns & Laird Lines Ltd and renamed *Lairdscastle*.

4.9.1940   On a voyage from Glasgow to Belfast she sank under tow, 20 miles south of Campbeltown between Cumbraes and Mull of Kintyre, following a collision with *Vernon City*.

263. *Lairdsburn* (1923) O.N. 144983

1,881 grt   84.42 × 11.58 × 4.57 m

B. Ardrossan Dockyard Ltd, Ardrossan. Yard No. 330.

Single screw, triple expansion, steam engine, 336 nhp, 4 cylinder. By J. G. Kincaid & Company Ltd, Greenock.

7.3.1923   Launched.

1923   Delivered to the British & Irish Steam Packet Company Ltd, Dublin as *Lady Louth*.

5.6.1930   Transferred to Burns & Laird Lines Ltd, Glasgow, renamed *Lairdsburn*.

21.10.1941 In collision with *King Edward* off Gourock.

1942   In collision with *Romsey* off Gourock, fifteen people lost their lives from *Romsey*.

22.5.1953   Arrived at Port Glasgow and broken up by Smith & Houston Ltd.

264. *Lairdshill* (1920) O.N. 143723

1,679 grt   83.51 × 11.58 × 5.18 m

B. Ardrossan Dockyard Ltd, Ardrossan. Yard No. 308.

Single screw, triple expansion, steam engine, 360 rhp, 553 nhp. By J. G. Kincaid & Company Ltd, Greenock.

11.8.1920   Launched as *Ardmore* for the City of Cork Steam Packet Company Ltd.

1921   Registered in Cork.

1923   Transferred to the British & Irish Steam Packet Company Ltd, renamed *Lady Longford*.

1930   Transferred to Burns & Laird Lines Ltd, Glasgow. Renamed *Lairdshill*.

1936   To the British & Irish Steam Packet Company Ltd, renamed *Lady Longford*.

To the British & Irish Steam Packet Company (1936) Ltd, Dublin.

1937   Transferred to Burns & Laird Lines Ltd, renamed *Lairdshill*.

9.7.1957   Arrived at Dublin and broken up by Hammond Lane Foundry.

265. *Lairdsben* (1893) O.N. 99959

726 grt   67.29 × 8.86 × 4.45 m

B. Harland & Wolff Ltd, Belfast. Yard No. 266.

Twin screw, triple expansion, steam engine, 219 hp, 225 nhp, 6 cylinder. By builder. 13½ knots.

4.2.1893	Launched as *Mystic* for the Belfast Steamship Company Ltd.
1910	City of Cork Steam Packet Company Ltd. Became *Carrickfergus*.
1917	Sold to the Sligo Steam Navigation Company Ltd.
1919	Sligo Steam Navigation Company Ltd acquired by Coast Lines Ltd.
1931	To Burns & Laird Lines Ltd. Renamed *Lairdsben*.
1936	Sold to Smith & Company for demolition.
1937	Broken up at Port Glasgow.

266. *Lairds Isle* (1911) O.N. 132546

1,675 grt   649 nrt   96.31 × 12.52 × 4.81 m

B. William Denny & Brothers Ltd, Dumbarton. Yard No. 937.

Three steam turbines, driving triple screws. By builder.

1.4.1911	Launched as *Riviera* for the South Eastern & Chatham Railway Company's Management Committee, London, for the Folkestone to Boulogne route.
8.1914	Requisitioned by the Admiralty as a seaplane carrier.
5.1919	Decommissioned and returned to owner.
1923	Southern Railway Company, London.
1932	J. B. Couper.
1933	Burns & Laird Lines Ltd. Renamed *Lairds Isle*.
1939	Requisitioned by the Admiralty and converted to an armed boarding vessel employed in the North Sea.
1940–44	Tender at the Torpedo School. Converted to a landing ship infantry for the Normandy landings (Juno Beach) and then employed as a troopship.
1946	Decommissioned and returned to owners.
6.8.1957	Final Ardrossan–Belfast sailing. Laid up at Albert Harbour, Greenock.
9.10.1957	Arrived at Troon and broken up by the West of Scotland Shipbreaking Company Ltd.

267. *Royal Ulsterman* (1936) O.N. 163225

3,290 grt   99.94 × 14.53 × 4.14 m

B. Harland & Wolff Ltd, Belfast. Yard No. 963.

Twin screw, 2SCSA, oil engine, 1,076 rhp, 1,077 nhp, 5,200 bhp. By builder. 17 knots.

10.3.1936	It was originally intended to name her *Laird of Ulster* but she was launched as *Royal Ulsterman* for the Burns & Laird Lines Ltd.
1940	Requisitioned by the Admiralty as HMS *Royal Ulsterman*.
1945	Returned to owner's service.
1968	Sold to Cammell Laird & Company Ltd, Birkenhead, renamed *Cammell Laird*.
1970	Sold to Med-Link Lines Shipping Company Ltd, Nicosia, Cyprus. Renamed *Sounion*.
3.3.1973	Sank at Beirut following an explosion.
10.9.1973	Arrived at Piraeus in tow and broken up at Perama, Greece.

268. *Royal Scotsman* (1936) O.N. 164080

3,288 grt   99.94 × 14.53 × 4.14 m

B. Harland & Wolff Ltd, Belfast. Yard No. 964.

Twin screw, oil engine, 1,076 rhp, 1,077 nhp, 5,200 bhp. By builder. 17 knots.

11.3.1936	Originally intended to be named *Laird of Scotia*, she was launched as *Royal Scotsman* for Burns & Laird Lines Ltd.
1940	Requisitioned by the Admiralty as HMS *Royal Scotsman*.
1945	Returned to owner's service.
28–29.9.1967	Final Glasgow–Belfast–Glasgow sailings.
1967	Sold to Hubbard Explorational Company Ltd, Freetown, Sierra Leone.
1969	Renamed *Apollo*.
1976	Sold to Richard Jaross with the intention of converting her to a floating restaurant at Brownsville, Texas.

10.1977   Auctioned and purchased by Zanzibar Incorporated, Panama. Renamed *Arctic Star.*

17.9.1980   Damaged at Brownsville.

1984   Broken up at Brownsville.

269. *Lairdswood* (2) (1936) O.N. 187106
789 grt   69.79 × 11.33 × 3.50 m
B. Harland & Wolff Ltd, Belfast. Yard No. 976.
Twin screw, oil engine, 2SCSA, 330 rhp, 332 nhp, 1,400 bhp. By builder.

21.7.1936   Launched as *Lairdswood* for Burns & Laird Lines Ltd, Glasgow.

1959   Transferred to the Belfast Steamship Company Ltd, renamed *Ulster Sportsman.*

1966   Sold to Transrodopi S. A., Burundi, and renamed *Transrodopi IV.*

1968   Sold to Navigation Maritime Bulgare, Bulgaria, and renamed *Alnilam.*

8.1970   Broken up at La Felguera.

270. *Lairdscrest* (1936) O.N. 164091
789 grt
B. Harland & Wolff Ltd, Belfast. Yard No. 977.
Twin screw, 2SCSA, oil engines, 1,400 bhp, 332 nhp, 2 × 5 cylinder. By builder. 13½ knots.

6.8.1936   Launched as *Lairdscrest* for the Ayr–Ardrossan–Belfast service with *Lairdswood.*

Above: *Royal Ulsterman* and *Irish Coast* (3) at Glasgow.

Below: *Royal Ulsterman.*

1968	Sold for £22,500 to Greek interests and renamed *San Marco*.
1975	Renamed *Kronos*.
1978	Broken up.

271. *Lairdsbank* (2) (1936) O.N. 164095
814 grt   69.79 × 11.27 × 3.65 m
B. Harland & Wolff Ltd, Belfast. Yard No. 978.
Twin screw, two 2SCSA, oil engine, 330 rhp, 332 nhp, 5 cylinder. By builder. 13½ knots.

3.9.1936   Launched as *Lairdsbank* for Burns & Laird Lines Ltd, Glasgow.

6.4.1937   On an voyage from Londonderry to Heysham with 200 cattle and 200 pigs, she ran aground at Barncorkrie, north of the Mull of Galloway, in fog. The Portpatrick lifeboat took off seven cattlemen and the tug *Flying Falcon* towed her into deeper water. She was then taken to Ayr, where the livestock were landed, and she was later towed to the Ailsa yard at Troon and repaired. The following day, *Lairdsmoor* was in collision with *Taranaki* in fog off Black Head, Wigtonshire, and sank.

1963   Transferred to the British & Irish Steam Packet Company Ltd, Dublin. Renamed *Glanmire*.

1969   Broken up at Dalmuir.

272. *Lairdsdale* (1930) O.N. 152236
891 grt   67.45 × 10.75 × 4.60 m
B. Dublin Dockyard Company, Vickers Shipyard, Dublin. Yard No. 146.
Twin screw, triple expansion, steam engine, 196 rhp, 249 nhp. By McKie & Baxter Ltd, Glasgow.

28.7.1930   Launched as *Sligo* for the Sligo Steam Navigation Company Ltd, Sligo.

1936   Burns & Laird Lines Ltd, Glasgow. Renamed *Lairdsdale*.

1954   Transferred to the Belfast Steamship Company Ltd, renamed *Ulster Drover*.

9.11.1959   Arrived at Troon and broken up.

273. *Lairds Loch* (1944) O.N. 169416
1,580 grt   80.16 × 12.55 × 3.81 m
B. Ardrossan Dockyard Ltd, Ardrossan. Yard No. 393.
Twin screw, twin M8 cylinder, 2SCSA, oil engine, 2,560 bhp. By British Auxiliaries Ltd.

9.3.1944   Launched as *Lairds Loch* for Burns & Laird Lines Ltd, Glasgow, for the Glasgow–Londonderry service.

1969   Sold to Sefinot Ltd, Eilat, Israel. Renamed *Hey Daroma*.

3.9.1970   On a voyage from Eilat to Sharm el-Sheikh she was damaged by a mine and beached in the Gulf of Aqaba, 7 miles from Sharm el-Sheikh. Abandoned and declared a constructive total loss.

274. *Kildare/Lairdsford* (2) (1919) O.N. 143218
1,389 grt   85.2 × 11.6 m
B. Caledon Shipbuilding & Engineering Company Ltd. Yard No. 267.
Single screw, triple expansion, steam engine, 277.5 rhp, 196 nhp. By builder. 12 knots.

1918   Ordered by the British Government as a war standard ship.

18.3.1919   Launched as *War Garry*.

21.5.1919   Delivered as *Lady Emerald* to the British & Irish Steam Packet Company Ltd, London.

1921   Registered in Dublin.

1936   Owners became the British & Irish Steam Packet Company (1936) Ltd, Dublin.

1938   Renamed *Carlow*. Owner renamed the British & Irish Steam Packet Company Ltd.

1939	To Coast Lines Ltd, Liverpool, renamed *Brittany Coast*.
1946	Transferred to Burns & Laird Lines Ltd, renamed *Kildare*.
1948	Registered under the British & Irish Steam Packet Company Ltd, Liverpool.
1952	To Burns & Laird Lines Ltd, renamed *Lairdsford*.
5.4.1960	Arrived at Troon and broken up.

275. *Lairdsoak* (2) (1937) O.N. 165124

606 grt   49.53 × 8.77 × 2.92 m

B. N. V. van Duivendijk, Netherlands. Yard No. 225.

Single screw, 6 cylinder, 2SCSA, oil engine. By Atlas-Diesel A/B, Stockholm.

1937	Delivered as *Ngarua* to William Wilson & Company Ltd, Southampton.
1939	Coast Lines Ltd (Merchants Line Ltd). Renamed *Silver Coast*.
3.1946	Burns & Laird Line Ltd. Renamed *Lairdsoak*.
4.1946	Registration changed from Southampton to Glasgow.
1960	Zillah Shipping Company Ltd. Renamed *Garthfield*.
1962	*Krios*.
1968	*Kyriakoula K.*
1974	*Dimitrios II.*
1992	Deleted from Lloyd's Register.

276. *Loch Aline* (1904) O.N. 119140

229 grt   41.69 × 6.43 × 5.02 m

B. Scott & Sons Ltd, Bowling. Yard No. 173.

Single screw, compound, steam engine, 2 cylinder. By builder.

17.5.1904	Launched as *Plover* for David MacBrayne Ltd. Engine and boiler from *Flowerdale* (488 grt/1878).
1934	Renamed *Loch Aline*.

1939–1945	Operated as an examination vessel based at Rothesay.
4.1946	Burns & Laird Lines Ltd,
1948	Thomas Heiton & Company Ltd, Dublin. Renamed *Saint Fintan*.
2.7.1951	Arrived at Llanelli and broken up by Edgar G. Rees Ltd. Her engines were seventy-three years old.

277. *Lairdsrock* (2) – See *Glen*, Tyne Tees Steam Shipping Company Ltd.

278. *Lairds Moor* (1948) O.N. 182101

990 grt   78.02 × 11.76 × 3.10 m

B. William Denny & Brothers Ltd, Dumbarton. Yard No. 1416.

Lairdsrock (2).

Single screw, oil engine, 2SCSA, 144 rhp, 1,200 bhp, 8 cylinder. By Sulzer Brothers Ltd, Winterthur, Switzerland, fitted by Rankin & Blackmore Ltd. 12 knots.

8.5.1948   Launched as *Lairds Moor* for Burns & Laird Lines Ltd, Glasgow.

22.3.1960   Transferred to the Belfast Steamship Company Ltd, Belfast. Renamed *Colebrooke* in Belfast, Mersey & Manchester Steamship Company colours.

1963   Lengthened by Grayson, Rollo & Clover Ltd at Birkenhead – 87.17 × 11.76 × 3.77 m.

1970   Sold to Losinjska Plovidba, Rijeka, Yugoslavia. Renamed *Mirna*.

3.11.1972   Grounded at Cephalonia island, Greece, and later refloated.

5.11.1972   Arrived Tunis.

1975   Owner restyled Losinjska Plovidba OOUR Brodarstvo.

1.12.1984   Scuttled off Nerezine, Mali Losinj, Yugoslavia.

279. *Lairds Ben* (1949) O.N. 182122

995 grt   77.60 × 11.79 × 3.10 m

B. William Denny & Brothers Ltd, Dumbarton. Yard No. 1434.

Single screw, oil engine, 2SCSA, 144 rhp, 1,200 bhp, 8 cylinder. By Sulzer Brothers Ltd, Winterthur, Switzerland, fitted by Rankin & Blackmore Ltd. 12 knots.

14.2.1949   Launched as *Lairds Ben* for Burns & Laird Lines Ltd, Glasgow.

25.3.1959   Transferred to the Belfast, Mersey & Manchester Steamship Company Ltd (John J. Mack & Sons Ltd, Belfast, as managers). Renamed *Brookmount*.

1960   Managed by the Belfast Steamship Company Ltd. Retained previous colours.

1970   Sold to Cia Naviera Viva S. A., London. Renamed *Ikaria*.

1971   Sold to Rosade Lines S. A. L., Beirut, Lebanon. Renamed *Pierre Rodolphe*.

1973   Purchased by Khodr Adel El-Hoss, Beirut, Lebanon. Renamed *Ziad*.

1979   Renamed *Sweet Waves*.

18/19.11.1983 When laid up at Tripoli, Lebanon, she was damaged and sank.

1984   Broken up where she lay.

280. *Lairdsfern* (1937) O.N. 164312

484 gr   9x 7.5 × 3 m

B. Scheeps de Noord Alblasserdam, Netherlands. Yard No. 562.

Single screw, oil engine, 94 nhp. By Klöckner Humboldt Deutz A. G., Köln, Germany.

1937   Delivered as *Denbigh Coast*.

18.12.1951   Transferred to Burns & Laird Lines, renamed *Lairdsfern*.

12.1958   Reverted to *Denbigh Coast*.

18.7.1960   On a voyage from Manchester to Belfast she sank in collision with *Irish Maple* in the Crosby Channel, Liverpool.

281. *Lairdscastle* (2) (1922) O.N. 143050

1,434 grt   82.60 × 11.61 × 4.93 m

B. Caledon Shipbuilding & Engineering Company Ltd, Dundee. Yard No. 265.

Single screw, triple expansion, steam engine, 278 rhp, 196 nhp. By builder. 12 knots.

17.1.1919   Launched as *War Leven* and completed for the shipping controller (J. Moss & Company Ltd, London) as *Limoges*.

Sold to Moss Steamship Company Ltd, Liverpool.

1922   Coast Lines Ltd, Liverpool. Renamed *Western Coast*.

1941   To Burns & Laird Lines Ltd.

1946	Renamed *Meath*.
1948	Transferred to the British & Irish Steam Packet Company Ltd.
1952	To Burns & Laird Lines Ltd. Renamed *Lairdscastle*.
5.6.1958	Arrived at Hendrik-Ido-Ambacht and broken up.

282. *Lairdscraig* (1936) O.N. 164098

1,599 grt   697 nrt   83.21 × 11.58 × 5.18 m

B. Alexander Stephen & Sons Ltd, Linthouse, Glasgow. Yard No. 550.

Single screw, triple expansion, steam, 210 rhp, 196 nhp, 3 cylinder by builder. 12 knots.

3.9.1936	Launched as *Rathlin* for the Clyde Shipping Company Ltd, Glasgow.
1941	Requisitioned by the Admiralty as a convoy rescue ship.
1945	Returned to commercial service with owners.
15.7.1953	Sold to Burns & Laird Lines Ltd, Glasgow. Renamed *Lairdscraig*.
6.1956	Transferred to the British & Irish Steam Packet Company Ltd, renamed *Glengariff*.
30.12.1963	Arrived at Passage West and broken up by Haulbowline Industries Ltd.

283. *Lairdsglen* (2) (1954) O.N. 185014

1,496 grt   1,875 dwt   472 nrt   90.79 × 13.13 × 5.39 m

B. Ardrossan Dockyard Company Ltd. Yard No. 415.

Twin screw, 2,860 bhp, 2SCSA, Sulzer diesel engines, 2 × 6 cylinder. By George Clark (1938) Ltd, Sunderland. 528 head of cattle or 3,264 cubic metres (115,300 cubic feet). 14 knots.

9.3.1954	Launched.
10.1954	Delivered as *Lairdsglen* for Burns & Laird Lines Ltd, Glasgow.
1969	Converted to a livestock carrier by Manchester Drydock Company Ltd.
26.2.1971	Burns & Laird Lines acquired by the P&O Steam Navigation Company Ltd.
1.10.1971	Managed by P&O Short Sea Shipping Ltd.
28.9.1973	Registered under the Belfast Steamship Company Ltd, Belfast.
29.3.1974	Sold to Frans Buitelaar Ltd, Boston, Lincolnshire, renamed *Devon Express*.
1974	Sold to Livestock Carriers Incorporated, Panama.
1981	Purchased by Kagitingan Shipping Corporation, Panama.
1982	Registered in the Philippines.

Managed by Vroon B. V.

Returned to Livestock Carriers Incorporated (Vroon B. V. as managers).

Devon Express. (Courtesy of Malcolm Cranfield)

1983   Transferred to Kagitingan Shipping Corporation, Panama (Vroon B. V. as managers).

Sold to Jose Navarro Frances, Spain, for demolition.

9.12.1983   Arrived at Cartagena.

2.1.1984   Demolition commenced.

284. *Lairdsburn* (2) – See *Beal/Sylvian Coast*, Tyne Tees Steam Shipping Company Ltd.

285. *Pointer* – See *Birchfield*, Zillah Shipping Company Ltd.

286. *Spaniel* – See *Brentfield*, Zillah Shipping Company Ltd.

Lairdsburn (2) berthed in the West Float at Birkenhead.

287. *Kelvin* – See *Ulster Premier*, Belfast Steamship Company Ltd.

288. *Talisker* – See *Ulster Pioneer*, Belfast Steamship Company Ltd.

289. *Tay* – See *Western Coast*, Coast Line.

290. *Lairdsfox* – See *Foxfield*, Zillah Shipping Company Ltd.

291. *Lairdsfield* – See *Greenfield*, Zillah Shipping Company Ltd.

292. *Lion* (1967) O.N. 307690

3,333 grt   932 dwt   1,024 nrt   111.03 × 17.73 × 11.21 m

B. Cammell Laird & Company Ltd, Birkenhead. Yard No. 1326.

Twin controllable pitch propellers, 11,000 bhp, 2 × 12 cylinder, 4SCSA, Vee diesel engines. By Crossley Brothers Ltd, Manchester.

Passengers: 1,200. 160 vehicles.

20.9.1966   Keel laid.

8.8.1967   Launched by Mrs N. Wright, wife of Burns & Laird General Manager.

21.12.1967   Delivered as *Lion* for Burns & Laird Lines Ltd, Glasgow.

3.1.1968   Maiden voyage Ardrossan–Belfast. Force 9 gales delayed the sailing for 90 minutes.

26.2.1971   Coast Lines Ltd were acquired by the P&O Steam Navigation Company Ltd.

1.10.1971   Managed by P&O Short Sea Shipping Ltd.

28.9.1973   Registered under the Belfast Steamship Company Ltd, Belfast.

31.3.1975   Managed by P&O Ferries who discussed operating her on the Aberdeen–Lerwick service.

20.2.1976   Registered under Southern Ferries Ltd.

22.2.1976   Withdrawn from the Ardrossan–Belfast service. Sent to Chantiers de l'Atlantique, Le Havre, and rebuilt for the Normandy Ferries service from Dover to Boulogne. A bow visor was fitted and she was remeasured – 3,987 grt, 1,395 nrt, 1,412 dead weight.

8.4.1976   First sailing on Normandy Ferries' Dover–Boulogne service.

1978   Painted in Normandy Ferries livery.

31.8.1978   Registered under P&O Ferries Ltd.

1984   Registered under P&O Normandy Ferries Ltd.

2.11.1984   Collided with the Dover breakwater.

4.1.1985   Sold to European Ferries Plc (Townsend Thoresen as managers).

1985   Sold to Thenamaris Shipping Incorporated, Limassol, renamed *Baroness M.*

1987   Owned by *Baroness M.* Ferries Services Ltd, Bahamas.

1987   Chartered to British Channel Islands Ferries Ltd, renamed *Portelet.*

1988   On completion of the charter she reverted to *Baroness M.* Operated on the Larnaca–Jounieh service.

1990   Operated on Piraeus–Larnaca–Israel service.

24.2.1990   On a journey from Larnaca to Greece she came under fire from a gunboat.

1991   Operated on the Brindisi–Korfu–Igoumenitsa–Patras service.

1997   Sold to Equestor Shipping Company N. V., Kingston, St Vincent and Grenadines.

1997   Operated in Indonesia.

Above: *Kelvin.*

Below: *Lion* leaving Ardrossan

Baroness M at Weymouth.

2002   Renamed *Adinda Lestari 101*.
3.2004   Sold for demolition.
12.4.2004   Arrived at Chittagong Roads, Bangladesh, and broken up.

British & Irish Steam Packet Company Ltd.

293. *Lady Cloe* (1916) O.N. 139129
1,581 grt   1,876 dwt   79.24 × 11.58 × 4.57 m
B. Sir Raylton Dixon & Company Ltd, Middlesbrough. Yard No. 592.

Single screw, triple expansion, steam engine, 220 rhp, 162 nhp by Richardsons, Westgarth & Company Ltd, Middlesbrough. 11 knots. Cargo capacity 94,960 cubic feet. 10 knots.
Passengers: 70.
17.4.1916   Launched.
1916   Delivered to the British & Irish Steam Packet Company Ltd and operated on Dublin–Cork–Falmouth–Plymouth–Torquay–Southampton–London route weekly in each direction.
1936   Owned by the British & Irish Steam Packet Company (1936) Ltd (Dublin).
1937   Registered at Dublin.
1938   Transferred to Coast Lines Ltd, Liverpool, renamed *Normandy Coast*.
11.1.1945   On a voyage from London to Liverpool she was torpedoed and sunk by the German submarine *U-1055* off Port Lynas, Anglesey.

294. *Lady Wimborne* (1915) O.N. 139074
1,542 grt   1,876 dwt   79.24 × 11.58 × 4.57 m
B. Clyde Shipbuilding & Engineering Company Ltd, Port Glasgow. Yard No. 314.
Single screw, triple expansion, steam engine, 134 rhp, 216 nhp, 3 cylinder. By builder. 11 knots.
27.5.1915   Launched.
1915   Delivered to the British & Irish Steam Packet Company Ltd.
1936   Owned by the British & Irish Steam Packet Company (1936) Ltd (Dublin).
1938   Renamed *Galway*.
1938   Owners renamed British & Irish Steam Packet Company Ltd.
1939   Transferred to Coast Lines Ltd, Liverpool, renamed *Galway Coast*.

1945   Sold to Virtu Steamship Company Ltd (Anthony & Bainbridge Ltd), Liverpool.

1946   Renamed *Virtu*.

1947   Registered at Malta.

27.2.1948   On a voyage from Port Said to Tobruk she grounded off Raz Azzaz lighthouse, between Bardia and Tobruk, Libya.

19.5.1948   Refloated, towed to Tobruk and laid up.

11.1950   Broken up at Tobruk.

295. *Lady Gwendolen* (1911) O.N. 132505

2,163 grt   1,336 nrt   91.44 × 12.19 × 5.48 m

B. Clyde Shipbuilding & Engineering Company Ltd. Yard No. 294.

Single screw, triple expansion, steam engine, 362 rhp, 3 cylinder. By builder.

13.5.1911   Launched.

1911   Delivered to the British & Irish Steam Packet Company Ltd (Dublin).

1917–1918   Renamed *Lyudmila* for use of the Governor of Arkhangelsk, Russia.

1918   Returned to the British & Irish Steam Packet Company Ltd. Sold to the Dundee, Perth & London Shipping Company Ltd, Dundee.

1919   Purchased by the New York, Newfoundland & Halifax Steam Ship Company Ltd (C. T. Bowring & Company Ltd), Liverpool. Renamed *Rosalind*.

1921   Registered in St John's, Newfoundland.

1923   Registered in Liverpool.

1929   Sold to the Bermuda & West Indies Steamship Company Ltd, Hamilton, Bermuda.

1936   Sold to Zetska Plovidba A. D., Koster, Yugoslavia, renamed *Lovcen*.

1940   Owned by Cia Centro Americana de Navegacion Ltda (Zetska Plovidba A. D.), Panama.

1941   Sold to the United States Government, renamed *Columbia*.

1942   Renamed *Brigadier General Harry E. Rethers*.

1946   Sold to Chan Kin Cheong, Canton, China, renamed *Wah Chung*.

1950   Sold to the Grande Shipping Corporation S. A., Panama, renamed *Teresa*.

1952   Broken up in China.

296. *Lady Emerald/Carlow* (1918) O.N. 143218

1,389 grt   85.2 × 11.6 m

B. Celedon Shipbuilding & Engineering Company Ltd. Yard No. 267.

Single screw, triple expansion, steam engine, 277.5 rhp, 196 nhp. By builder. 12 knots.

1918   Ordered by the British Government as a war standard ship.

18.3.1919   Launched as *War Garry*.

21.5.1919   Delivered as *Lady Emerald* to the British & Irish Steam Packet Company Ltd, London.

1921   Registered in Dublin.

1936   Owners became the British & Irish Steam Packet Company (1936) Ltd, Dublin.

1938   Renamed *Carlow*.

Owner renamed the British & Irish Steam Packet Company Ltd.

1939   To Coast Lines Ltd, Liverpool, renamed *Brittany Coast*.

1946   Transferred to Burns & Laird Lines Ltd, renamed *Kildare*.

1948   Registered under the British & Irish Steam Packet Company Ltd, Liverpool.

1952   To Burns & Laird Lines Ltd, renamed *Lairdsford*.

5.4.1960   Arrived at Troon and broken up.

297. *Lady Patricia/Kerry* (1918) O.N. 143158

1,391 grt   82.5 × 11.6 m

B. Caledon Shipbuilding & Engineering Company Ltd. Yard No. 266.

Single screw, triple expansion, steam engine, 280 rhp, 196 nhp. By builder. 12 knots.

1918   Ordered by the British Government as a war standard ship.

18.2.1919   Launched as *War Spey*, delivered as *Lady Patricia* to the British & Irish Steam Packet Company Ltd, London.

1921   Registered in Dublin.

1936   Owned by the British & Irish Steam Packet Company (1936) Ltd (Dublin).

1938   Renamed *Kerry*.

Owner became the British & Irish Steam Packet Company Ltd.

1939   To Coast Lines Ltd, Liverpool, renamed *Kerry Coast*.

1941   To Burns & Laird Lines Ltd, Liverpool.

11.3.1944   Sunk following a collision with *Mosdale* in the Mersey.

20.5.1945   Raised and salvaged.

1945   Sold to Henry P. Lenaghan & Sons Ltd, Belfast, renamed *Bangor Bay*.

1946   Purchased by the Burns & Laird Lines Ltd, Liverpool, renamed *Kerry*.

1947   Transferred to the British & Irish Steam Navigation Company Ltd.

6.1959   Broken up at Passage West.

298. *Lady Louth/Lady Galway/Galway* (1894) O.N. 99760

1,249 grt   79.55 × 10.36 × 4.87 m

B. Blackwood & Gordon Ltd, Port Glasgow. Yard No. 229.

Single screw, triple expansion, steam engine, 400 rhp, 330 nhp. By builder. Two masts. 14 knots.

Passengers: 70 First Class. 500 cattle.

24.5.1894   Launched as *Louth*.

Delivered to the City of Dublin Steam Packet Company, Dublin.

1919   Sold to London Maritime Investment Company Ltd, Dublin.

To the British & Irish Steam Packet Company Ltd, Dublin.

1920   Renamed *Lady Louth*.

To the City of Cork Steam Packet Company Ltd, Liverpool. Renamed *Bandon*.

1921   Registered in Cork.

1931   To the British & Irish Steam Packet Company Ltd, Dublin. Renamed *Lady Galway*.

1936   Owners became the British & Irish Steam Packet Company (1936) Ltd, Dublin.

1938   Renamed *Galway*.

Broken up at Port Glasgow by Smith & Houston Ltd.

299. *Lady Wicklow/Wicklow* (1895) O.N. 104963

1,032 grt   79.24 × 10.36 × 4.87 m

B. Blackwood & Gordon Ltd, Port Glasgow. Yard No. 230.

Single screw, triple expansion, steam engine, 258 rhp, 330 nhp. By builder. 14 knots.

28.3.1895   Launched as *Wicklow* for the City of Dublin Steam Packet Company, Dublin.

1918   Requisitioned by the Shipping Controller.

1919   Returned to the City of Dublin Steam Packet Company.

Sold to the London Maritime Investment Company Ltd, Dublin.

Owned by the British & Irish Steam Packet Company Ltd, Dublin.

1920   Renamed *Lady Wicklow*.

1936   Owner became the British & Irish Steam Packet Company (1936) Ltd, Dublin.

1938   Renamed *Wicklow*.

Owner restyled the British & Irish Steam Packet Company Ltd.

1947   Transferred to the Belfast, Mersey & Manchester Steamship Company Ltd, Belfast.

22.8.1948   Arrived at Llanelly and broken up by Rees Shipbreaking Company Ltd.

300. *Lady Kerry* (1897) O.N. 104976

1,199 grt   79.24 × 10.36 × 4.87 m

B. Blackwood & Gordon Ltd, Port Glasgow. Yard No. 237.

Single screw, triple expansion, steam engine, 398.7 rhp, 330 nhp. By builder. 15 knots.

6.2.1897   Launched as *Kerry* for the City of Dublin Steam Packet Company, Dublin.

1919   Sold to London Maritime Investment Company Ltd, Dublin. To the British & Irish Steam Packet Company Ltd, Dublin.

1920   Renamed *Lady Kerry*.

1924   Broken up at Birkenhead.

301. *Lady Carlow* (1896) O.N. 104968

1,250 grt   493 nrt   79.24 × 10.36 × 4.87 m

B. Blackwood & Gordon Ltd, Port Glasgow. Yard No. 232.

Single screw, triple expansion, steam engine, 398.7 rhp, 330 nhp. By builder. 15 knots.

3.3.1896   Launched as *Carlow* for the City of Dublin Steam Packet Company, Dublin.

1919   Sold to London Maritime Investment Company Ltd, Dublin. Owned by the British & Irish Steam Packet Company Ltd, Dublin.

1920   Renamed *Lady Carlow*.

23.3.1925   Arrived at Troon and broken up by J. J. King Ltd.

302. *Belfast* (1884) O.N. 88994

457 grt

B. Irvine & Company Ltd, West Hartlepool. Yard No. 52.

Iron, single screw, compound steam, 110 hp, 134 nhp. By Blair & Company Ltd, Stockton-on-Tees.

1884   Ordered by the Dublin & Liverpool Screw Steam Packet Company Ltd.

4.10.1884   Launched as *Belfast* and delivered to the City of Dublin Steam Packet Company Ltd, Dublin.

1919   Sold to London Maritime Investment Company Ltd, Dublin. Owned by the British & Irish Steam Packet Company Ltd, Dublin.

1922   Sold to Latvijas Kugneezibas Sabeedriba Austra, Riga, Latvia. Renamed *Austra*.

1924   Purchased by Schifffahrts Ges. 'Austra', Riga, Latvia.

1927   Broken up.

303. *Lady Killiney* (1917) O.N. 140454

1,145 grt   77.60 × 11.00 m

B. Caledon Shipbuilding & Engineering Company Ltd, Dundee. Yard No. 245.

Single screw, triple expansion, steam engine, 206.4 rhp, 347 nhp. By builder. 14 knots.

2.10.1917   Launched as *Killiney*.

1918   Delivered to Tedcastle, McCormick & Company Ltd, Dublin.

1919   Tedcastle, McCormick & Company Ltd acquired by the British & Irish Steam Packet Company Ltd.

1920   Renamed *Lady Killiney*.

1923   To the City of Cork Steam Packet Company Ltd, Cork.

1924   Renamed *Ardmore*.

1936   To the British & Irish Steam Packet Company (1936) Ltd, Cork.

1938   Owners restyled the British & Irish Steam Packet Company Ltd.

11.11.1940   On a voyage from Cork to Fishguard with livestock she was reported missing off Ballycotton Lighthouse. All on board were lost. It was later confirmed that she was mined and sank.

1998   Wreck located off Great Saltee Island, Co. Wexford.

304. *Eblana* (1892) O.N. 99746
808 grt   64.92 × 9.75 × 4.57 m
B. Ardrossan Dockyard Company, Ardrossan. Yard No. 175.
Single screw, compound steam engine, 185 hp, 204 nhp. By Hutson & Corbett Ltd, Glasgow. 13 knots.

22.10.1892   Launched for Robert Tedcastle & Company, Dublin.

1897   Owned by Tedcastle, McCormick & Company Ltd, Dublin.

1919   Tedcastle, McCormick & Company Ltd acquired by the British & Irish Steam Packet Company Ltd.

1923   Broken up.

305. *Blackrock* (1892) O.N. 99743
789 grt
B. Naval Construction & Armaments Company Ltd, Barrow. Yard No. 216.
Single screw, triple expansion, steam engine, 360 hp, 297 nhp. By builder. 14 knots.

10.10.1892   Launched as *Blackrock* for F. McCormick & Company, Dublin

1895   Owned by J. McCormick & Company Ltd, Dublin.

1897   Owned by Tedcastle, McCormick & Company Ltd, Dublin.

1919   Tedcastle, McCormick & Company Ltd, Dublin acquired by the British & Irish Steam Packet Company Ltd.

1923   Broken up at Ardrossan.

306. *Dublin* (1904) O.N. 117516
711 grt
B. John Fullerton & Company Ltd, Paisley. Yard No. 175.
Single screw, triple expansion, steam engine, 155 rhp, 156 nhp. By Ross & Duncan Ltd, Govan, Glasgow. 11 knots.

17.2.1904   Launched as *Dublin* for Tedcastle, McCormick & Company Ltd, Dublin.

1919   Tedcastle, McCormick & Company Ltd, Dublin, acquired by the British & Irish Steam Packet Company Ltd.
Owned by Coast Lines Ltd.

1920   Transferred to the British & Irish Steam Packet Company Ltd.

1922   Transferred to Coast Lines Ltd, renamed *Cardigan Coast*.

1928   Sold to R. & D. A. Duncan Ltd, Belfast, renamed *Dublin*.

1940   Purchased by S. Instone & Company Ltd, London. Renamed *Themston*.

1950   Sold to Tyson, Edgar Shipping Ltd, London.

1952   Broken up at Rosyth.

307. *Cumbria* (1896) O.N. 104971
694 grt   179 nrt   60.35 × 9.14 × 4.26 m
B. Ailsa Shipbuilding Company, Troon. Yard No. 58.
Single screw, triple expansion, steam engine, 175 rhp, 174 nhp by Dunsmuir & Jackson Ltd, Glasgow. 12 knots.

12.8.1896   Launched as *Cumbria* for Robert Tedcastle & Company, Dublin.

1897   Owned by Tedcastle, McCormick & Company Ltd, Dublin.

1919   Tedcastle, McCormick & Company Ltd, Dublin, acquired by the British & Irish Steam Packet Company Ltd.

1920   Transferred to the City of Cork Steam Packet Company Ltd, Liverpool.

1921   Registered in Cork.

25.2.1925   Sold for breaking up at Granton by the Granton Shipbreaking Company Ltd.

308. *Lady Kildare* (1920) O.N. 144200
1,217 grt   74.67 × 10.36 × 4.87 m
B. William Beardmore & Company Ltd, Dalmuir. Yard No. 613.
Single screw, triple expansion, steam engine, 265 nhp. By builder.

26.1.1920   Launched as *Setter* (Originally planned to name her *Whippet*) for G. & J. Burns Ltd, Glasgow. G. & J. Burns Ltd were acquired by Coast Lines Ltd.

1920   To the British & Irish Steam Packet Company Ltd, renamed *Lady Kildare*.

1931   Transferred to the Belfast Steamship Company Ltd, Belfast.

1932   Renamed *Ulster Castle*.

8.6.1950   Arrived at Preston and broken up.

309. *Lady Meath* (1906) O.N. 124134
862 grt   68.58 × 10.05 × 4.87 m
B. Scott's Shipbuilding & Engineering Company Ltd, Greenock. Yard No. 409.
Single screw, triple expansion, steam engine, 247 rhp. By builder. 13 knots.

19.7.1906   Launched as *Lurcher* for G. & J. Burns Ltd, Glasgow.

1920   G. & J. Burns Ltd were acquired by Coast Lines Ltd.
To the British & Irish Steam Packet Company Ltd, Dublin. Renamed *Lady Meath*.

1925   Transferred to the City of Cork Steam Packet Company Ltd, Cork. Renamed *Inniscarra*.

1935   Sold to Wexford Steamships Company Ltd, Wexford. Renamed *Menapia*.

7.1939   Broken up by Smith & Houston Ltd, Port Glasgow.

310. *Lady Martin* (1913) O.N. 133548
1,189 grt   76.50 × 10.97 m
B. Raylton Dixon & Company Ltd, Middlesbrough. Yard No. 585.
Single screw, triple expansion, steam engine, 178 rhp, 138 nhp. By Richardsons, Westgarth & Company Ltd, Middlesbrough. 10½ knots.

13.12.1913 Launched as *Northern Coast* for Powell, Bacon & Hough Lines Ltd, Liverpool.

1917   Coast Lines Ltd.

1920   Transferred to the British & Irish Steam Packet Company Ltd, renamed *Lady Martin*.

1921   Registered in Dublin.

1936   Company restyled British & Irish Steam Packet Company (1936) Ltd, Dublin.

1938   Sold to A/S Eastis Laevandus, Tallinn, Estonia. Renamed *Pearu*.

6.1940   Seized by the USSR in the Baltic, renamed *Vodnik*.

14.8.1941   On a voyage from Kronstadt to Tallin she was lost, east of Prangh Island.

311. *Lady Tennant/Kilkenny* (1903) O.N. 119083
452 grt   50.29 × 7.92 × 3.04 m
B. Napier & Miller Ltd, Glasgow. Yard No. 132.
Single screw, triple expansion, steam engine, 93 rhp. By D. Rowan & Company Ltd, Glasgow. 10¾ knots.

7.12.1903   Launched as *Lady Tennant* for Nobel's Explosives Company Ltd, Glasgow.

1904   Completed.

1914   Sold to the Stornoway Shipping Company Ltd, Stornoway.

1916   Sold to M. Langlands & Sons (Stornoway) Ltd.

1918   M. Langlands & Sons (Stornoway) Ltd acquired by Coast Lines Ltd.

1920	Transferred to the British & Irish Steam Packet Company Ltd, Liverpool.
1921	Registered in Dublin.
1923	To Coast Lines Ltd, renamed *Elgin Coast*.
1930	Renamed *Kilkenny*.
1936	Sold to Captain H. W. B. Ohlmeyer, Hamburg, Germany. Renamed *Lisa*.
1950	New oil engine, 500 bhp, fitted by Klöckner-Humboldt Deutz A. G., Köln, Germany.
1962	Sold to Theodoros O. Vavatsioulas and Helene T. Vavatsioulas, Salonica, Greece. Renamed *Orestis*.
1969	Sold to A. Pastrikos and G. and D. Papageorgiou, Thessaloniki, Greece. Renamed *Mario*.
1974	Broken up in Greece.

312. *Lady Valentia* (1920) O.N. 144976

1,211 grt   73.15 × 10.97 × 4.57 m
B. A. & J. Inglis Ltd, Glasgow. Yard No. 600.
Single screw, triple expansion, steam engine, 203 nhp. By builder. 11¼ knots.

29.11.1920	Launched as *Northern Coast* (Originally intended to be *Ayrshire Coast*).
1921	Delivered to the British & Irish Steam Packet Company Ltd as *Lady Vatentia*.
1922	Transferred to Coast Lines Ltd, renamed *Northern Coast*.
1954	Broken up at Passage West by Haulbowline Industries Ltd.

313. *Lady Longford* (1920) O.N. 143723

1,679 grt   83.51 × 11.58 × 5.18 m
B. Ardrossan Dockyard Ltd, Ardrossan. Yard No. 308.
Single screw, triple expansion, steam engine, 360 rhp, 553 nhp. By J. G. Kincaid & Company Ltd, Greenock.

11.8.1920	Launched as *Ardmore* for the City of Cork Steam Packet Company Ltd.
1921	Registered in Cork.
1923	Transferred to the British & Irish Steam Packet Company Ltd, renamed *Lady Longford*.
1930	Transferred to Burns & Laird Lines Ltd, Glasgow. Renamed *Lairdshill*.
1936	To the British & Irish Steam Packet Company Ltd, renamed *Lady Longford*.

To the British & Irish Steam Packet Company (1936) Ltd, Dublin.

1937	Transferred to Burns & Laird Lines Ltd, renamed *Lairdshill*.
9.7.1957	Arrived at Dublin and broken up by Hammond Lane Foundry.

314. *Lady Brussels* (1902) O.N. 109884

1,090 grt
B. Gourlay Brothers & Company Ltd, Dundee. Yard No. 202.
Twin screw, triple expansion, steam engine, 350 rhp, 350 nhp. By builder. 15 knots.

26.3.1902	Launched as *Brussels* for the Great Eastern Railway Company, Harwich.
28.3.1915	Attempted to ram a German submarine.
22.6.1916	Captured by the German navy and Captain Fryatt executed. Renamed *Brugge* and operated as a submarine depot ship at Zeebrugge.
5.10.1918	Scuttled in an attempt to block the entrance to Zeebrugge harbour.
1918	Requisitioned by the Belgium Government.
4–6.8.1919	Raised.
1920	Responsibility of the British Government, renamed *Brussels*.

1921   Purchased by the Dublin & Lancashire Shipping Company Ltd, Dublin (Joseph Gale, Preston), converted to a cattle carrier.

1922   Dublin & Lancashire Shipping Company Ltd acquired by the British & Irish Steam Packet Company Ltd.

1923   Renamed *Lady Brussels*.

1929   Broken up at Port Glasgow.

315. *Lady Louth* (2) (1923) O.N. 144983
1,881 grt   84.42 × 11.58 × 4.57 m
B. Ardrossan Dockyard Ltd, Ardrossan. Yard No. 330.
Single screw, triple expansion, steam engine, 336 nhp. By J. G. Kincaid & Company Ltd, Greenock.

7.3.1923   Launched.

1923   Delivered to the British & Irish Steam Packet Company Ltd, Dublin, as *Lady Louth*.

1930   Transferred to Burns & Laird Lines Ltd, Glasgow, renamed *Lairdsburn*.

21.10.1941   In collision with *King Edward* off Gourock.

1942   In collision with *Romsey* off Gourock; fifteen of the people on board the *Romsey* lost their lives.

22.5.1953   Arrived at Port Glasgow and broken up by Smith & Houston Ltd.

316. *Lady Limerick* (1924) O.N. 146419
1,945 gr   84.42 × 11.58 × 4.57 m
B. Ardrossan Dockyard Ltd, Ardrossan. Yard No. 329.
Single screw, triple expansion, steam engine, 178 rpm, 336 nhp. By J. G. Kincaid & Company Ltd, Greenock. 14 knots.

25.3.1924   Launched as *Lady Limerick* for the British & Irish Steam Packet Company Ltd, Dublin.

1930   Transferred to the Burns & Laird Lines Ltd, Glasgow, renamed *Lairdscastle*.

4.9.1940   On a voyage from Glasgow to Belfast she was in collision with *Vernon City*. An attempt was made to tow her to port but she sank.

317. *Lady Iveagh* (1892) O.N. 98274
598 grt   57.91 × 8.83 × 4.26 m
B. A. & J. Inglis Ltd, Glasgow. Yard No. 224.
Single screw, triple expansion, steam engine, 148 nhp. By builder.

7.7.1892   Launched as *Iveagh* for the Dundalk & Newry Steam Packet Company Ltd, Newry.

1926   Dundalk & Newry Steam Packet Company Ltd acquired by the British & Irish Steam Packet Company Ltd.

1930   Broken up at Port Glasgow.

318. *Lady Meath* (2)/*Meath* (1929) O.N. 146429
1,598 grt   97.9 × 12.2 × 4.87 m
B. Ardrossan Dockyard Company Ltd. Yard No. 341.
Twin screw, triple expansion, steam engine, 195 rhp, 222 nhp. By J. G. Kincaid & Company Ltd, Greenock.

2.2.1929   Launched.

1929   Delivered as *Lady Meath*.

1936   British & Irish Steam Packet Company (1936) Ltd, Dublin.

1938   Renamed *Meath*.

16.8.1940   On a voyage from Dublin to Birkenhead with cattle and sheep she was sunk by a mine off Beamer Rock Lighthouse, Holyhead.

319. *Lady Kerry* (2) O.N. 104466
877 grt   71.93 × 9.44 × 4.57 m
B. Harland &Wolff Ltd, Belfast. Yard No. 306.

Twin screw, triple expansion, steam engine, 263 rhp. By builder. 13 knots.

9.6.1896	Launched as *Comic* for the Belfast Steamship Company Ltd, Belfast.
1921	Transferred to Laird Line Ltd, Glasgow, renamed *Cairnsmore*.
1922	To Burns & Laird Lines Ltd, Glasgow.
1929	Transferred to the British & Irish Steam Packet Company Ltd, Dublin. Renamed *Lady Kerry*.
1934	Broken up at Preston.

320. *Lady Carlow* (2) O.N. 108619

883 grt   71.93 × 9.44 × 4.87 m

B. Barclay, Curle & Company Ltd, Glasgow. Yard No. 410.

Twin screw, triple expansion, steam engine, 263 rhp. By builder. 14 knots.

26.10.1897	Launched as *Logic* for Thomas Gallaher (Belfast) Ltd and chartered to the Belfast Steamship Company Ltd.
1904	Sold to the Belfast Steamship Company Ltd, Belfast.
1921	Transferred to Laird Line Ltd, Glasgow, renamed *Culzean*.
1922	Burns & Laird Lines Ltd, Glasgow.
1929	Transferred to the British & Irish Steam Packet Company Ltd, renamed *Lady Carlow*.
1936	Sold to Smith & Company Ltd to be broken up.
20.2.1937	Resold to the West of Scotland Shipbreaking Company Ltd and arrived at Troon to be broken up.

321. *Lady Munster/Lough* (1906) O.N. 120714

1,915 grt   71.93 × 9.44 × 4.57 m

B. Harland & Wolff Ltd, Belfast. Yard No. 379.

Twin screw, quadruple expansion, steam engine, 824 rhp. By builder. 18 knots.

27.2.1906	Launched as *Graphic* for the Belfast Steamship Company Ltd, Belfast.
1923	In collision with the *Balsam* in the Victoria Channel, Belfast.
3.6.1923	Salvaged and later returned to service. New engines, 660 nhp.
1929	Transferred to the British & Irish Steam Packet Company Ltd, renamed *Lady Munster*.
1936	British & Irish Steam Packet Company (1936) Ltd.
1938	Renamed *Louth*.
1939	Registered in Liverpool.
1948	Transferred to the Belfast Steamship Company Ltd, renamed *Ulster Duke*.
1951	Sold to be broken up in Italy.
15.5.1951	Sank under tow to La Spezia, Italy.

322. *Lady Leinster/Lady Connaught* (2) (1911) O.N. 132019

2,254 grt   99.06 × 12.49 × 4.87 m

B. Harland & Wolff Ltd, Belfast. Yard No. 424.

Twin screw, triple expansion, steam engine, 840 rhp by builder. 18 knots.

7.9.1911	Launched as *Patriotic* for the Belfast Steamship Company Ltd, Belfast.
1930	Transferred to the British & Irish Steam Packet Company Ltd, Dublin, renamed *Lady Leinster*.
1936	British & Irish Steam Packet Company (1936) Ltd.
1938	Renamed *Lady Connaught*.
1940	Registered in Liverpool.
26.12.1940	Sustained damage by mines and laid up.
1941	Abandoned by insurance underwriters.
1942	Converted to a livestock carrier by the Dublin Dockyard Company Ltd.

1944   Converted to a hospital ship.

1946   Returned to builders at Belfast and converted to a cruise vessel.

1947   Owned by Coast Lines Ltd, Liverpool, renamed *Lady Killarney.*

1956   Broken up at Port Glasgow.

323. *Lady Connaught/Longford* (1906) O.N. 120712

1,869 grt   97.53 × 12.49 × 5.18 m

B. Harland & Wolff Ltd, Belfast. Yard No. 378.

Twin screw, quadruple expansion, steam engine, 824 rhp. By builder. 18 knots.

13.1.1906   Launched as *Heroic* for the Belfast Steamship Company.

1914   Requisitioned by the Admiralty as HMS *Heroic.*

1920   Returned to commercial service.

1930   Transferred to the British & Irish Steam Packet Company Ltd, renamed *Lady Connaught.*

1936   British & Irish Steam Packet Company (1936) Ltd.

1938   Renamed *Longford.*

1940   Registered in Liverpool.

1953   Broken up at Barrow.

324. *Lady Lough* (3) (1906) O.N. 123124

1,389 grt   83.82 × 11.27 × 4.87 m

B. Caledon Shipbuilding & Engineering Company Ltd, Dundee. Yard No. 187.

Single screw, quadruple expansion, steam engine, 282 rhp, 310 nhp. By builder.

10.4.1906   Launched as *Duke of Montrose* for the Dublin & Glasgow Sailing & Steam Packet Company Ltd, Dublin.

1908   The Dublin & Glasgow Sailing & Steam Packet Company Ltd, Dublin acquired by Burns Steamship Company Ltd. Renamed *Tiger.*

1922   To Burns & Laird Lines Ltd, Glasgow.

1929   Renamed *Lairdsforest.*

1930   Transferred to the British & Irish Steam Packet Company Ltd and converted to carry cattle, renamed *Lady Louth.*

1934   Broken up at Port Glasgow.

325. *Staveley/Lady Glen* (1891) O.N. 99173

1,034 grt   492 nrt   73.15 × 9.75 × 4.57 m

B. C. S. Swan & Hunter Ltd, Newcastle. Yard No. 166.

Single screw, triple expansion, steam engine, 248 nhp, 3 cylinder. By Westgarth, English & Company Ltd, Middlesbrough. 12½ knots.

1.5.1891   Launched as *Staveley* for the Manchester, Sheffield & Lincolnshire Railway Company Ltd, Grimsby.

1897   Owner became the Great Central Railway Company, Grimsby.

1923   London & North Eastern Railway Company, Grimsby.

1932   Purchased by Manuel Swift, Liverpool, and sold to the British & Irish Steam Packet Company Ltd.

1933   Renamed *Lady Glen.*

8.1933   Broken up at Preston.

326. *Lutterworth* (1897) O.N. 99169

1,002 grt   73.15 × 9.75 × 4.87 m

B. Earle's Shipbuilding & Engineering Company Ltd, Hull. Yard No. 343.

Single screw, triple expansion, steam engine, 249 nhp. By builder. 15 knots.

8.4.1891   Launched as *Lutterworth* for the Manchester, Sheffield & Lincolnshire Railway Company Ltd, Grimsby.

1897	Owner became the Great Central Railway Company, Grimsby.
1912	New engines, 249 rhp, 250 nhp.
1923	London & North Eastern Railway Company, Grimsby.
1932	Sold to the British & Irish Steam Packet Company Ltd.
1933	Broken up at Preston.

327. *Lady Cavan/Cavan* (1906) O.N. 123248

602 grt   54.25 × 9.14 × 4.26 m

B. Earle's Shipbuilding & Engineering Company Ltd, Hull. Yard No. 517.
Single screw, triple expansion, steam engine, 79.5 nhp. By builder.
9 knots.

5.3.1906	Launched as *Fido*, for Thomas Wilson, Sons & Company Ltd, Hull.
1917	Owner became Ellerman's Wilson Line Ltd.
1922	Sold to H. H. Poole & Company Ltd, London. Renamed *Poolmina*.
1930	Sold to Wexford Steamships Company Ltd, J. J. Stafford, Wexford, renamed *Wexfordian*.
1933	Purchased by the British & Irish Steam Packet Company Ltd, Dublin. Renamed *Lady Cavan*.
1936	British & Irish Steam Packet Company (1936) Ltd.
4.4.1937	In collision with *Alder* in fog at the entrance to Strangford Lough. *Adler* sank.
1938	Renamed *Cavan*.
1939	Sold to Michael A. Karageorgis, Piraeus, Greece, renamed *Marios*.
25.4.1941	Sank by aircraft at Aiyion in the Gulf of Corinth, Greece.

328. *Ardmore* – See *Lady Killiney* (1918).

329. *Kenmare* (1921) O.N. 143487

1,675 grt   83.82 × 11.58 × 5.18 m

B. Ardrossan Drydock Company, Ardrossan. Yard No. 278.
Single screw, triple expansion, steam engine, 360 rhp, 553 nhp. By
J. G. Kincaid & Company Ltd, Greenock.

24.2.1921	Launched as *Kenmare* for the City of Cork Steam Packet Company Ltd, Cork.
1936	British & Irish Steam Packet Company (1936) Ltd.
11.6.1956	Arrived at Passage West and broken up by Haulbowline Industries Ltd.

330. *Innisfallen* (1930) O.N. 152222

3,071 grt   97.84 × 14.02 × 4.57 m

B. Harland & Wolff Ltd, Belfast. Yard No. 870.
Twin screw, oil engine, 1,192 rhp, 1,193 nhp. By builder.

4.3.1930	Launched as *Innisfallen* for the City of Cork Steam Packet Company Ltd, Cork.
1936	British & Irish Steam Packet Company (1936) Ltd, Cork.
21.12.1940	Sunk in the River Mersey.

331. *Finola* (1920) O.N. 143533

879 grt   60.96 × 9.44 × 3.96 m

B. Dublin Dockyard Company Ltd, Dublin. Yard No. 105.
Single screw, triple expansion, steam engine, 120 rhp, 155 nhp. By Ross & Duncan Ltd, Glasgow.

27.11.192	Launched as *Finola* for Michael Murphy Ltd, Dublin.
1921	Registered in Cardiff.
1926	Michael Murphy Ltd acquired by the British & Irish Steam Packet Company Ltd.
1936	British & Irish Steam Packet Company (1936) Ltd.

1939   Transferred to Coast Lines Ltd, Liverpool. Renamed *Glamorgan Coast*.

1947   Transferred to British Channel Traders Ltd, London. Renamed *Stuart Queen*.

To Queenship Navigation Ltd, London.

1952   To Zillah Shipping Company Ltd (W. A. Savage Ltd), Liverpool. Renamed *Caldyfield*.

1955   Broken up at Preston.

332. *Kilkenny* (1937) O.N. 159788
1,320 grt   80.46 × 12.19 × 4.26 m
B. Dublin Dockyard Company Ltd, Dublin. Yard No. 169.
Single screw, oil engine, 404 rhp. By Harland & Wolff Ltd, Belfast.
14.4.1937   Launched as *Kilkenny* and towed to Belfast for the engine to be installed.
Delivered to the British & Irish Steam Packet Company (1936) Ltd.
1971   Sold to Patrick J. O'Connor & Company, Dublin. Renamed *Cork*.
1974   Broken up at Dalmuir.

333. *Leinster* (1937) O.N. 164343
4,302 grt   107.59 × 15.24 × 4.57 m
B. Harland & Wolff Ltd, Belfast. Yard No. 995.
Twin screw, oil engine, 1,348 rhp, 1,347 nhp. By builder. 17 knots.
24.6.1937   Launched as *Leinster* for the British & Irish Steam Packet Company (1936) Ltd.
Completed for Coast Lines Ltd, Liverpool.
1938   Chartered to the British & Irish Steam Packet (1936) Ltd.
1940   Returned to Coast Lines Ltd, Liverpool.

Kilkenny.

1946   Transferred to the Belfast Steamship Company Ltd, renamed *Ulster Prince*.
1966   Sold and renamed *Ulster Prince I*.
1967   Sold to Van Heyghen Frères, Belgium to be broken up.
Sold to Epirotiki Lines (George Potamianos Ltd), Greece, and renamed *Adria*.
1969   To Epirotiki Steamship Company Ltd, Famagusta, Cyprus. Renamed *Adria*.
1969   Renamed *Odysseus*.
1979–1980   Broken up at Faslane.

334. *Munster* (1937) O.N. 166226
4,305 grt   107.59 × 15.24 × 4.57 m
B. Harland & Wolff Ltd, Belfast. Yard No. 996.
Twin screw, oil engine, 1,348 rhp, 1,347 nhp by builder. 17 knots.
3.11.1937   Launched as *Munster*.
1938   Delivered to Coast Lines Ltd, Liverpool.
To the British & Irish Steam Packet Company (1936) Ltd.
1939   Transferred to the Belfast Steamship Company Ltd.
7.2.1940   On a voyage from Belfast to Liverpool she was mined and
sank near the Mersey Bar lightship.

335. *Dundalk* (1938) O.N. 159826
699 grt   56.69 × 10.66 × 3.96 m
B. Ardrossan Dockyard Ltd, Ardrossan. Yard No. 372.
Single screw, oil engine, 113 rhp, 218 nhp, 7 cylinder. By British Auxiliaries
Ltd, Glasgow.
10.11.1938   Launched as *Dundalk*.
1939   Delivered to the British & Irish Steam Packet Company Ltd,
Dublin.
1966   Sold to Varverakis & Company, Greece. Renamed *Alexis*.
5.9.1966   On a voyage from Constantza to Beirut with a cargo of
sheep and eggs she sank, 35 miles west of Paphos, Cyprus.

336. *Meath* (2) (1919) O.N. 143050
1,434 grt   82.60 × 11.58 × 4.87 m
B. Caledon Shipbuilding & Engineering Company Ltd, Dundee. Yard No. 265.

Above: Odysseus.

Below: Munster.

Single screw, triple expansion, steam engine, 278 rhp, 196 nhp. By builder. 12 knots.

1918   Ordered as a war standard ship.

17.1.1919   Launched as *War Leven* for the Shipping Controller, (J. Moss & Company Ltd, London, as managers).

Delivered as *Limoges* and purchased by Moss Steamship Company Ltd, 351. Liverpool.

1922   Sold to Coast Lines Ltd, Liverpool. Renamed *Western Coast*.

1941   Transferred to Burns & Laird Lines Ltd and it was proposed to rename her *Lairdsvale* but this did not occur.

1946   Renamed *Meath*.

1948   Operated by the British & Irish Steam Packet Company Ltd.

1952   Transferred to Burns & Laird Lines Ltd, renamed *Lairdscastle*.

1958   Broken up at Hendrik-Ido-Ambacht, Netherlands.

337. *Innisfallen* (2) (1969) O.N. 159848

3,705 grt   99.66 × 15.24 × 4.57 m

B. William Denny & Brothers Ltd, Dumbarton. Yard No. 1405.

Twin screw, Sulzer oil engine, 1,589 nhp, 6,400 bhp. By builder. 17 knots.

12.12.1947   Launched as *Innisfallen* for the British & Irish Steam Packet Company Ltd, Cork.

1969   Renamed *Innisfallen I*.

Sold to Isthmian Navigation Company Ltd (The Hellenic Mediterranean Lines Company Ltd), Famagusta, Cyprus, for £65,000. Renamed *Poseidonia*.

8.7.1985   Arrived at Brindisi and broken up.

338. *Leinster* (2) (1947) O.N. 159877

4,088 grt   107.59 × 15.24 × 4.57 m

B. Harland & Wolff Ltd, Belfast. Yard No. 1352.

Twin screw, oil engine, 698 rhp, 1,590 nhp, 5,600 bhp. By builder. 17½ knots.

Innisfallen (2).

20.5.1947   Launched.

1968   Renamed *Leinster I*.

Sold to Med Sun Ferry Lines Ltd, Famagusta, Cyprus. Renamed *Aphrodite*.

1975/76   Registered at Limassol, Cyprus.

1987   Broken up at Aliaga, Turkey.

339. *Munster* (2) (1947) O.N. 159871

4,088 grt   107.59 × 15.24 × 4.57 m

B. Harland & Wolff Ltd, Belfast. Yard No. 1349.

Twin screw, oil engine, 698 rhp, 1,590 nhp, 5,600 bhp. By builder. 17½ knots.

25 3.1947   Launched as *Munster* for the British & Irish Steam Packet Company Ltd, Dublin.

Leinster (2).

1968   Renamed *Munster I.*
Sold to Epirotiki Steamship Navigation Company (George Potamianos) S. A., Piraeus, Greece. Renamed *Theseus.*
1969   Became *Orpheus.*
1996   Operated for Royal Olympic Cruises Ltd.
28.12.2000   Arrived at Alang and broken up.

340. *Inniscarra* (1948) O.N. 182867
584 grt   675 dwt   51.81 × 8.53 × 3.04 m
B. Burntisland Shipbuilding Company Ltd, Burntisland, Fife. Yard No. 310.

Single screw, oil engine, 184 nhp, 800 bhp. By British Polar Engines Ltd, Glasgow.
20.5.1948   Launched for British Channel Islands Shipping Company Ltd, London.
1948   Delivered as *Brittany Coast.*
1950   Transferred to the British & Irish Steam Packet Company Ltd, renamed *Inniscarra.*
1952   Registered in Dublin.
1969   Sold to Oldham Brothers, Liverpool, to be broken up.
1970   Sold to Kassos Maritime Enterprises Ltd, Greece, and renamed *Elni.*
1971   Purchased by Vassilios and Gerassimos Zavitsanos, Piraeus, Greece.
Sold to Theodoros and Vassilios Zavitsanos and Theodoros Argiris, Piraeus, Greece.
1972   Sold to Mrs Kyriaki D. Kallimassia and Mrs Evangelia B. Dimopoulou, Piraeus, Greece. Renamed *Ria.*
2.1982   Broken up at Naples.

341. *Glengariff* (1936) O.N. 164098
1,599 grt   697 nrt   83.21 × 11.58 × 5.18 m
B. Alexander Stephen & Sons Ltd, Linthouse, Glasgow. Yard No. 550.
Single screw, triple expansion, steam engine, 210 rhp, 196 nhp. By builder. 12 knots.
3.9.1936   Launched as *Rathlin* for the Clyde Shipping Company Ltd, Glasgow.
1941   Requisitioned by the Admiralty as a convoy rescue ship.
1945   Returned to commercial service with owners.
1953   Sold to Burns & Laird Lines Ltd, Glasgow. Renamed *Lairdscraig.*

1956   Transferred to the British & Irish Steam Packet Company Ltd, renamed *Glengariff*.

30.12.1963   Arrived at Passage West and broken up by Haulbowline Industries Ltd.

342. *Wicklow* (2) – See *Sandhill* (1938), Tyne Tees Steam Shipping Company Ltd.

343. *Meath* (3) (1959) O.N. 400281

1,590 grt   84.12 × 12.80 × 4.57 m

B. Liffey Dockyard Ltd, Dublin. Yard No. 180.

Single screw, oil engine, 446 rhp, 2,500 bhp. By George Clark & North East Marine Ltd, Sunderland.

4.11.1959   Launched as *Meath* for the British & Irish Steam Packet Company Ltd, Dublin.

1974   Sold to Vickers Ltd, London.

1975   Converted to a submarine support and oceanographic research vessel by the Manchester Dry Dock Company Ltd at Manchester. Renamed *Vickers Viscount*.

1978   Managed by James Fisher & Sons Ltd.

1979   Sold to British Oceonics Ltd, Leith (Premier Shipping & Engineering Ltd, Barrow as managers). Renamed *British Viscount*.

1980   Purchased by J. H. Food Machinery Ltd, Hull.

1981   Sold to Fairfield Industries (Bermuda) Ltd, Hamilton, Bermuda (J. Marr & Son Ltd, Hull, as managers).

1984   Owned by Fairfield Industries Panama S. A. (Johnasia (S) Pte Ltd as managers).

1990   Renamed *British* and broken up in India.

344. *Glanmire* (1936) O.N. 164095

814 grt   69.79 × 11.27 × 3.65 m

B. Harland & Wolff Ltd, Belfast. Yard No. 978.

Twin screw, oil engine, 330 rhp, 332 nhp. By builder. 13½ knots.

3.9.1936   Launched as *Lairdsbank* for Burns & Laird Lines Ltd, Glasgow.

1963   Transferred to the British & Irish Steam Packet Company Ltd, Dublin. Renamed *Glanmire*.

1969   Broken up at Dalmuir.

345. *North of Scotland*, Orkney & Shetland Shipping Company Ltd.

Glanmire.

346. *Earl of Zetland* (2) (1939) O.N. 165251

548 grt   144 dwt   50.7 × 8.9 × 3.66 m

B. Hall, Russell & Company Ltd, Aberdeen. Yard No. 749.

Single screw, 840 bhp/618k W, two stroke, single acting, oil engine, 6 cylinder. By British Auxilliaries Ltd, Glasgow. 12 knots.

Passengers: 218.

20.5.1939   Launched.

8.1939   Delivered.

1960   Coast Lines Ltd acquired the North of Scotland, Orkney & Shetland Shipping Company Ltd.

26.2.1971   Coast Lines acquired by the P&O Steam Navigation Company Ltd.

1.10.1971   Managed by P&O Short Sea Shipping Ltd.

6.3.1975   Sold to J. Turner, Middlesbrough Ocean Surveys Ltd.

1976   Renamed *Celtic Surveyor* and converted to a diving support vessel.

1980   Purchased by Cosag Marine services Ltd.

1982   Sold to Celtic Surveyor Ltd (Hydrosphere Ltd as managers) and adapted for use as a floating restaurant at Eastbourne.

1988   Sold and used as a restaurant ship at Lowestoft.

2013   Restaurant/bar at the Royal Quays, North Shields, River Tyne, reverted to *Earl of Zetland.*

347. *St Magnus* (4) (1936) O.N. 165247

1,641 grt   76.20 × 11.58 × 4.87 m

B. Hall, Russell & Company Ltd, Aberdeen. Yard No. 742.

Single screw, triple expansion, steam engine, 2,100 ihp. 14 knots.

Passengers: 420.

29.12.1936   Launched as *St Clair* (2).

6.5.1937   Maiden voyage.

Celtic Surveyor.

8.1939   Special return voyage from Leith to Lyness, on the island of Hoy.

7.1940–45   Requisitioned by the Admiralty as HMS *Baldur*, participating in the British occupation of Iceland and based at Reykjavik until October 1943. She was then converted at Aberdeen as a convoy rescue ship.

1943   *St Clair.*

6.1945   Returned to owners and placed on the direct Aberdeen–Lerwick route.

7.1946   Returned to service after conversion to oil burning.

8.1954   It was discovered that one of the boilers had developed a crack that necessitated immediate repairs and she was unable to maintain the Monday evening sailing. However, the repairs were completed quickly and she was able to sail on Thursday evening.

12.1959   Renamed *St Clair II*.

11.1960   *St Magnus* (4).

10.1966   *St Magnus II*.

30.3.1967–1.4.1967   Final voyage for the North of Scotland, Orkney & Shetland Shipping Company Ltd.

8.4.1967   Sold and left Leith under her own steam. Broken up at Bruges, Belgium.

348. *St Clement* (2) (1946) O.N. 181006

815 grt   590 dwt   454 nrt 57.27 × 9.47 × 5.63 m

B. Hall, Russell & Company Ltd, Aberdeen. Yard No. 791.

Passengers: 12.

Single screw, 840 bhp, 2SCSA, oil engine, 6 cylinder. By British Polar Engines Ltd, Glasgow.

26.6.1946   Launched by Mrs Littlejohn Smith.

9.1946   Delivered as *St Clement* to the North of Scotland, Orkney & Shetland Steam Navigation Company Ltd.

1953   Owners restyled to North of Scotland, Orkney & Shetland Shipping Company Ltd.

1955   Operated from Leith to Aberdeen and Kirkwall and Stromness until 1960.

1960   Company acquired by Coast Lines Ltd.

1966–1974   Replaced *St Ola* during her surveys and also as a supplemental vessel during summer excursions.

26.2.1971   Coast Lines Ltd acquired by the P&O Steam Navigation Company Ltd.

1.10.1971   Managed by P&O Short Sea Shipping Ltd.

31.3.1975   P&O Ferries as managers.

8.12.1976   Sold to E. G. Loukedes, Piraeus, Greece, renamed *Grigoris*.

1977   Registered under Co-ownership Grigoris (E. G. Loukedes as managers).

1980   Sold to Chrysoula Panagopoulou S. A. (Olympios Zeus Shipping Company Ltd as managers), Greece, renamed *Melina*.

1982   Sold to Lotus Maritime Company, Greece.

19.4.1984   Arrived at Eleusis, Greece, and broken up by N. K. Savas.

349. *St Ninian* (2) (1950) O.N. 182025

2,242 grt   935 dwt   1,217 nrt 87.05 × 14.02 × 7.68 m

B. Caledon Shipbuilding & Engineering Company Ltd, Dundee. Yard No. 478.

Twin screw, 2,620 bhp, 4SCSA, Polar oil engine, 2 × 8 cylinder. 14 knots.

6.3.1950   Launched.

6.1950   Delivered as *St Ninian* to the North of Scotland, Orkney & Shetland Steam Navigation Company Ltd, Aberdeen.

1953   Owners restyled as North of Scotland, Orkney & Shetland Shipping Company Ltd.

1960   Company acquired by Coast Lines Ltd.

26.2.1971   Coast Lines Ltd acquired by the P&O Steam Navigation Company Ltd.

26.4.1971   Sold to Atlantique Cruise Lines Ltd, North Sydney, Nova Scotia, and placed on the North Sydney Island to St Pierre and Miquelon service.

1979   Purchased by the Galápagos Tourist Corporation, Ecuador, renamed *Bucanero* following Atlantique Cruise Lines declaring bankruptcy. The ship was seized, sold and refitted by Shelburne Marine Ltd Shipyard prior to entering service around the Galápagos Islands.

1991   Broken up at Guayaquil, Ecuador, by Acerias Nacionales del Ecuador S. A.

ROYAL MAIL TWIN SCREW MOTOR VESSEL "ST. NINIAN"

350. *St Ola* (2) (1951) O.N. 183843

750 grt   389 dwt   350 nrt   54.28 × 10.08 × 6.03 m

B. Alexander Hall & Company Ltd, Aberdeen. Yard No. 733.

Single screw, 1,025 bhp, 2SCSA, oil engine, 7 cylinder. By British Polar Engines Ltd, Glasgow. 11 knots.

Passengers: 345; 14 berths.

23.2.1951   Launched.

5.1951   Delivered to the North of Scotland, Orkney & Shetland Steam Navigation Company Ltd, Aberdeen, and operated mainly on the Pentland Firth service between Scrabster and Stromness and occasional excursion cruises.

1953   Owners restyled North of Scotland, Orkney & Shetland Shipping Company Ltd.

1960   North of Scotland, Orkney & Shetland Shipping Company Ltd acquired by Coast Lines Ltd.

26.2.1971   Coast Lines Ltd acquired by P&O Steam Navigation Company Ltd.

1.10.1971   Managed by P&O Short Sea Shipping Ltd.

1974   Renamed *St Ola II*.

28.1.1975   Final voyage Stromness–Scrabster–Stromness. Berthed with the new *St Ola* (3) at Scrabster.

30.1.1975   Sold to Aquatronics International Ltd, Bermuda, renamed *Aqua Star* and converted to an oceanographic survey vessel for North Sea oil operations. (J. Marr & Sons Ltd as managers).

1977   Owners restyled Fairfield Industries (Bermuda) Ltd.

1983   Managed by J. Marr & Son Ltd, Fleetwood.

Above: Official company photograph of *St Ninian* (2).

Below: *St Ninian* (2).

Owners restyled as Fairfield Aquatronics Ltd and later Aquatronics Ltd.

1987   Sold to José Oliveira Gomez, Spain.

15.1.1987   Arrived at Vigo to be broken up.

25.6.1987   Demolition commenced.

18.8.1987   Demolition completed.

351. *St Rognvald* (3) (1954) O.N. 183846

941 grt   1,052 dwt   355 nrt   74.37 × 11.91 × 6.55 m

B. Alexander Hall & Company Ltd, Aberdeen. Yard No. 745.

Single screw, 2,100 bhp, 2SCSA, Sulzer oil engine, 7 cylinder. By William Denny & Brothers Ltd, Dumbarton. 13 knots.

14.10.1954   Launched by Mrs Mackie, wife of the manager of the North of Scotland, Orkney & Shetland Shipping Company Ltd.

3.1955   Delivered as *St Rognvald*.

1960   North of Scotland, Orkney & Shetland Shipping Company Ltd acquired by Coast Lines Ltd.

26.2.1971   Coast Lines Ltd acquired by P&O Steam Navigation Company Ltd.

1.10.1971   P&O Short Sea Shipping Ltd as managers.

4.5.1973   Aground on Thieves Holm, off Kirkwall, on a voyage from Aberdeen. Later refloated.

18.5.1973   Refloated and anchored in Kirkwall Bay.

25.6.1973   Returned to service.

31.3.1975   Managed by P&O Ferries.

23.5.1978   Sold to Ramajim Shipping Company Ltd, Gibraltar, renamed *Winston*.

1982   Sold to Clyde Shipping International Company Inc., Panama.

1986   Purchased by International Trading & Shipping Company, Banjul, The Gambia, renamed *Washington*.

1990   Sold to Trasatlantique, renamed *Radia 10*.

St Rognvald (3).

1991   Purchased by the Centuri International Shipping Company, renamed *Ras-Halague*.

24.7.1993   Laid up at Las Palmas.

28.7.1998   Broken up at Las Palmas.

352. *St Clair* (3) (1960) O.N. 301600

2,864 grt   1,030 dwt   1,570 nrt   90.31 × 15.36 × 8.22 m

B. Ailsa Shipbuilding Company Ltd, Troon. Yard No. 507.

Single screw, 3,750 bhp, 2SCSA, Sulzer oil engine, 10 cylinder. By Sulzer Brothers Ltd, Winterthur. 15 knots.

Passengers: 450.

29.2.1960   Launched by Ms Mary M. Dixon.

6.1960   Delivered.

1960   Company acquired by Coast Lines Ltd.

1970–1971   Chartered by the Belfast Steamship Company Ltd to relieve their passenger/car ferries during their winter overhauls.

26.2.1971   Coast Lines Ltd acquired by the P&O Steam Navigation Company Ltd.

1.10.1971   Managed by P&O Short Sea Shipping Ltd.

31.3.1975   P&O Ferries as managers.

3.3.1977   Renamed *St Clair II*.

17.6.1977   Sold to Meat & Foodstuffs Company (W. L. L., Kuwait), renamed *Al Khairat* and converted to a livestock carrier.

1987   Sold to A. R. Mohammad Farooq, Pakistan, to be broken up.

20.6.1987   Arrived at Gadani Beach.

19.7.1987   Demolition commenced.

353. *St Magnus* (5) (1955) O.N. 303225

871 grt   1,240 dwt   355 nrt   73.82 × 11.58 × 6.73 m

B. N. V. Terneuzensche Scheepv Maats, Ternauzen, Netherlands. Yard No. 58. Single screw, 1,190 bhp, 4SCSA, oil engine, 7 cylinder. By Masch. Augsburg-Nürnberg, Augsburg, West Germany.

15.1.1955   Launched.

5.1955   Delivered as *City of Dublin* to Palgrave Murphy Ltd (Palgrave Murphy (Shipowners) Ltd as managers), Dublin.

1960   Company acquired by Coast Lines Ltd.

9.1966   Purchased by the North of Scotland, Orkney & Shetland Shipping Company. Sailed to Ardrossan for conversion, costing £100,000, to carry refrigerated cargo and cattle and sheep.

15.3.1967   Renamed *St Magnus*.

24.3.1967   Sailed from Ardrossan.

26.3.1967   Arrived Leith.

30.3.1967   Maiden voyage to Aberdeen and Kirkwall.

26.2.1971   Coast Lines Ltd acquired by P&O Steam Navigation Company Ltd.

1.10.1971   Managed by P&O Short Sea Shipping Ltd.

31.3.1975   Managed by P&O Ferries.

3.6.1977   Sold to Sunstar Lines Ltd, Cyprus, renamed *Mitera Eirini*.

1977   Purchased by Dery Shipping Lines, Lebanon, renamed *Dragon*.

12.1.1979   On a voyage from Bourgas to Aden with a cargo of timber and canned goods she sank off Anadolu Kayak at the Black Sea entrance to the Bosporus after colliding with *Hakan*.

St Magnus (5).

Tyne Tees Steam Shipping Company Ltd.

354. *Craster/Caspian Coast* (1935) O.N. 161583
733 grt   341nrt   63.39 × 9.75 × 3.65 m
B. Swan Hunter & Wigham Richardson Ltd, Wallsend. Yard No. 1482.
Single screw, triple expansion, steam engine, 144 nhp, 3 cylinder. By builder.
6.1935   Delivered as *Craster* to the Tyne Tees Steam Shipping Company Ltd.
1946   Renamed *Caspian Coast.*
1947   Sold to London Scottish Line Ltd, renamed *London Merchant.*
1959   Purchased by Maldive interests, renamed *Maldive Crescent.*
28.6.1967   On a voyage from East Pakistan to Rangoon, with a cargo of jute, she was wrecked near Cape Negrais on the Bassein coast.
29.6.1967   Abandoned.

355. *Newminster/Dorian Coast* (1925) O.N. 148131
967 grt   406 nrt   70.40 × 10.66 × 4.26 m
B. Hawthorn, Leslie & Company Ltd, Hebburn. Yard No. 538.
Single screw, triple expansion, steam engine, 240 nhp, 3 cylinder. By builder.
7.1925   Delivered as *Newminster.*
1946   Renamed *Dorian Coast.*
1947   Sold to Eastern Navigation Company (Shariff Hassum & Company), Bombay, renamed *Azadi.*
11.1951   Arrived at Bombay and broken up.

356. *Bilton* (1920) O.N. 144936
746 grt
B. J. Samuel White & Company Ltd, Cowes, Isle of Wight. Yard No. 1545.
Single screw, triple expansion, steam engine. 9 knots.

14.7.1920   Launched.
8.1920   Delivered as *Bilton* to Coombes, Marshall & Company, Middlesbrough.
1929   Sold to Tyne Tees Shipping Company Ltd, same name.
1946   Purchased by J. Kelly Ltd, Belfast, renamed *Coleraine.*
1951   Renamed *Ballyhalbert.*
1.1958   Aground at Ardrossan, refloated.
16.6.1959   Arrives at Troon and broken up.
25.11.1959   Breakup completed.

357. *Alnwick/Cyprian Coast* (1936) O.N. 161595
508 grt   50.4 × 8.3 m
B. Hawthorn, Leslie & Company Ltd, Hebburn. Yard No. 608. 9 knots.
50.29 × 8.22 × 3.06 m.
Single screw, 4SCSA, oil engine. By Humbolt-Deutzmotoren AG, Köln-Deutz.
20.4.1936   Launched.
5.1936   Delivered as *Alnwick.*
1946   Renamed *Cyprian Coast.*
23.12.1955   In collision, sank and later raised and repaired.
1968   Transferred to British Channel Island Shipping Ltd.
19.5.1968   Arrived at Antwerp and broken up at Boom.

358. *Beal/Sylvian Coast* (1936) O.N. 161591
504 grt   249 nrt   50.29 × 8.22 × 3.06 m
B. R. & W. Hawthorn Leslie & Company Ltd, Hebburn. Yard No. 603.
Single screw, 82 nhp, oil engine, 7 cylinder. By Humboldt-Deutzmotoren AG, Köln-Deutz.
8.1.1936   Launched.
2.1936   Delivered as *Beal.*

1946   Renamed *Sylvian Coast.*

1959   Burns & Laird Lines, renamed *Lairdsburn.*

1966   Sold to Michael Koutlakis, Piraeus, renamed *Agia Sofia.*

1973   Sold to Elpis & Company Ltd, Piraeus.

1975   Purchased by M. Athanasiou, Piraeus, renamed *Friendship III.*

1976   Sold to East Mediterranean Lines Shipping Enterprises Company Ltd, Piraeus, renamed *Ariadne.*

5.3.1970   On a voyage from Kephalonia to Barcelona in ballast she was wrecked after striking Augusta breakwater.

359. *Cragside/Elysian Coast* (1935) O.N. 149158

496 grt   49.07 × 8.53 m

B. Furness Shipbuilding Company Ltd, Haverton Hill-on-Tees. Yard No. 245.

Single screw, triple expansion, steam, 3 cylinder engine. By North East Marine Engineering Company, Newcastle.

1935   Delivered as *Cragside.*

1946   Renamed *Elysian Coast.*

1952   *Westfield.*

30.6.1956   Arrived at Preston and broken up.

360. *Gateshead/Persian Coast* (1919) O.N. 143040

744 grt   58.2 × 8.9 m

B. Forth Shipbuilding Company Ltd, Aberdeen. Yard No. 29.

Single screw, triple expansion, steam engine. 9 knots.

1919   Ordered as *War Colne* and delivered as *Catherine Annie* to J. Leete & Company, London.

1922   Sold to J. Hay & Sons, Glasgow, renamed *The President.*

1933   Purchased by the Tyne Tees Steam Shipping Company Ltd, renamed *Gateshead.*

1946   *Persian Coast.*

1951   Sold to Mersey Ports Stevedoring Company, Liverpool, renamed *Celia Mary.*

1955   Purchased by Glynwood Navigation Company, Hull, becoming *Cupholder.*

26.4.1956   Arrived at Hendrik-Ido-Ambacht and broken up.

361. *Glen/Belgian Coast* (1935) O.N. 161584

471 grt   234 nrt   50.29 × 8.22 × 3.06 m

B. Hawthorn, Leslie & Company Ltd, Hebburn. Yard No. 598.

Single screw, 82 nhp, oil engine, 7 cylinder. By Humboldt-Deutzmotoren AG, Köln-Deutz.

14.6.1935   Launched.

7.1935   Delivered as *Glen.*

1946   Renamed *Belgian Coast.*

1947   Burns & Laird Lines, renamed *Lairdsrock.*

10.1966   Sold to Pericles K. Varvates & N. Kavarnicoloau, Piraeus, renamed *Giorgis.*

1979   Co-owned by 'Lefteris D' (Thira Shipping), Piraeus, renamed *Lefteris D.*

1980   Sold to Etna Maritime Company S. A., Panama, renamed *Tenaron S.*

10.12.1980 On a voyage from Italian ports with a cargo of cigarettes she stranded off Karpathos island and sank.

362. *Lowick/Frisian Coast* (1937) O.N. 161610

586 grt   978 dwt   57.79 × 9.63 × 3.32 m

B. Scheeps Gideon Koster, Groningen. Yard No. 157.

Single screw, oil engine, 4SCSA, 880 bhp, 6 cylinder. By Humboldt-Deutzmotoren.

1937	Delivered as *Lowick*.
1946	Renamed *Frisian Coast*.
4.10.1967	Sold and renamed *Agia Eleni*.
26.11.1977	Wrecked off Mandraki Point, Rhodes.

363. *Sandhill/Durham Coast/Valerian Coast/Hebridean Coast* (1937) O.N. 165759

586 grt   57.91 × 9.75 × 3.35 m

B. Scheeps Gideon Koster, Groningen. Yard No. 158.

Single screw, oil engine, 144 nhp, 825 bhp. By Humboldt-Deutzmotoren AG, Köln, Germany.

18.11.1937	Launched as *Sandhill* for the Tyne Tees Steam Shipping Company Ltd.
1943	Tyne Tees Steam Shipping Company Ltd acquired by Coast Lines Ltd.
1946	Renamed *Valerian Coast*.
1948	Transferred to the Aberdeen Steam Navigation Company Ltd, Aberdeen. Renamed *Hebridean Coast*.
1951	Transferred to the Tyne Tees Steam Shipping Company Ltd.
1953	Transferred to the Belfast Steamship Company, renamed *Ulster Chieftain*.
1956	To the Tyne Tees Steam Shipping Company Ltd, renamed *Durham Coast*.
1960	Transferred to the British & Irish Steam Packet Company Ltd, Dublin. Renamed *Wicklow*. New oil engine fitted by Humboldt-Deutzmotoren AG, Köln, Germany.
1970	Sold to Sistallic Shipping Company Ltd, Famagusta, Cyprus, and renamed *Sinergasia*.
1973	Sold to Aghios Sostis Maritime Company Ltd, Cyprus. Renamed *Sonia*.

1974	Purchased by the Fortitude Maritime Company, Greece, became *Margarita P.*
1976	Sold to Cia de Nav. Scotia S. A., Panama.
1980	Broken up at Baia, Italy.

364. *Thornaby/Northumbrian Coast* (1935) O.N. 160745

1,174 grt   504 nrt   69.18 × 10.05 × 4.26 m

B. Hawthorn Leslie & Company Ltd, Hebburn. Yard No. 596.

Single screw, oil engine, 148 nhp, 3 cylinder. By Hawthorn, Leslie & Company Ltd.

1.5.1935	Launched.
6.1935	Delivered as *Thornaby*.
1946	Renamed *Northumbrian Coast*.
1.1963	Broken up at *Dunston*.

365. *Wooler/Novian Coast* (1936) O.N. 163048

507 grt   50.29 × 8.22 m

B. Smiths Dock Company, Middlesbrough. Yard No. 1000.

Single screw, oil engine, 4SCSA, 370 bhp, 7 cylinder. By Humboldt-Deutzmotoren, Köln.

8.4.1936	Launched.
5.1936	Delivered as *Wooler*.
1946	Renamed *Novian Coast*.
12.1968	Broken up at Willebroek.

366. *Olivian Coast* (1946) O.N. 169215

749 grt   965 dwt   64.61 × 10.05 × 4.26 m

B. Ardrossan Dockyard Company. Yard No. 405.

Single screw, oil engine. By British Polar Engines Ltd.

| 4.9.1946 | Launched. |

Olivian Coast.

1946   Delivered as *Olivian Coast.*

1967   British Channel Islands Shipping Company Ltd.

3.1968   Broken up at Ghent.

367. *Belgian Coast* (2) (1929) O.N. 161129

1,600 grt   946 nrt   76.20 × 11.27 × 4.87 m

B. D. & W. Henderson & Company Ltd, Glasgow. Yard No. 880.

Single screw, triple expansion, steam engine, 232 nhp, 3 cylinder. By McKie & Baxter Ltd.

31.10.1929   Launched.

11.1929   Delivered as *Dorothy Rose* to Richard Hughes & Company (Liverpool) Ltd.

1947   Purchased by the Tyne Tees Steam Shipping Company Ltd, renamed *Belgian Coast.*

11.1957   Arrived at Belgium and broken up.

368. *Virginian Coast* (1930) O.N. 162328

1,599 grt   76.20 × 11.28 × 4.87 m

B. D. & W. Henderson & Company Ltd, Glasgow. Yard No. 907.

Single screw, triple expansion, steam engine. 10½ knots.

14.10.1930   Launched.

11.1930   Completed as *Dennis Rose* for Richard Hughes & Company (Liverpool) Ltd.

1947   Sold to the Tyne Tees Steam Shipping Company Ltd, renamed *Virginian Coast.*

10.1953   Sold to Aniceto Urain & Lucio Zatica, Puerto Limón, Bilbao, renamed *Julian Presa.*

31.1.1958   Arrived at Briton Ferry and broken up by T. W. Ward Ltd.

369. *Grampian Coast* (1937) O.N. 165464

481 grt   49.9 × 8 m

B. N. V. Indust. Maats De Noord, Alblasserdam, Netherlands. Yard No. 566.

Single screw, oil engine. 9 knots.

1937   Ordered as *Welsh Coast*, delivered as *Emerald Queen* for the British Channel Islands Shipping Company.

1947   Transferred to the Tyne Tees Steam Shipping Company Ltd, renamed *Grampian Coast.*

1963   Renamed *Gilda.*

1977   Converted to a floating restaurant at Porto Garibaldi, Italy.

370. *Iberian Coast* (1949) O.N. 169224

1,188 grt   1,503 dwt   67.05 × 10.97 × 4.57 m

B. George Brown & Company Ltd, Greenock. Yard No. 250.

Single screw, 2SCSA, 1190 bhp, oil engine, 7 cylinder. By British Polar Engines Ltd.

21.12.1949   Launched as *Sandringham Queen* for Queenship Navigation Ltd.

1950   Delivered as *Iberian Coast* to the Tyne Tees Steam Shipping Company Ltd.

1966   Sold to Spiridione Lucchi, Venice, Italy, renamed *Pupi*.

1976   Purchased by Amnivas Maritime Hellas Ltd, Piraeus, renamed *Agios Nicolaos*.

26.8.1978   On a voyage from Bareltta to Mozambique with a cargo of wheat she suffered an engine room fire and sank 20 miles west of Crete.

371. *Suffolk Coast* (3) (1938) – See Coast Lines Ltd.

372. *Hampshire Coast* (3) (1940) O.N. 168075

1,224 grt   625 nrt   72.84 × 10.36 × 4.26 m

B. Ardrossan Dockyard Ltd, Ardrossan. Yard No. 378.

Single screw, triple expansion, steam engine, 850 bhp, 3 cylinder. By J. G. Kincaid & Company Ltd.

14.11.1940   Launched as *Stuart Queen* for Queenship Navigation Ltd.

1946   Renamed *Hampshire Coast*, Coast Lines Ltd.

1952   Transferred to the Tyne Tees Steam Shipping Company Ltd.

3.1959   Broken up in Holland.

373. *Netherlands Coast* (1953) O.N. 169248

867 grt   1,008 dwt   331 nrt   68.88 × 10.66 × 3.96 m

B. George Brown & Company Ltd, Greenock. Yard No. 256. 12 knots.

Single screw, 2SA, 1330 bhp, oil engine, 8 cylinder. By British Polar Engines Ltd.

6.1953   Delivered as *Netherlands Coast*.

1968   Sold to Bat Harim Mediterranean Lines Ltd, Ashdod, Israel, renamed *Bat Harim*.

1974   Purchased by the Woodcock Shipping Corporation, Panama, renamed *Woodcock*.

Lau Ka Nung, Penang, Malaysia, and later to Leong Shen Shipping (Singapore) Pte, Panama, renamed *Hong Leong*.

7.9.2010   Deleted from Lloyd's Register.

374. *Yorkshire Coast* (2) (1959) O.N. 186896

785 grt   967 dwt   355 nrt 59.9 × 10.2 × 4.63 m

B. George Brown & Company Ltd, Greenock. Yard No. 272.

Single screw, 2SA, oil engine, 900 bhp, 6 cylinder. By British Polar Engines Ltd. 11 knots.

18.6.1959   Launched.

8.10.1959   Delivered to Coast Lines Ltd.

26.2.1971   Coast Lines acquired by the P&O Steam Navigation Company Ltd.

1.10.1971   Management transferred to P&O Short Sea Shipping Ltd.

14.4.1972   Sold to J. & A. Gardner & Company Ltd, Glasgow, renamed *Saint Enoch*.

1976   Purchased by Galwave Navigation Ltd (Stewart Chartering Ltd, managers), Cyprus, renamed *Galwave*.

1980   Sold to Ugarit Navigation Company Ltd, Cyprus, renamed *Saer*.

13.3.1986   On a voyage from Beirut to Limassol with empty containers, she was in collision with *Omar B* off Cyprus and sank in position 34013'N 34016'E.

375. *Stormont* (2) – See *Fife Coast* (3), Coast Lines Ltd.

376. Zillah Shipping Company Ltd.

377. *Amy Summerfield* (1921) O.N. 143718

407 grt   43.6 × 7.7 m

B. Day, Summers & Company Ltd, Southampton. Yard No. 187.

Single screw, compound steam engine. 9 knots.

11.1.1921	Launched.
1921	Delivered to Summerfield Company Ltd, Liverpool.
12.1922	Abandoned and sank in Irish Sea. Salvaged and returned to service.
3.1927	Sold to W. A. Savage & Company Ltd, same name.
23.3.1949	Collided with *Pass of Liny* in the Ribble Estuary in dense fog.

23.3.1951   Stranded off Caernant Quarry, Nant Gwrtheyrn, North Wales. She was a regular visitor to the berth but because of the stormy weather she was forced to return to Liverpool without her cargo of stone sets. However, the company sent the ship straight back to Caernant to load, but on arrival the wind caught hold of the mooring line and it became entangled in her propeller. She was quickly blown onto the beach and, following inspection, the insurance company declared her a total loss. Plans to tow her to Port Dinorwig on the Menai Straits to be broken up were soon abandoned and it was clear that she would have to be demolished on the beach where she lay. Because of the location of the vessel the scrap dealer, William Williams, was forced to purchase a multi-terrain vehicle to transport the remains of the vessel up from the beach.

378. *Aquilla* (1907) O.N. 124059

450 grt   172 nrt   47.24 × 7.92 × 3.35 m

B. Ailsa Shipbuilding Company Ltd, Troon. Yard No. 171.

Single screw, compound engine, 2 cylinder. By Ross & Duncan.

2.3.1907   Launched.

Amy Summerfield.

12.1915–1.1920	Requisitioned by the Admiralty as an RFA stores carrier.
1941–1945	Requisitioned by the Admiralty as a cable ship.
1949	Sold to the Zillah Shipping Company Ltd, Coast Lines Ltd, Liverpool.
27.11.1953	Sold to Richard Abel & Sons Ltd, renamed *Alladale*.
1956	Purchased by the Fleetwood Sand & Gravel Company Ltd.
9.1967	Broken up at Fleetwood by C. & J. Davies Ltd.

379. *Ashfield* (1914) O.N. 137401

436 grt   43.4 × 7.9 m

B. Lytham Shipbuilders Ltd. Yard No. 490.

Single screw, triple expansion, steam engine.

1914	Delivered as *Ashfield*.
3.4.1954	Broken up at Llanelli by Rees Shipbreaking Company Ltd.

380. *Beechfield* (1921) O.N. 145912
449 grt   43.3 × 7.9 m
B. Lytham Shipbuilders Ltd, Lytham. Yard No. 590.
Single screw, triple expansion, steam engine. 8½ knots.

17.11.1921	Launched as *Oakfield*.
1949	Renamed *Beechfield*.
12.1955	Broken up at Troon by the West of Scotland Shipbreaking Company Ltd.

381. *Briarfield* (1902) O.N. 143669
446 grt   43.3 × 7.9 m
B. Lytham Shipbuilders Ltd, Lytham. Yard No. 579.
Single screw, triple expansion, steam reciprocating engine. 8½ knots.

20.5.1920	Launched.
13.9.1920	Delivered.
11.6.1955	Arrived at Troon and broken up by the West of Scotland Shipbreaking Company Ltd.

382. *Broomfield* (1937) O.N. 166230
657 grt   773 dwt   53.8 × 8.8 m
B. Lytham Shipbuilders Ltd, Lytham. Yard No. 841.
Single screw, triple expansion, steam engine. 8½ knots.

18.11.1937	Launched as *Broomfield*.
1955	Renamed S. E. Cooper.
9.1965	Broken up at Silloth by Ardmore Steel of Cumberland Ltd.

383. *Dransfield* (1921) O.N. 145595
652 grt   48.76 × 9.14 × 3.35 m
B. Ailsa Shipbuilding Company, Troon. Yard No. 381.
Single screw, triple expansion, steam engine, 81 nhp, 3 cylinder. By builder.

20.5.1921	Launched as *Arclight* for Light Shipping Company Ltd (Ross & Marshall Ltd), Greenock.
1921	Delivered.
1933	Sold to Gilchrist Traders (Steamships) Ltd (F. B. Johnston Ltd,), Liverpool, renamed *Fire Queen*.
1943	Sold to Coast Lines Ltd, Liverpool.
1945	Renamed *Orkney Coast*.
1949	Transferred to the Zillah Shipping Company Ltd, renamed *Dransfield*.
10.11.1955	Arrived at Troon and broken up by the West of Scotland Shipbreaking Company Ltd.

384. *E Hayward* (1908) O.N. 127944
444 grt   47.85 × 7.92 × 3.35 m
B. Ailsa Shipbuilding Company Ltd, Ayr. Yard No. 211.
Single screw, compound steam engine, 64 nhp, 2 cylinder.

10.10.1908	Launched.
1949	Sold to the Zillah Shipping Company Ltd.
1957	Sold to Richard Abel & Sons Ltd, Liverpool.
1959	Renamed *Ennisdale*.
8.10.1960	Arrived at Passage West and broken up by Haulbowline Industries Ltd.

385. *Gorsefield* (1922) O.N. 147177
628 grt   53.3 × 8.6 m

B. Lytham Shipbuilders Ltd, Lytham. Yard No. 605.
Single screw, triple expansion, steam engine. 9 knots.

1922   Delivered as *Gorsefield*.
6.1958   Broken up at Preston by T. W. Ward Ltd.

386. *Larchfield* O.N.168803
493 grt   43.4 × 8.3 m
B. Lytham Shipbuilding Company Ltd, Lytham. Yard No. 865.
Single screw, triple expansion, steam engine. 9 knots.
20.2.1957   Arrived at Barrow and broken up by T. W. Ward Ltd.

387. *Mayflower* (1905) O.N. 120889
396 grt   149 nrt   43.89 × 7.92 × 3.04 m
B. Ailsa Shipbuilding Company Ltd. Yard No. 139.
Single screw, compound steam engine, 94 nhp, 2 cylinder. By Ross &
Duncan Ltd.
16.9.1905   Launched.
1949   Purchased by the Zillah Shipping Company Ltd.
21.12.1953   Sold to Richard Abel & Sons Ltd.
1954   Renamed *Mallowdale*.
13.11.1956   Arrived at Troon and broken up by the West of Scotland
Shipbreaking Company Ltd.

388. *Ophir* (1907) O.N. 124102
469 grt   172 nrt   47.24 × 7.92 × 3.35 m
B. Ailsa Shipbuilding Company Ltd, Troon. Yard No. 194.
Single screw, compound steam engine, 130 lbs, 94 nhp, 2 cylinder by
Ross & Duncan Ltd. 8 knots.
9.11.1907   Launched.
12.12.1907   Delivered as *Ophir*.

Ophir.

30.12.1917   Requisitioned by the Admiralty as a fleet messenger,
renamed HMS *Opulent*.
18.6.1919   Reverted to *Ophir*.
10.1940   Requisitioned as an armed store carrier.
1943   Operated as a cable ship, renamed *Eldorado*.
3.1946   Returned as *Ophir*.
1949   Sold to the Zillah Shipping Company Ltd.
39.7.1954   Arrived at Llanelli and broken up by the Rees Shipbreaking
Company.

389. *Rowanfield* (1938) O.N. 166248
495 grt   43.4 × 8.3 m

B. Lytham Shipbuilders Ltd. Yard No. 849.
Single screw, triple expansion, steam engine. 9 knots.

1938	Delivered as *Rowanfield*.
1957	Sold and renamed *Rowan*.
1964	*Antonio Miguel*.
1976	*Nicola*.
1977	*Leros I*.
1981	*Cap Christos*.
10.1983	Broken up at Messina.

390. *Silverfield* (1915) O.N. 137436
426 grt   43.4 × 7.9 m
B. Lytham Shipbuilding & Engineering Company Ltd, Lytham. Yard No. 508.
Single screw, triple expansion, steam engine. 10 knots.

2.2.1915	Launched.
4.5.1954	Arrived Preston and broken up by T. W. Ward Ltd.

391. *Hazelfield* (1959) O.N. 182412
692 grt   56 × 8.8 m
B. Lytham Shipbuilding & Engineering Company Ltd, Lytham. Yard No. 889.
Single screw, triple expansion, steam engine.

1959	Sold to John S. Monks Ltd, renamed *Sprayville*.
1963	Sold to Greek interests and renamed *Fouli*.
1964	*Aghios Gerassimos*.
1976	*Agios Gerassimos*.
2.10.1979	Foundered in rough seas off Palmorola Island, Naples. It was reported that she was smuggling cigarettes.

392. *Fairfield* (1925) O.N. 147311
801 grt   58.1 × 9.8 m
B. J. Duthie & Sons Ltd, Aberdeen. Yard No. 464.
Single screw, triple expansion, steam engine. 10 knots.

1925	Delivered to R. Gilchrist & Company Ltd as *Portia*.
1943	Sold to Coast Lines.
1945	Renamed *Shetland Coast*.
1946	Sold to Michael Murphy Ltd, renamed *Portia*.
1950	Purchased by the Zillah Shipping Company Ltd, renamed *Fairfield*.
13.11.1955	Arrived at Troon and broken up by the West of Scotland Shipbreaking Company Ltd.

393. *Caldyfield* (1920) O.N. 143533
879 grt   61 × 9.4 m
B. Dublin Dockyard Company. Yard No. 105.
Single screw, triple expansion, steam engine. 9½ knots.

27.11.1920	Launched as *Finola*.
1939	Renamed *Glamorgan Coast*.
1947	*Stuart Queen*.
1952	*Caldyfield*.
9.1955	Broken up at Preston by T. W. Ward Ltd.

394. *Westfield* (1935) O.N. 149158
496 grt   49.07 × 8.53 m
B. Furness Shipbuilding Company Ltd, Haverton Hill-on-Tees. Yard No. 245.
Single screw, triple expansion, steam engine, 3 cylinder. By North East Marine Engineering Ltd, Newcastle.

30.4.1935	Launched.
5.1935	Delivered as *Cragside*.

1946	Renamed *Elysian Coast*.
1952	Renamed *Westfield*.
30.6.1956	Arrived at Preston and broken up by T. W. Ward Ltd.

395. *Northfield* (1933) O.N. 163319
781 grt   59.4 × 9.4 m
B. Burntisland Shipbuilders Ltd. Yard No. 174.
Single screw, triple expansion, steam engine. 10 knots.
26.1.1933   Launched as *London Queen*.
1948   Transferred to the Belfast, Mersey & Manchester Steamship Company Ltd, renamed *Stormont*.

Foxfield.

1950	*Cavan*.
1953	*Northfield*.
31.3.1956	Arrived at Preston and broken up by T. W. Ward Ltd.

396. *Foxfield* (1951) O.N. 185508
562 grt   864 dwt   272 nr   57.60 × 9.32 × 4.11 m
B. Ferus Smit v/h Smit & Zoon, Foxhol, Netherlands. Yard No. 112.
Single screw, 650 bhp, 4SCSA, oil engine, 6 cylinder. By N. V. Werkspoor, Amsterdam, Netherlands. 10 knots.
13.10.1951   Launched.
19.1.1952   Delivered as Leemans to N. V. Scheepv-Onderneming Kustverkeer (W. H. James & Company Scheepv. en Handel Maats N. V. as managers), Netherlands.
11.1954   Sold to the Zillah Shipping Company Ltd (W. A. Savage Ltd as managers), Liverpool, renamed *Foxfield*.
1963   Registered as owned by W. A. Savage Ltd.
6.4.1966   Sold to Burns & Laird Lines Ltd, Glasgow, renamed *Lairdsfox*.
26.2.1971   Burns & Laird Lines Ltd acquired by the P&O Steam Navigation Company Ltd.
1.10.1971   Managed by P&O Short Sea Shipping Ltd.
28.9.1973   Transferred to the Belfast Steamship Company Ltd, Belfast.
31.3.1975   Owned by P&O Ferries.
15.11.1977   Sold to J. H. Ramagee, Panama, renamed *Lilaida*.
1978   Registered under Naviera Lilaida S. A., Panama.
27.8.1989   Arrived at Cádiz, Spain, and broken up.

397. *Oatfield* (1952) O.N. 185496
538 grt   635 dwt   53.5 × 8.3 m
B. Scheeps De Waal, Zaltbommel. Yard No. 647.

Single screw, oil engine. 10 knots.

10.4.1952	Launched as *Pieter Hubert*.
1954	Renamed *Oatfield*.
20.7.1966	Sold to Y. & G. Vamounis and renamed *Sophia*.
1974	*Pavlina*.
1975	*Thalis*.
1977	*Linta* and later *Saraa*.
1984	*Tarek M*, *Amani* and *Fawaz*.
1985	*Gloria I*.
10.8.1985	On a voyage from Beirut to Limassol, she sank 9 miles off Beirut.

398. *Freshfield* (1954) O.N. 185488
517 grt   864 dwt   56.5 × 8.7 m
B. Scheeps Ijsselwerf. Yard No. 103.
Single screw, oil engine. 10 knots.

4.3.1954	Launched as *Freshfield*.
10.10.1961	On a voyage from Par to Runcorn with 760 tons of china clay, she sank in the Crosby Channel, Liverpool, following a collision with the Guinness motorship *The Lady Gwendolen*. She was later salvaged and taken to Egerton Dock, Birkenhead. At the subsequent inquiry into the collision, held in Liverpool in March 1962, the master of *The Lady Gwendolen* was held to blame for excessive speed and bad look-out. The master of *The Lady Gwendolen*, Cecil Henry Meredith, had his certificate suspended for a period of six months from 10 November 1961.
1962	Sold and renamed *Joika*.
1965	*Arnholt*.
1971	*Byrding*.
1989	*Maly*.

Fallowfield and *Cambrian Coast* at Liverpool.

1991	*Bird*.
1993	*Seabec*.
1.10.1993	On a voyage with a cargo of containers from Barcelona to Genoa, she sank 30 miles south-west of Almería.

399. *Fallowfield* (1953) O.N. 185509
566 grt   851 dwt   60.35 × 9.02 × 3.68 m
B. Scheeps Gebr. van Diepen, Waterhuizen. Yard No. 927.
Single screw, oil engine, 4SCSA, 5 cylinder. By Appingedammer-Brons.
11 knots.

15.8.1953	Launched as *Medusa*.
1954	Renamed *Fallowfield*.

6.1971   *Arklow Bay.*

22.9.1973   On a voyage from Antwerp to Arklow with potash and bromine she sank 40 miles south-west of Milford Haven.

400. *Greenfield* (1953) O.N. 185518

504 grt   760 dwt   53.2 × 8.6 m

B. Scheeps van der Werf, Deest. Yard No. 249.

Single screw, 4SCSA, 8 cylinder. By Motoren 'De Industrie', Alphen. 11 knots.

4.4.1953   Launched as *Pieter Maarten.*

1953   Delivered as *Coolsingel.*

1955   Renamed *Greenfield.*

1966   *Lairdsfield.*

6.2.1970   On a voyage from the Tees to Cork with a cargo of steel she capsized in the Tees Estuary. She was later refloated and broken up at Middlesbrough by Tees Marine Services Ltd.

401. *Grangefield* (1954) O.N. 187101

309 grt   762 dwt   53.3 × 8.5 m

B. Scheeps van der Werf, Deest. Yard No. 251.

Single screw, oil engine, 4SCSA, 660 bhp, 8 cylinder by builder.

22.5.1954   Launched as *Statensingel.*

1955   Renamed *Grangefield.*

1964   W. A. Savage, Liverpool. Same name.

12.1967   To Coast Lines Ltd, same name.

1968   Tyne Tees Steam Shipping Company Ltd, same name.

8.1969   To Transen Shipping Corporation Ltd, Panama.

1973   To Trans Sea Shipping Corporation, Panama. Renamed *Sea Goblin.*

1978   Sold to Terra Investment & Trading Company, Panama.

Brentfield.

1979   Renamed *Julianna.*

1998   Deleted from Lloyd's Register.

402. *Brentfield* (1955) O.N. 187114

1,262 grt   68.28 × 11.58 m

B. George Brown & Company Ltd, Greenock. Yard No. 262.

Single screw, Sulzer, 2SCSA, oil engine, 7 cylinder. By G. Clark & N. E. Marine (Sunderland) Ltd.

21.6.1955   Launched as *Brentfield.*

1959   Renamed *Spaniel.*

1965   Transferred to Burns & Laird Line.

1968   To Coast Lines Ltd, Liverpool.

1970   Coast Lines (Services) Ltd.

1971	Managed by P&O Short Sea Shipping Ltd.
1972	To the Belfast Steamship Company Ltd.
11.1973	Sold to the Isle of Man Steam Packet Company Ltd, renamed *Conister*.
29.9.1981	Arrived at Avilés and broken up by Desguaces y Salvamentos S. A.

403. *Birchfield* (1956) O.N. 187140

1,265 grt   1,151 dwt   611 nrt   68.27 × 11.27 m

B. Ardrossan Dockyard Company, Ardrossan. Yard No. 422.

Single screw, 2SCSA, oil engine, 7 cylinder. By George Clark & North Eastern Marine (Sunderland) Ltd. 10 knots.

2.2.1956	Launched.
1956	Delivered as *Birchfield*.
12.1958	Transferred to Coast Lines Ltd, Liverpool.
1959	Converted to carry containers, renamed *Pointer*.
1965	Transferred to Burns & Laird Lines Ltd, Glasgow.
1971	Managed by P&O Short Sea Shipping Ltd.
1972	Transferred to the Belfast Steamship Company Ltd.
1975	Managed by P&O Ferries.
1975	Sold to Isthmian Navigation Company Ltd and renamed *Taurus III*.
1984	Purchased by Larnaca Project S de R L., Honduras, renamed *Larnaca Town*.
1985	*Mina*.
16.5.1986	Arrived at Perama and broken up.

404. *Edgefield* (1955) O.N. 187129

500 grt   945 dwt   61.8 × 9.6 m

B. Scheeps Noord Nederlandsche, Groningen. Yard No. 278.

Single screw, oil engine. 10½ knots.

26.11.1955	Launched as *Spolesto* and later renamed *Edgefield*.
4.2.1965	Sold to Marine Transport Services Ltd.
1965	Renamed *Sarsfield*.
1970	*Valerie B.*
1973	*Rosemary D.*
1974	*Silloth Trader.*
1980	*Radcliffe Trader.*
1983	*Mirabelle.*
2.3.1984	On a voyage from Aruba to Cartagena, she grounded off the Macuira National Park, Colombia.

405. *Earlsfield* (1952) O.N. 169238

635 grt   967 dwt   60.92 × 9.20 × 3.68 m

B. Scheeps Bodewes, Martenshoek. Yard No. 396.

Single screw, oil engine, 4SCSA, 6 cylinder. By builder. 10½ knots.

28.6.1952	Launched as *Coquetdyke*.
1956	Renamed *Earlsfield*.
1969	*Katie H.*
7.3.1972	On a voyage from Rotterdam to London with a cargo of fertilizer she was in collision with *Zeeparel* in the North Sea and sank.

406. *Holmfield* (1956) O.N. 187157

488 grt   640 dwt   49.62 × 8.29 × 3.04 m

B. Scheeps Haarlemsche, Haarlem. Yard No. 546.

Single screw, oil engine, 4SCSA, 395 bhp, 6 cylinder. By builder. 9 knots.

8.12.1956	Launched as *Ooster Eems*.
1957	*Holmfield.*
1967	Sold and renamed *Prodromos*.

1974	*Dimitrios F.*
1974	*Constantinos TZ* and later *Kostas Tzamtzis*.
1982	Broken up in Greece.

407. *Fernfield* (1954) O.N. 301284
561 grt   851 dwt   266 nrt   60.41 × 9.05 × 4.17 m
B. Gebr van Diepen, Waterhuizen, Netherlands. Yard No. 930.
Single screw, oil engine, 4SCSA, 650 bhp, 6 cylinder. By N. V. Werkspoor, Amsterdam, Netherlands. 1,000 cubic metres (35,000 cubic feet). 10 knots.

25.9.1954	Launched.
11.1954	Delivered as *Haaksbergen* to N. V. Zuid-hollandsche Scheepv. Maats, Netherlands.
1958	Sold to the Zillah Shipping Company Ltd (W. A. Savage Ltd as managers), Liverpool, renamed *Fernfield*.

Fernfield passing New Brighton.

1963	Transferred to W. A. Savage Ltd.
12.1967	Transferred to Coast Lines Ltd.
1970	Registered under Coast Lines (Management) Ltd.
6.1971	Registered under Coast Lines (Services) Ltd.
26.2.1971	Coast Lines Ltd acquired by the P&O Steam Navigation Company Ltd.
1.10.1971	Managed by P&O Short Sea Shipping Ltd.
8.12.1971	Sold to James Tyrrell Ltd, renamed *Shevrell*.
5.1972	Purchased by Enterprise de Navigation de L'Isle Incorporated, Canada, renamed *Courdre de L'Ile*.
15.6.1988	On a voyage from Sept-Iles, Québec, to Cote Ste Catherine, Quebéc, with a cargo of scrap metal, she met the eastbound bulk carrier *Algowest* off Les Escoumins, Québec, in dense fog. At 06.00 a.m. the two vessels collided nearly head on. Within minutes, the *Courdre de L'Ile* sank in around 30 m (100 feet) of water off Pointe au Boisvert, Québec. *Algowest* sustained minor damage and was able to proceed to Baie Comeau to discharge her cargo. Nine of *Courdre de L'Ile*'s crew were rescued by the *Algowest* and the ship's cook was declared missing and presumed drowned.

408. *Glenfield* – See *Channel Queen* (2), British Channel Islands Shipping Company Ltd.

409. *Garthfield* (1938) O.N. 165124
608 grt   49.5 × 8.8 m
B. N. V. van Duivendijk, Netherlands. Yard No. 225.
Single screw, oil engine. 9 knots.

1938	Delivered as *Ngarua* for W. A. Wilson & Company Ltd.
1940	Sold to Merchants Ltd, renamed *Silver Coast*.
1943	Purchased by British Channel Traders Ltd.
1946	Renamed *Lairdsoak*.

1960	*Garthfield.*
1962	Sold to Greek interests, renamed *Krios.*
1968	*Kyriakoula.*
1974	*Dimitrios II.*
1992	Deleted from Lloyd's Register.

410. *Fordfield* (1954) O.N. 301348
561 grt   61 × 9.1 m

B. Scheeps Gebr. van Diepen N. V., Groningen, Netherlands. Yard No. 928. Single screw, oil engine. 10 knots.

1954	Delivered as *Eibergen.*
1960	Purchased by the Zillah Shipping Company Ltd, renamed *Fordfield.*
11.1.1962	On a voyage from the River Neath to Amsterdam with a cargo of coal she capsized and sank in the English Channel 10 miles south-east of Owers Light Vessel off Selsey Bill.

ACKNOWLEDGEMENTS AND BIBLIOGRAPHY

Books

McRonald, Malcolm, *The Irish Boats. Volume 1: Liverpool – Dublin* (The History Press, 2005).

McRonald, Malcolm, *The Irish Boats. Volume 3: Liverpool – Belfast* (The History Press, 2008).

Duckworth, Christian and Langmuir, Graham, *Clyde and other Coastal Steamers* (T. Stephenson & Sons, 1978).

Middlemiss, Norman L., *Coast Lines* (Shield Publications, 1998).

Sinclair, Robert C. *Across the Irish Sea, Belfast-Liverpool Shipping Since 1819* (Conway Maritime Press, 1990).

Robins, Nick, *Tyne-Tees Steam Shipping Company and its Associates* (Bernard McCall, 2014).

Magazines and Journals

Sea Breezes
The Journal of Commerce
The Motor Ship
The Syren & Shipping Illustrated
Marine News (World Ship Society)

Photographers

Dave Crolly
Malcolm Cranfield

All images are by the author or from his collection unless otherwise credited.